HOW GOOD IS GOD!

Coaching Church

BEYOND THE GATES OF HELL, TO TRULY EXPERIENCE HEAVEN

Also by *Kristen Wambach*

HOW GOOD IS GOD! | Available in Paperback, Hardback, and Audible

HOW GOOD IS GOD! The Redemptive Activation Journal —The Strategic Playbook for Hearing God's Voice and Executing Your Heavenly Design.

The UnFinished Book
Scan to Shop The UnFinished Book

Interviewing Jesus Podcast
Scan to listen to the most recent episode

KristenWambach.com

Kristen Wambach

HOW GOOD IS GOD!

"Step into the presence of a God
whose Goodness is an active override
to every religious limit you've ever known
—and discover
a destiny that doesn't just leave the building;
it rewrites the earth."

Rabbitrail Publishing

Copyright Page

Rabbitrail Publishing

HOW GOOD IS GOD! Coaching Church-BEYOND THE GATES OF HELL, TO TRULY EXPERIENCE HEAVEN.
Copyright © 2026 by Kristen Wambach
This title is also available Hardback, Paperback, eBook, and Audible. Visit https://www.kristenwambach.com/
Requests for information should be addressed to: Rabbitrail Publishing 2365 NE Merloy Ave. Corvallis, Oregon 97330
https://www.kristenwambach.com/
rabbitrailpublishing.html

Library of Congress Cataloging-in-Publication Data
Wambach, Kristen, 2026 Copyright ©

New International Version (NIV)
Scripture quotations marked (NIV) are taken from the Holy Bible, New International Version®, NIV®. Copyright © 1973, 1978, 1984, 2011 by Biblica, Inc.™ Used by permission of Zondervan. All rights reserved worldwide. www.zondervan.com. The "NIV" and "New International Version" are trademarks registered in the United States Patent and Trademark Office by Biblica, Inc.™

The Message (MSG)
Scripture quotations marked (MSG) are taken from THE MESSAGE, copyright © 1993, 2002, 2018 by Eugene H. Peterson. Used by permission of NavPress. All rights reserved. Represented by Tyndale House Publishers, Inc.

Amplified Bible (AMP)
Scripture quotations marked (AMP) are taken from the Amplified® Bible (AMP), Copyright © 2015 by The Lockman Foundation. Used by permission. www.Lockman.org.

The Living Bible (LBT / TLB)
Scripture quotations marked (TLB) or (LBT) are taken from The Living Bible copyright © 1971. Used by permission of Tyndale House Publishers, Carol Stream, Illinois 60188. All rights reserved.

The Free Agents (Public Domain)
King James Version (KJV)
Scripture quotations marked (KJV) are taken from the King James Version of the Bible. Public domain.

The KJV is subject to Crown Copyright there
New Heart English Bible (NHEB)
Scripture quotations marked (NHEB) are taken from the New Heart English Bible. Public domain.

Weymouth New Testament (WNT)
Scripture quotations marked (WNT) are taken from the Weymouth New Testament (The New Testament in Modern Speech). Public domain.

ISBN: 979-8-9950858-1-2 Hardback
ISBN: 979-8-9950858-0-5 Paperback
ISBN 979-8-9950858-2-9 ePub
ISBN: 979-8-9950858-3-6 HOW GOOD IS GOD! The Redemption Activation Journal
Book Cover Design: Kristen Wambach
Co-editor Laure Fabre
Co-editor John Bugni
First printing April 1st 2026
Printed in the United States of America

"Kindness is the ultimate override for confusion.

It's a conversation 2,000 years in the making."
—Kristen Wambach

Dedication

For the Fathers in my life...

Dad,
I will never forget the day you pointed to an article hidden in the ink and photos of your beloved newspaper — a prophetic word regarding this book. And that was the miracle, Dad; you had no idea what a *"Prophetic Word"* was.
That word was the second-best thing you ever said to me.
I love you, Dad. *See? Yes, I Am!*
George Arthur Richards July 20, 1927 – October 5, 2020

Father God,
"Call to me and I will answer you and tell you great and unsearchable things you do not know."
— Jeremiah 33:3
I heard You... *Kisses.*
Abba. Alpha. Omega.

My Game Plan

PRE-GAME ASSESSMENT

MY STARTING LINE (Where I am right now. The area of my life where I feel "benched," stuck, or ready for a new season.)

____

____

____

____

THE END ZONE (If God is truly as good as this book promises, what does my life look like on the other side of these pages?)

____

____

____

____

THE ONE BIG PLAY

MY DIRECT QUESTION ("Jesus, the one thing I ask You to reveal to me in our time together is...")

____

____

____

____

MY COMMITMENT: I am choosing to be Spiritually BRAVE. I am trading my history for His mystery. I am ready to get off the sidelines and into the game.

____

____

____

____

"I am suiting up. I am Spirit-ready. Let's run the play."

Date: ___________________________

Signed: _________________________________

HOW GOOD IS GOD!

"Kindness and Goodness don't just answer doubt—they melt it. This isn't a lecture; it's the conversation He literally died to have with you."

CONTENTS

CONTENTS

CONTENTS

THE STARTING LINE-UP
The Redemptive Gifts

Every championship team relies on a roster of specialized athletes. You wouldn't put a Linebacker at Quarterback, and you wouldn't ask a Kicker to block on the offensive line.

The kingdom of Heaven is no different.

God designed the human spirit with seven distinct "positions," known in scripture as the *Redemptive Gifts* (Romans 12). These are not just personality traits; they are the spiritual DNA that determines how you see the field, how you overcome the enemy, and how you bring victory to the team.

MEET THE ROSTER:

THE PROPHET: *The Eyes of the Team.* Designed to see the future and repair the breach.

THE SERVANT: *The Hands of the Team.* Designed to heal the land and empower the family.

THE TEACHER :*The Mind of the Team.* Designed to ground the truth and preserve the history.

THE EXHORTER: *The Voice of the Team.* Designed to bridge the gap and ignite the party.

THE GIVER :*The Heart of the Team.* Designed to resource the vision and birth the new.

THE RULER: *The Shoulders of the Team.* Designed to build the empire and expand the territory.

THE MERCY: *The Spirit of the Team.* Designed to host the presence and worship the King.

17

The Pre-Game

HOW GOOD IS GOD!

THE FIELD CONDITIONS

Subject: TIME vs. ETERNITY

We often live our lives watching the clock, afraid of running out of time. But the kingdom doesn't run on a clock; it runs on a "Love" rhythm.

Timeline 101 is not just a history lesson. It is a map of the heartbeat of God.

"History is not just what happened. It is the blueprint of what is coming."

Eyes up. Check the scoreboard. We are closer to the end zone than you think.

Timeline 101

Do not carry the memory of yesterday's failures, nor postpone your inheritance for tomorrow's striving. The work is finished, and the kingdom is at hand—your eternal history is activated by the simple and present act of being the Beloved Son, Beloved Daughter, today. — Jesus

Inspired | **Jesus,** *the Famous Only Begotten Son, walking the Emmaus road with* **Vince Lombardi** *and* **Bill Belichick**...
Two of the most successful and revered head coaches in the history of the NFL walking with the Savior?

Now that is a conversation I want to hear.

For the love of great motivational quotes! We all need the "Dream & Do" voices that get inside our heads. We need the leaders, the team players, the fans, the concession stands, and the tailgate groupies. We even need the contender who challenges our crown. Together, they push the "pigskin" of our life down the field.

(And yes, I am using Coaching as a football metaphor: a team sport of transition and adaptation to move the ball of life into the End Zone.)

Definition of End Zone: God's "Super Bowl" intent for you—realized, released, and resulting in victory.

Now, the Author's first long pass: **The TIMELINE.**

We begin our journey not in the present age, but by gazing across the Timeline—the Generational Line established by God's very finger. This Timeline is the ledger of inspired works, the words that moved millions in our own lifetime.

I use this foundational continuity (from 1959 to the present) to demonstrate God's Goodness relentlessly moving across the entire age of our spiritual understanding. We are ensuring that our breakthrough is built upon where *He* pointed His finger, and where we—the Readers—responded by being moved.

As a podcaster, I know listeners can't wait to get past the "who's who" of introductions to find the gold. So let's cut to the chase.

I am certain that God is "Gooder" than the bandwidth of this book. I am certain that the testimony of Jesus' humanity is the only doctrine worth its salt. I am certain in my ability to convey a spiritual story. I am also certain Holy Spirit will fill in the blanks for me.

I am certain this book stumbled into your day divinely. I am certain you will disagree with me. I am certain your disagreement will result in a choice.

I am certain Jesus caught every tear shed on our journey to this conversation. I am certain that Jesus gave **US** the Keys to the kingdom. I am certain I am purposed to courageously turn those ancient keys and dismantle the spiritual decay that has hidden the Divine passages—opening the doors Jesus commissioned for access since His ascension.

And finally... I am certain you will feel a deep inner smile, a spontaneous outer giggle, and perhaps even dance a jig, as the assurance already revealed in your spirit is confirmed: **God is truly that good!**

And you knew it all along.

TIMELINE: This is my Hail Mary pass... are you a wide receiver or a tight end?

"Are you open to catch it?"

@God Text Message Delivered

The world speaks in broadcasts; God speaks in whispers. But the miracle of your divine connection is that His whisper is a text message—instant, personal, and always delivered. — Kristen Wambach

1 Kings 19:11–12 (NIV) "The Lord said, 'Go out and stand on the mountain in the presence of the Lord, for the Lord is about to pass by.' Then a great and powerful wind tore the mountains apart and shattered the rocks before the Lord, but the Lord was not in the wind. After the wind there was an earthquake, but the Lord was not in the earthquake. After the earthquake came a fire, but the Lord was not in the fire. And after the fire came a gentle whisper."

Jeremiah 33:3 (NIV) "Call to me and I will answer you and tell you great and unsearchable things you do not know."

1 John 2:27 (TMT) "I am convinced that the effect of His touch within you is permanent; this is the Christ-anointing that teaches you all things, so that you do not need any teacher whose doctrine does not resonate with truth. Deception cannot compete with spirit-resonance."

The Hail Mary is thrown...

We are now in the realm of metaphorical senses and intuitive language. I know, cowboys only get 8 seconds too! (American Rodeo shtick: In professional bull riding, the rider must stay on the bull for exactly 8 seconds to qualify. Any longer is unnecessary; any shorter is a failure.)
The throw - Desperate. Deep. Hope. Leaping. Blocking. Catching. My. Beloved. Now.

The Experience: What a blustery night. November came in with a gust, and God did a little re-arranging in my night season. Seven times He moved the "Book" furniture around. A "Text message"—so easy to hear God in that lucid place.

"This is the Rhema Mind receiving a message while the Logos Mind is still hitting the snooze button."

Here are the messages I received.

"PHONE"—TEXT MESSAGES FROM HEAVEN
Text #1: From the Movie *Secretariat* Subject: Redemption via Golf
Lucien Laurin: *(As he hits the ball poorly)* "Fore!"
Penny Tweedy: "I'm Mrs. Tweedy. I need a trainer."
Lucien Laurin: *(Exasperated)* "Lady, I can't train you to play golf! Now if you'll excuse me, I'm trying to save my soul here!"

The Download: Their meeting—a frantic shout of "Fore!" over a disastrous golf swing—is the chaotic preamble to a shared destiny. Lucien is a washed-up trainer trying to save his reputation; Penny is an inexperienced owner making desperate moves. Neither knows that the foal soon to be born, *Secretariat*, is the agent of their redemption. The horse will pull Lucien out of obscurity and validate Penny's audacious faith, saving both their legacies from the disappointment of their present circumstances.
Secretariat (2010) Walt Disney Pictures. Screenplay by Mike Rich. Directed by Randall Wallace.

Text #2: From the Movie *Seabiscuit* Subject: The Value of Broken Things

Tom Smith: *(Regarding a beautiful but injured racehorse)* "You don't throw a whole life away just 'cause it's banged up a little."

The Download: This quiet wisdom is the foundational principle for the entire *Seabiscuit* team. The owner was grieving a son, the trainer was marginalized, and the jockey was damaged. Their meeting wasn't chaotic, but a mutual recognition of shared brokenness. *Seabiscuit*, the "banged up" race horse, was the agent of their redemption. By refusing to throw away the horse's life, these men found their own lives, careers, and dignities restored.

Seabiscuit (2003) Universal Pictures / DreamWorks Pictures. Screenplay by Gary Ross. Based on the book *Seabiscuit: An American Legend* by Laura Hillenbrand.

Text #3: The Yellow Footprints Protocol Time: 2:30 AM | Subject: The Initiation

Son: "I think I want to paint the yellow footprints in front of my house."

The Context: A father (Vietnam-era Marine) receives this text from his son (medically retired Afghanistan-era Marine). The "yellow footprints" are the official starting point at boot camp—the threshold where civilians die and recruits are born.

The Download: The father understands. This isn't about remembrance; it's about rededication. It is a signal that the old life must be ritually acknowledged before the new life can begin. This mirrors the challenge for the Church today. We cannot move forward without standing on our own yellow footprints—an intentional vigil of self-assessment, sacrificing our civilian comfort to embrace our identity in Christ. This painful step is the agent of our redemption.

Text #4: From the coming of age Baseball Movie: The "Sandlot" Confrontation

Subject: The "F-Word" (Offense)

At first, I thought, "Oh my... I need to write the F-word?" The font was so large it took up the entire page. Then Holy Spirit interpreted it.

Ham Porter vs. Phillips

Phillips: "You play with a bunch of rejects."

Ham: "What'd you say, crapface?!"

Phillips: "You ain't good enough to lick the dirt off our cleats."

Ham: "Watch it, jerk!"

Phillips: "Shut up, idiot!"

Ham: "Moron!"

Phillips: "Scab eater!"

Ham: "Butt sniffer!"

Phillips: "Pus licker!"

Ham: "Fart smeller!"

Phillips: "You eat dog crap for breakfast, geek!"

Ham: "You mix your Wheaties with your mama's toe jam!"

Phillips: "You bob for apples in the toilet! And you like it!"

Ham: *(The devastating blow)* "YOU PLAY BALL LIKE A GIRL!"

Phillips *(Stunned)* "What did you say?"

Ham Porter "You heard me."

Phillips "Tomorrow. Noon, at our field. Be there, buffalo-butt breath."

Ham Porter "Count on it, pee-drinking crap-face!"

The Download: This confrontation—the insults, the posturing, the sting—is the human operating system's default setting. It is the primal Logos Mind engaging in defense. This confrontation is the "F-Word" (Offense). Offense is the fence where we stop playing in freedom and start defending our turf. You cannot experience Oneness (the true field of play) until you drop the need to defend your ego.

The Sandlot (1993). Directed by David Mickey Evans. Distributed by 20th Century Fox. Known for the quote: "Heroes get remembered, but legends never die."

Text #5: The Hidden Figure Subject: Find Him

offense ojesus offense

Did you find Him? (Hint: 249 times "offense," 1 time "Jesus.") Cheat Sheet in Film Room & Locker Room Notes Page 400.

The Download: Why do we seek Him? Because the chaos of this overwhelming world reflects our own sensory overload. The simple act of finding His fixed, recognizable pattern is a cognitive victory. It is a call to action: override the noise to find the Person.

Text #6: The Delivery System Subject: Communion & Connection

"Truly, truly, I say to you, unless you eat the flesh of the Son of Man and drink his blood, you have no life in you." — John 6:53

The Download: This is one of the most "offending" statements Jesus ever made. But this is **How Good God Is!** His Communion is not just remembrance; it is the delivery system for His perfect health.
   • **Pastor Joseph Prince:** "Communion is God's ordained delivery system... If disease came through Adam's eating, then by another act of eating, we can eat our way back to health."
   • **The Mirror Translation:** "You have no real life in yourselves until you consume the flesh of the Son of man... fully assimilating and realizing our co-association and oneness."
   In short: These words are a radical call to union.

Text #7: The Final Instruction

—Napoleon Hill

Think

And

Grow

Rich

Thus Concludes God's Text Message.

You didn't just read seven text messages from heaven; you ran a series of drills. *"The communication of your faith becomes effective in the accurate knowledge of every good thing that is in us in Christ."* Philemon 1:6 MTB. You do not need to "attract" the win. You need to acknowledge the inheritance. Wealth is not just what you have. It is knowing Who has you.

Did you intuitively hear what God was communicating to you? Every scene—from Secretariat's redemption to the Sandlot's fence confrontation—was a divine play call confirming one thing: Spiritual Growth isn't about striving for an external victory. It is about assimilating and consuming the finished work of Jesus until your very thoughts mirror His.

The ball is now in your hands.

Words that Moved Millions

"When you die, if you get up to the Pearly Gates and they ask you, 'What did you do with your dash?'... The dash is that little line between the year you were born and the year you died."

—**Linda Ellis** (often quoted by coaches like **Paul "Bear" Bryant**)

— TIMELINE —

WHY IS IT THAT THE FIRST TIME we remember God speaking to us—or the first time we truly hear His voice—is often when we are at our most broken?

Was our hearing also broken? Did our brokenness actually serve to open our ears to a divine whisper we couldn't hear before?

Did God all of a sudden decide to speak to us after years of silence? Or is there something about the distance felt in brokenness that seems to "finally" connect the Bluetooth device we call *self*?

"God has gone to great lengths to protect our ability to say no, because without it, love simply cannot exist."

— **Wm. Paul Young**

Free will... is it really free?

Words that Move Millions... How God moved me! There wasn't anything like it—the measure of excitement that pushed me out of my comfort zone and into the End Zone.

The Football Metaphor

The scoring areas at each end of the playing field, bounded by the goal lines, end lines, and sidelines, are known as the end zones. A player must carry the ball into, or catch the ball in, this area to score a touchdown. Each NFL end zone measures 10 yards by 53 ⅓ yards. — NFL Operations

(Can I have a T-shirt, please, that says "10 x 53 ⅓ yards"?)

Imagine standing on the threshold of the "football game of life." Each play represents the trials and triumphs you face. You're in the huddle, eyes fixated on victory, feeling the electric anticipation and gravity of your part.

Throughout the game, as the clock ticks down, there's a sense of urgency. But pause for a moment to listen.

In the End Zone (10 x 53 ⅓ yards), a whisper echoes. It is the voice of God, urging you to remain steadfast and true. His guidance is not just a distant call heard in moments of triumph; it's woven through every play, every decision, reminding you that He is present in the struggle and the celebration alike.

"Hearing the Pulse of Sonship"

My friend, a next-door neighbor and committed "Bible-thumper," invited me, purchased the tickets, and drove me to my first-ever "Christian Artist" concert. We entered a large hall on a Portland university campus. The room was packed. We squeezed down the aisle, into hard, straight-backed chairs we barely sat down in.

This was nothing like the sanctuary or worship music my John 3:16 Bible church hymnals offered. Our choir history included one "Special Music" and three songs—verses one, two, and four—themed by John W. Peterson and Horatio Spafford.

"Supposedly—and I say that with attitude—when peace like a river attends your soul..." when peace like a river attends your soul in the midst of billowing sorrows, It Is Well. But my broken soul knew it wasn't well. *Heaven came down and glory filled my soul, when at the cross my Savior made me whole.* But my life was anything but whole.

Then, she entered the stage.

Larger than life. The praise applause ignited. Electric guitar strapped to her side and a head full of unruly auburn curls. I don't think heaven came down; I'd suggest we met glory in the air.

Margaret Becker lifted her hands with the crowd as people moved in freedom. The music escorted you in rhythm and toe-tapping song; sitting in your seat was impossible. The air was effervescent and loudly electrified.

I had never heard anyone, let alone a woman's voice, act like noise-canceling headphones, removing everyone from the room except God and me. Captivated and focused, my heart began to ascend. The burdens I walked in with had been dismantled. In a state of overwhelm and "oh my goodness," I noted the artist. She was amazing—an inspiration. His sound through her saturated my inhale, filling the airstream on the inside of me.

As clearly as the day He said them, or the moment I heard them:

God said, *"Kristen, you could be up there."*

Aghast with knowing, He was right! The cheerleader in me knew this was my team! I think God also re-downloaded the playbook in my DNA, but that is only hindsight suggesting.

Over and over again in this season, He beckoned me to mirror His voice in my head, until the day I stopped taking off the 10 x 53 ⅓ yards T-shirt He continued to clothe me with.

I live for His End Zone.

My husband Don had his "come to Jesus" moment on the beaches of Hawaii in the final months of his Marine Corps service (Vietnam Era)—travesty and homeland dishonor wreaking havoc on the heart of our nation's servicemen. We all have a moment in time where Time notarizes His signature and Fatherhood in our understanding.

I'll add a "but" here: *His signature on our life is timeless.*

Free will does not override or govern His signature of love; it supports your decision in time. Eternity is without a line of time!

This chapter is dedicated to the words that caught our—yours and mine—*Pulse of Sonship* attention on the timeline of pen and paper, to digital ink. Moves of God are like an arrow bound to the bullseye mark. They are communal and not walled within the structure of the church.

Finally, I had tasted the End Zone.

"Just as writers employ myriad styles to share their gifts and written works, so too does God utilize every means to communicate the singular gift of redemption to mankind."

My prayer: 10 x 53 ⅓ yards.

A Divine Re-tuning: What is a Redemptive Gift?

A Redemptive Gift is a collection of seven divine attributes found nestled inside Romans 12: **Prophet, Servant, Teacher, Exhorter, Giver, Ruler, and Mercy.**

God the Father embeds into our design, according to the grace given us, one prominent or "lead" gift and recognizable secondary gifts.

"Before I shaped you in the womb, I knew you intimately. I had divine plans for you before I gave you life, and I set you

apart and chose you to be mine. You are my prophetic gift to the nations."— Jeremiah 1:5 (TPT)

Jesus embodies all seven.

God's intimate knowledge of us and His individual divine plan reminds me of the umbilical cord between mother and child—fully supported, nurtured, a conduit providing intrinsic nourishment of your worth and wonder to the world around you.

Rob Lacey described the ministry gifts brilliantly from Ephesians 4:11: *"What God has in us, is gift wrapped to the world: some are commissioned to pioneer, others are gifted prophetically, some as announcers of good news, some as shepherds with a real gift to care and nurture, and others have a gift to ignite instruction through revelation knowledge."* (Couriers, Communicators, Counsellors, and *Coaches*).

In years of ministry, I have noticed that the "Ministry" gifts (Ephesians 4) function as edifiers to serve our spheres of influence. However, *Redemptive Gifts* (Romans 12) function inside and outside the church—babes or mature, developed or undeveloped, sanctified or not. They are hard-wired into us, allowing free movement around spirit, soul, and body.

This is similar to how the brain acts as the body's command center. A "light" gift (a sustainable source of divine creative energy) comes with spiritual packaging and personality liken to yours.

Remember the movie *Inside Out*? It is a wonderful prophetic picture of how Redemptive Gift Personalities take on a "person" inside you. They are wondrous made-from-God entities sewn into your DNA. Their sole purpose is fulfilling Christ's redemption in *ALL OF YOU*. No time stamp!

We learned through community and divine inner healing permissions that your spirit can communicate with an individual's redemptive gift to bring forth healing. Each of the seven gifts moves independently but always supports the whole. All seven will be present in you because of Jesus.

(Great resources for study: Nancy Benz, Mike Parsons, and Arthur Burk with special honorable mention.)

Unlocking "Redemption"

Ephesians 1:7-10 (Mirror):*"Since we are [fully represented] in Him, His blood is the ransom that secures our redemption... His grace communicates a wisdom and discernment of our worth that completely surpasses any definition."*

Romans 5:12 (Mirror, Commentary):*"Sin is to live out of context with the blueprint of one's design; to behave out of tune with God's original harmony."*

Jesus has tuned every instrument in the symphony of mankind. Whether you play within His *"Opus"* today or show up tomorrow, Redemptive Gifts facilitate your ability to read your *Sonship* notes on the music.

The Symphony of Gifts
1. Prophet / Perceiver: The Conductor
• **In the Symphony**: The conductor stands before the orchestra with the entire musical score laid out. With intense focus, they lead the ensemble, ensuring every instrument is in tune.

• **Redemptive Power:** They are the voice of spiritual awakening. Like the conductor, they bring clarity and truth to a messy world, challenging hypocrisy and ensuring our "music" is in perfect harmony with God's original score.

2. Servant / Minister: The Rhythm Section (Percussion)
• In the Symphony: The drums and timpani provide the foundational beat that holds the entire orchestra together. Without this reliable pulse, the music would fall apart.

- **Redemptive Power:** This gift redeems life by making God's love tangible. They are the hands and feet of Christ, creating a supportive foundation (authority) where others can find healing.

3. Teacher: The First Chair Violin
- **In the Symphony:** The first chair leads the string section, playing the primary melody with technical precision and a deep understanding of musical theory.
- **Redemptive Power:** The Teacher's power is building a strong, unshakable foundation of faith. They bring order to complex spiritual concepts, freeing people from confusion.

4. Exhorter / Encourager: The Trumpet or Horn
- **In the Symphony:** The trumpet plays bold, inspiring fanfares that uplift the entire piece, calling the listener to attention.
- **Redemptive Power:** This is a high-energy, "party" gift. Like the trumpet, they boldly proclaim messages of hope, revealing the nature of God and motivating others to action.

5. Giver: The Harp
- **In the Symphony:** The harp's sound adds a beautiful, rich texture that quietly supports the other instruments, adding vital depth and harmony.
- **Redemptive Power:** The Givers are a quiet but powerful force, bringing beauty from a place of generous overflow. They redeem life by fueling Kingdom impact and making all other gifts possible.

6. Ruler / Leader: The Cellos and Basses
- **In the Symphony:** The lower strings provide the powerful structure upon which the rest of the music is built. They bring deep, resonant order.
- **Redemptive Power:** Rulers are fearless visionaries who bring order to chaos. They redeem life by creating structures for growth, leading others with a combination of love and wisdom.

7. Mercy-Giver: The Flute or Oboe
• **In the Symphony:** The flute plays a soft, gentle melody that speaks directly to the heart.
• **Redemptive Power:** The Mercy-givers hear God with their heart. They define the ambiance and redeem life by offering profound healing, providing a safe space for authentic connection.

The Archer's Stance: A Time to Aim (Kairos)

The purpose of writing *Words that Moved Millions* is to explore how God reveals redemptive gifts through seasons. It mirrors the disciplined act of an archer.

An archer takes a careful stance, then nocks an arrow (the Redemptive Gift). With a controlled motion, they pull the bow to full draw, anchoring their hand. In this moment of intense focus, they aim.

That aim represents a Season.

Then comes the *Release*. The archer lets the arrow fly, holding their stance until it hits the target.

In a particular season of our corporate growth, God's aim was perfect. He released a "written revival"—books that acted like flashing lights on a marquee, all proclaiming: *"This way."*

The Opera: Vox Dei: Revelatio Ultima (Latin for "Voice of God: The Final Revelation")
The stage is set.
7 Characters = 7 Redemptive Gifts. 7 Books that Moved Millions within their published timeline. And God's timeline-arrow pointing to **Today**.

The Finger of God: Aiming Your Hard-Wired Purpose

"THE FINGER OF GOD" — that is the released arrow.

This is a beautiful and comprehensive way to see how God orchestrates a timeless symphony through the unique "light gifts" He has hard-wired into each of us. By blending the biblical foundations of Psalm 119, the real-world impact of these written revivals, and the calls to action found in "Coaching Quotes," we can see how His love story—*the Restoration of All Things*—is unfolding.

It moves through every generation, like a beacon, flashing a singular message:

"This way."

Before you go...

Consider,

How Good is God? (Pause and answer that for yourself right now.)

Your Timeline... (Where has the arrow of His purpose landed in your life?)

HOW GOOD IS GOD!

HARD-WIRED

Definition: *Inherent. Innate. Unchangeable. Connected permanently to a power source.*

You are not a random assembly of parts. You are a deliberate design.

The Finger of God did not just form you; **It pointed you.**

Next page. The game is about to begin.

The Conductor: Prophet

Coaching Church | Calling the Symphony to Order

"A good coach will make his players see what they can be,

rather than what they are."

— **Ara Parseghian** | *Legendary College Football Coach*

THE PROPHET'S GIFT CHALLENGES US to see with divine sight.

It is a spirit perfectly captured in the opening stanzas of Psalm 119. The psalmist embodies this zeal, declaring, "*My soul is consumed with longing for your judgments at all times.*"

This same passion for truth was the heartbeat of *The Shack (2007),* a prophetic work that challenged traditional views of God, much like the unexpected outcome of Super Bowl XLII (2008). In that game, the underdog New York Giants prophetically overthrew the undefeated Patriots' seemingly unassailable perfect season.

Both the book and the game functioned like a beacon, helping readers and fans see what could be, rather than what they had always assumed.

The Pressure of Prophetic Truth

The Prophet's gift lives under the fierce pressure of truth, challenging hypocrisy and demanding alignment with the original score of God's heart.

This contrasts sharply with the Mercy-Giver's gift, which carries the divine mandate to comfort, defining the ambiance and prioritizing emotional safety.

While the Mercy-Giver creates the safe room for healing, the Prophet must often walk in first and shine the blinding light that reveals the unhealed wound. It's the difference between the *Conductor* demanding perfect harmony and the *Flute* ensuring the music reaches the heart.

Both are essential, but the Prophet will always risk offense to deliver the breakthrough truth needed to move the ball forward.

The Shack by William P. Young

Redemptive Gift & Time: As a **Prophet's** gift, *The Shack* was a book for its time, emerging in 2007 when many were feeling disillusioned with organized religion and institutional hurt. Its message was a timely challenge to a rigid, distant image of God, daring to be a beacon of light in a dark moment for many.

History, Core Value & Takeaways: Originally a self-published work shared among friends, it swiftly became a "written revival" that moved millions. Its **Core Value** is the unshakeable truth that God, in the form of the relational Trinity, is deeply present in our deepest pain.

How Good is God? He is so good that He would rather offend tradition than lose relationship.

This book was a beacon, declaring that God desires an intimate connection with us that exists entirely beyond the confines of doctrine and institutional hurt. The breakthrough it offered was the blueprint of a relational God, accessible to anyone.

"Like the Conductor, the Prophet brings clarity and truth to a messy world..."

Final Summary

For many, the blueprint of a relational God has been a lasting and healing force. The book opened their Rhema thought, to a divine voice they couldn't hear before.

For others, it was a momentary conversation piece or a point of theological contention rather than a permanent change in their relationship with God.

But regardless of the reception, this book served as a prophetic wake-up call. Its blueprint for healing through a personal connection to the Trinity has endured, helping a generation find a way back to God's love and acceptance.

Before you go...

Consider: Did the blueprint remain for you? (Has your view of the Trinity shifted from "Doctrine" to "Relationship"?)

HOW GOOD IS GOD!

THE HEARTBEAT

The Invisible Engine

In a stadium band, you watch the Drum Major, but you *feel* the percussion.

If the lead singer misses a note, it's a mistake. If the rhythm section drags, the whole song falls apart.

The Servant Gift is not a "doormat" for the team. They are the **Metronome** of the Kingdom.

Their Authority: To set the pace. To cleanse the atmosphere. To make sure the rest of the team is playing in time.

"You don't just do the work. You set the tone."

The Rhythm Section: Servant

Coaching Church | Setting the Pace of Purpose

"The first thing a coach needs to know is that he's a servant."

— **Bill Parcells** | *Hall of Fame NFL coach known as "The Big Tuna," who won two Super Bowls with the New York Giants and specialized in turning around struggling franchises.*

THE SERVANT'S GIFT IS ONE OF HUMBLE, diligent obedience—a practical application of God's commands that is beautifully captured in the psalm's verses.

The psalmist reflects this spirit by pleading, "My soul clings to the dust; give me life according to your word!" and promising, "I will run in the way of your commandments when you enlarge my heart!"

This foundational obedience was the heartbeat of *The Purpose Driven Life* (2002), which provided a clear, step-by-step path for millions to serve God.

Its message resonated with the essence of Super Bowl XXXVI (2002). In that game, the New England Patriots, a team of disciplined, humble servants, defeated the star-studded St. Louis Rams through a unified, purposeful game plan. It was that very playbook of a servant-led life, guiding them into the end zone.

The Servant's breakthrough is the *enlargement of the heart* that allows them to live with intention, not just follow a checklist.

The Servant's Authority

The Servant's authority is the highest because God trusts their humility. This reveals *How Good is God!*—He empowers the meek to be the indispensable foundation.

Unlike the Prophet who calls us to see a new truth, the Servant calls us to do the next right thing. The *Rhythm Section* holds the beat, even if the Conductor is demanding a difficult tempo change. Without the Servant, the symphony has no pulse.

The Purpose Driven Life *by Rick Warren*
Redemptive Gift & Time: As a Servant's gift, *The Purpose Driven Life arrived in 2002,* a time when many were searching for meaning and stability after the 9/11 attacks. It provided a clear, purposeful roadmap in a chaotic world, serving humanity in its most urgent spiritual need.

History, Core Value & Takeaways: The book became one of the best-selling non-fiction books in history. Its **Core Value** is that life is not about us; it's about God. Our purpose is found in a life of humble service to His plan.

Did the Blueprint Remain?

The 40-day challenge provided a powerful, hands-on blueprint for a generation of readers. The blueprint has remained for those who continued to live with a servant's heart. But for many, it was a temporary spiritual exercise that did not fully transform their understanding of their **IAMness.**

Final Summary

This book's servant-led blueprint for finding purpose resonated with a generation in search of meaning. It offered a practical and enduring plan for living life with intention and a foundation for a Christian life lesson.

Before you go...

Consider: Are you holding the beat? (Is your service a checklist, or is it the rhythm of a heart enlarged by God?)

HOW GOOD IS GOD!

THE CONCERTMASTER

The Guardian of the Pitch

Before the symphony plays a single bar of music, one violin stands up.

They don't play a melody. They play a standard. **The "A".**

If the First Chair is sharp, the orchestra screams. If the First Chair is flat, the orchestra drags. If they wobble, the masterpiece becomes a mess.

The **Teacher Gift** holds the frequency of Truth. They don't make up the notes; they ensure we are playing the ones the Composer wrote.

We don't tune to the crowd. We tune to the King.

The First Chair Violin: Teacher

Coaching Church | The Discipline of Truth

"Winning is a habit. Unfortunately, so is losing."
— **Vince Lombardi** | *Legendary NFL Coach*

THE TEACHER'S GIFT BUILDS AN UNSHAKABLE foundation of faith through methodical and loyal study.

The psalmist embodies this by declaring, "The law of your mouth is better to me than thousands of gold and silver pieces" and asking God to "teach me your statutes."

This meticulous nature was at the core of *The Prayer of Jabez* (2002), a book that took a single, obscure verse and built a powerful, foundational teaching around it.

This spiritual work mirrors the re-downloaded playbook in our DNA. It's simple, repeatable practice mirrored the disciplined, fundamental execution of Quarterback Tom Brady at Super Bowl XXXVIII (2004). In that game, Brady methodically led his team to a game-winning field goal.

The victory was not a result of a Hail Mary, but of a methodical process—just as the Teacher's gift helps us build winning habits in our faith.

How Good is God? He provides the unshakable framework so our breakthrough isn't accidental, but disciplined. While the Servant is the steady Rhythm Section, the Teacher is the First Chair Violin—demanding technical precision and accuracy to ensure the entire symphony is played without error or confusion.

The Prayer of Jabez by Bruce Wilkinson
Redemptive Gift & Time: The **Teacher's** gift took aim with bow, arrow and target in the early 2000s. It was a time of widespread interest in self-improvement and "unlocking" one's potential. This book provided a simple, concise teaching that gave readers a foundational principle for expanding their influence for God's glory.

History, Core Value & Takeaways: A short, accessible book, it became a massive success for its promise of a simple, biblical prayer for blessing and favor. Its **Core Value** is not the prayer itself, but the discipline of teaching it represents.

The book powerfully demonstrates that a simple, repeatable spiritual practice, when applied with meticulous focus (the Teacher's gift), acts as the foundational key to enlarging our lives. It proves that spiritual expansion is achieved through consistent, disciplined habit, not complex ritual.

Did the Blueprint Remain? The blueprint of a specific prayer technique was easy to adopt. Its lasting impact depended on whether readers saw it as a starting point for a deeper prayer life or a "quick fix" for blessings. For many, it laid a powerful foundation for continued prayer and a deeper faith journey.

Final Summary

This book offered a methodical entry point into the power of prayer. It taught a generation that God's blessings are accessible, provided we have the discipline to ask and the foundation to receive.

Before you go...

Consider: Are you practicing a habit or a ritual? (Is your faith built on a "Hail Mary" hope, or the winning habit of daily love—ignited discipline?)

The Trumpet: Exhorter

Coaching Church | Igniting the Call

"Coaching is the universal language of change and learning."
— **Pat Summitt** | *Hall of Fame Basketball Coach*

THE EXHORTER'S GIFT— THE "TRUMPET"— uplifts and inspires with words of hope, igniting a powerful, in-motion faith.

This energy is perfectly reflected in Psalm 119: "Oh, how I love your law! It is my meditation all the day."

This same spirit was embodied in *Jesus Calling* (2004), a book that provided a daily, personal dose of encouragement and inspiration to millions of readers, helping them to hear their own *Heavenly-Origin.*

Its message echoed the thrilling climax of Super Bowl XLIII (2009). In the fourth quarter, Larry Fitzgerald's last-minute, exhilarating touchdown run gave a powerful, exhorted moment of hope. It spoke the universal language of change, electrifying the stadium and making the crowd believe that victory was within reach.

The Ignition of Faith

If the *Teacher* provides the necessary meticulous structure for faith, the *Exhorter* provides the ignition and spontaneous energy needed to run the play.

The Exhorter does not just study the playbook; they scream, *"We can do this!"* and rally the team when the clock is winding down.

Jesus Calling by Sarah Young

Redemptive Gift & Time: As an **Exhorter's** gift, *Jesus Calling* arrived in 2004, a time when many were seeking intimacy and personal connection with a God who felt distant. The book's personal, first-person format provided a direct, encouraging antidote to this spiritual hunger.

History, Core Value & Takeaways: Based on the author's personal journals, this devotional became a global phenomenon for its direct, loving, and reassuring tone. Its **Core Value** is that God is an ever-present comforter who desires intimate, daily conversations with us.

How Good is God? He is so relentlessly good that He speaks personally every morning just to ensure you feel seen.

Did the Blueprint Remain? The daily devotional format provided a sustainable blueprint for many. The blueprint remained for those who were encouraged to listen for God's voice and to trust that He desires to speak to them personally, bridging heaven and earth.

Final Summary

This book stripped away the complexity of religion and replaced it with the simplicity of a voice. It taught a generation that God is not just to be studied (Teacher) or served (Servant), but to be *heard*.

Before you go...

Consider: Is your faith a monologue or a conversation? (Do you only speak to God, or do you pause long enough to let the Trumpet speak back?)

The Harp: Giver

Coaching Church | Fueling the Kingdom

"The difference between a successful person and others is not a lack of strength, not a lack of knowledge, but a lack of will."
— **Vince Lombardi** | *Legendary NFL Coach*

THE GIVER'S GIFT IS A SPIRIT of profound provision, leveraging resources to fuel the Kingdom. The psalmist captures this by declaring, "I love your commandments more than gold, more than fine gold."

This spiritual generosity was the heart of *Heaven Is for Real* (2010), a book that served as a gift of tangible hope and evidence of heaven's reality. This work was like an arrow released to its intended target, a sentiment that resonated with Super Bowl XLIV (2010).

In that game, the New Orleans Saints claimed victory. For a city still rebuilding from the devastation of Hurricane Katrina, their win was not just a sports statistic; it was a unifying, collective gift of healing and joy that was willed into existence.

The Quiet Power of Provision
The Giver's gift often operates quietly, like the **Harp** in the orchestra, but leverages the necessary resources to fuel the entire Kingdom.

If the **Prophet** provides the *vision* for where we need to go, the **Giver** provides the *fuel* that makes the journey possible, sustaining the other gifts in their work.

Heaven is for Real by Todd Burpo

Redemptive Gift & Time: As a **Giver's** gift, *Heaven is for Real* emerged in 2010, at a time when personal stories—particularly those with extraordinary claims—were highly sought after. It gave the world a simple, faith-affirming story that functioned as a divine gift of provision.

History, Core Value & Takeaways: A family's account of their son's near-death experience became a global sensation. Its **Core Value** is that heaven and the divine are real, tangible places.

How Good is God? He uses the Giver's gift to provide the necessary fuel—whether emotional, spiritual, or material—to sustain the lives of others. It reminded people that God is present in our lives in powerful ways.

Did the Blueprint Remain? The blueprint of tangible hope was a powerful, emotional gift. Its impact has remained for those who needed a profound sign of hope and comfort in a time of questioning. For others, it was a passing fad that didn't fundamentally change their worldview, but for a season, it provided a much-needed provision.

Final Summary

As a Giver's gift, this book provided a simple, powerful story of hope that functioned as a divine provision for millions. It left a blueprint of assurance about the reality of heaven and the presence of God that has endured as a source of comfort for many.

It fulfilled the Giver's role as the **"Harp"**—the quiet force that adds depth and harmony—to maintain the Symphony.

Before you go...

Consider: What is your fuel? (Are you hoarding your resources, or are you the Giver leveraging them to fuel the Kingdom?)

The Cellos and Basses: Ruler

Coaching Church | Building the Empire

"I'm a great believer in luck, and I find the harder I work the more I have of it."

— **Thomas Jefferson**

THE RULER'S GIFT BRINGS ORDER TO CHAOS, establishing a logical, structured foundation for others to stand on.

The psalmist reflects this conviction: *"Your righteousness is forever, and your law is truth."*

This same spirit was embodied in *More than a Carpenter* (1977), a work of apologetics that provided a powerful, evidenced-based framework for faith.

This approach mirrored the dominant Pittsburgh Steelers dynasty at Super Bowl XIII (1979). Their victory was not accidental; it was the result of a powerful, well-ordered system built on foundational principles of excellence. It was a testament to the ruler's ability to use the playbook effectively to build a dynasty.

How Good is God! He is so good that He provides the unshakeable order (the Rule) necessary to break through the chaos of "Hell, Pew, and Pulpit."

A Story Within a Story

This solid evangelical outreach holds a special place in my timeline. It was the only book on this list I had not read before entering into this writing project.

Though I am not naturally persuaded by logic or science to underscore my faith, I found Josh McDowell's testimonial research confirmed my years of transformational experience. I will forever remember God's signature on that day.

I purchased this pocket sized paperback, tagged in bright yellow letters **"MORE THAN 10,000,000 IN PRINT WORLDWIDE!"**— from the local used bookstore.

Inside, I found a penciled inscription:

To Morris, "2008." Hoping God will speak to you! Love Ben and Nora.

That same afternoon, I received a curious text message from my eldest son, Joseph. A retired Marine who served two tours of Afghanistan, he is currently enjoying a season of serving people as a shuttle driver for a local car dealership.

He sent me an image.

Lying on the passenger seat of his shuttle van was a hardback copy of *More than a Carpenter*—a random thank-you gift from a customer that very day.

Science can explain this simultaneous occurrence as chance. I prefer to describe it as God *quantum entangling Himself* in my heart, the heart of my children and now the value of this chapter.

More than a Carpenter *by Josh McDowell*
Redemptive Gift & Time: As a **Ruler's** gift, *More Than a Carpenter* was first published in 1977 and revised for decades. Its longevity speaks to a perennial need for intellectual arguments for faith, particularly during times of academic and cultural skepticism. It brought order to the chaos of doubt.

The Symphony Connection: The Ruler *(Cellos and Basses)* provides the powerful, foundational structure and harmony that the Exhorter *(Trumpet)* plays upon, ensuring the entire symphony has stability and direction.

History, Core Value & Takeaways: A classic work of Christian apologetics, its **Core Value** is that the case for Jesus's deity is not based on blind faith but on historical evidence.

Did the Blueprint Remain? The book's blueprint for a rational faith has remained foundational for generations of believers. It provided a clear, ordered system for thinking about Christianity. Its impact is long-lasting, continuing to be a go-to resource for finding purpose through faith.

Final Summary

This book, a testament to the Ruler's gift, established a lasting blueprint for a logical and evidence-based faith. It provided an ordered system of thinking that has ruled over the chaos of doubt for decades.

This "ordered system" is the very mechanism that allows the Ruler to receive and recognize supernatural phenomena—like the synchronized text message from a son.

Before you go...

Consider: Is your faith built on chaos, or a firm foundation? *(Do you have the structure in place to recognize when God is quantum entangling your life?)*

HOW GOOD IS GOD!

THE BREATH

The Sound of Intimacy

Percussion is struck. Strings are plucked. Brass is buzzed. But the Woodwind must be **breathed** into.

The Mercy gift lives closest to the mouth of God. They operate on the exhale of the Father.

While the Prophet shouts the warning and the Ruler builds the wall, the Mercy gift does something far more dangerous to the enemy:

They invite the King into the room.

WITHOUT THE SPIRIT, THE LETTER KILLS.

The Flute or Oboe: Mercy

Coaching Church |The Atmosphere of Healing

"You can accomplish anything you want in life

if you don't care who gets the credit."

— **Zig Ziglar** | *Motivational Coach*

THE MERCY—GIFT—THE FLUTE OR OBOE—offers a compassionate framework for healing relationships, bringing a beautiful, tender sound to the symphony of mankind.

The psalmist's plea in Psalm 119 reflects this, crying, *"Let my cry come before you, O Lord; give me understanding according to your word!"*

This compassionate spirit was at the heart of *The Five Love Languages*(1995), a book that offered a practical system for healing and restoring relationships.

Its success paralleled the well-oiled machine of the San Francisco 49ers dynasty at Super Bowl XXIX (1995). Their victory was built on the atmosphere of respect and harmony. It proved that a team that cares about the community—and not the individual glory—creates something truly amazing.

The Safe Room of the Spirit
Unlike the **Prophet** who brings truth through confrontation, the **Mercy-Giver** brings truth through understanding.

They hear God with their heart, ensuring the spiritual climate is safe enough for the Prophet's word to land without causing trauma. They define the ambiance of the Kingdom.

The Five Love Languages by Gary Chapman

Redemptive Gift & Time: As a **Mercy-Giver's** gift, *The Five Love Languages* was released in 1995, a period marked by rising divorce rates and a growing recognition of the need for relational health. It offered a practical, compassionate solution to common relationship problems.

History, Core Value & Takeaways: Based on a relational framework discovered in counseling, its **Core Value** is that understanding and speaking your partner's primary "love language" is key to a healthy relationship.

How Good is God? He provides the tender framework that defines the ambiance of love, making sure no one is unseen or unheard.

Did the Blueprint Remain? The blueprint of the Five Love Languages has become a cultural touchstone and has remained a foundational tool for countless couples. Its impact is enduring and continues to be used widely in counseling, ministry, and daily life, as it provides a practical way to show compassion and understanding.

Final Summary
As a Mercy-giver's guide, this book provided a compassionate, healing blueprint for relational health. Like the Flute/Oboe moving in a gentle melody, its timeless wisdom has remained as a guide for couples and families for decades.

It proves that the most enduring impact often comes not from the loudest noise, but from the safest sound.

Before you go…

Consider: What does your life sound like? (Does your presence sound like a clashing cymbal, or a healing melody?)

HOW GOOD IS GOD!

THE SIGNATURE

The Seal of Authenticity

Mass production has no soul. Factory lines create copies, but they do not create art.

Value is determined by one thing: **Who signed the work.**

The ridges on your fingertips are not random lines. They are the evidence that the Artist touched the clay while it was still wet.

You are not a reprint. You are a *bespoke* creation.

The Fingerprint of God is the only ID you need.

He Left His Fingerprint: Opus

Coaching Church | Your Divine Design

"Talent is God-given. Be humble. Fame is man-given. Be grateful.

Conceit is self-given. Be careful."

— **John Wooden** | *Legendary UCLA Basketball Coach*

OPUS (Latin for 'work'): This is the divine, complete musical work—God's masterpiece—which includes your unique design.
Words that Moved Millions + Redemptive Gifts + Your Timeline = OPUS.

This section invited you to confront the profound connection between your unique design and the timeless wisdom of God's "Arrow" Words. It encourages you to experience your **End Zone** by listening for His voice in the chronological details of your life.

Now, let's allow Jesus's questions to lead you into a deeper conversation about your own journey and the words He is speaking to you.

A Direct Conversation with Jesus
   1. **"Do you believe that I am able to do this?" (Matthew 9:28)**
Jesus asked this of two blind men seeking healing, getting to the heart of their faith and His power to act on their behalf. God is pointing out the gifts He's sent for our generation—each one a "light gift" with the power to transform.
   "As this settles in your spirit, lean into the headset and ask:

   'Jesus, do I truly trust that You are the Architect of my expansion? Am I ready to be coached past my own limits and into the weight of Your sovereign plan?'

   Stay in the huddle; listen for the compassionate Truth that silences the crowd of doubt and activates your faith for the field."

   2. **"What are you thinking in your hearts?" (Luke 5:22)**
When religious leaders were silently questioning Him, Jesus asked this question, revealing that He knows our every thought. The gifts God gave you are hard-wired into your innermost being.
   In a quiet moment, ask Jesus:
   "What are the thoughts in my heart about my own identity and purpose?"

   Be still and listen to what He reveals about how He sees you, far beyond the noise and opinions of the world.

   3. **"What are you talking about?" (Luke 24:17)**
Jesus asked this of the disciples on the road to Emmaus, inviting them to share the story of their sorrow and confusion. This is an invitation for you to have an open conversation about your own journey.

Ask Jesus:
"What is the story of my life that I want to share with You? Where have I seen You at work in my personal end zone, and where have I missed Your voice?"

Use this as an opportunity to be completely honest with Him.

Reflect and Respond
Activation for the Reader: Take a moment to write down what you heard from Jesus in this conversation. What did you learn about the path He has had you on and your own unique design? What is one step you can take today to act on what He has revealed?

____

____

____

____

Next Step

Over the coming week, pay close attention to the intuitive nudges and ideas that arise within you. Holy Spirit is flooding your spirit. Practice honoring those urges, knowing they are guiding you to your personal End Zone.

God is always talking through the entire game.

Prayer and Contemplation

Father, thank you for the divine plan You have woven into my true-I-am-ness. Thank you for never giving up on me and for continuing to speak to me.

I surrender my will to Yours and ask for the courage to act on what I hear. Show me how to live anchored in I AM, adopt a spirit of growth, and partner with Our light gifts to bring glory to Your name. In Jesus' name, Amen.

The Snap: Crossing the Line of Scrimmage

"You don't play to the crowd; you play to the clock. And when the clock runs out on doubt, the only voice that matters is the Coach's voice in your headset."

— Kristen Wambach

I TOLD YOU THAT WAS A HAIL MARY.

It was the reach of a spirit that refuses to settle for the "mysterious ways" of a distant God. Now, we are standing at the line of scrimmage.

Remembering what He has placed on the corporate table of communion isn't a history lesson; it is the fuel that supports us in our Oneness.

Your faith has brought you here. It has made it possible to usher in the presence of God and witness, for yourself, how utterly Good He is. The Holy Spirit is reaching out to help us arrive on the same page—not a page of religious agreement or legal doctrine, but the page where the Rhema conversation is finally at hand.

The clock has run out on the manmade ways of "doing, leaving, returning and loving" His church. It's time to listen to the only Voice that matters.

May I have the privilege of introducing you to:

HOW GOOD IS GOD?

Coaching Church *Beyond the Gates of Hell, to Truly Experience Heaven.*

Introduction

DEATH, HEAVEN, AND HELL. We *got* it wrong. We don't just *have* it wrong; we were taught a version that entirely missed the audacious goodness of God.

There is a difference between "getting" it and "having" it. To *get* implies it was attained or achieved by us. To *have* means we are simply in possession of it. The Author started life out spiritually blind; I failed to recognize **How Good God Is**, and therefore, I was not in possession of the truth.

And this is my *letter*—a manifesto, so to speak. It is not a fiction story or a memoir, though those journeys are written in *The UnFinished Book.*

At its foundation, a letter is simply an epistle. The Greek word is *epistolē* (ἐπιστολή), which literally means "message" or "letter."

The difference lies in the message's weight and purpose. Historically, an epistle carries the authority of a formal blueprint, designed for teaching and enduring impact. While this book conveys foundational truth with that same weight, my intent is to offer you both: the powerful philosophy of an epistle delivered through the relational intimacy of a personal letter.

This is a direct conversation, designed not to keep you at a distance, but to draw you into the heart of realizing **How Good is God!**

"I've observed that if individuals who prevail in a high competitive environment have any one thing in common besides success, it is failure —and their ability to overcome it."

—**Bill Walsh** | *Head Coach, San Francisco 49ers (1979-88)*

My intent of this "*letter*" is to point True North and believe in you, the reader, even if you find my words challenging or hard to understand. I exercise the **"One Faith | One Body | One Baptism | One Spirit"** belief, trusting that the genuine heart of the *letter* will sustain a conversation rooted in our mutual love of God.

This letter is written in freedom, remembering the religious prison I once inhabited, and honoring the individuals who encouraged me not to conform.

To believe God in the unusual. To see Jesus in simplicity. To ask many questions. To ask for forgiveness as often as the room fills with tension. To follow the passions in my heart.

For every cause, there is a reason or effect. Jesus paid for it all. He is the guarantee to every right thought we choose to employ. And that guarantor lives inside of us, regardless of our permissions.

"So our guarantee is the Christ-Likeness in you, me, and us.

How Good is God? This is your answer— He secured the truth inside you."

THE GAME PLAN
There are many different conquests or sporting themes in which to move a ball into play—a concert of strength, agility, and partnership. I have played many.

In most, I have better-than-average competence and fiercer competitiveness.

Bowling and Corn Hole seem to be my biggest challenge; my feminine curves distract my swing in more ways than one. But this is not bowling or Corn Hole!

"Ability is what you're capable of doing. Motivation determines what you do. Attitude determines how well you do it."

—**Lou Holtz** | *Head coach, New York Jets (1976)*

WHAT IF REVELATION WAS THE BALL?
| **Revelation is** gentle strength to heal the Mom whose son committed suicide.

| **Revelation's brilliance** reaches back into the depths of Sheol to change a stage-four cancer patients behavior from shutting off to opening up to their family for support.

| **The wonder of Revelation** stands as a living bridge for every aborted or miscarried child to speak redemption's "Hello," love, forgiveness, humility, changing the life of the mother who walks in known or unknown grief.

| **The spirit of Revelation** climbs across religious boundaries and the strongholds of man, declaring: Neither death or life or angels or principality, nor powers, nor things present, nor things to come, nor height, nor depth, nor any other creature, shall be able to separate us from the love of God. Not even ourself!

| **Revelation inspires** those who encounter love's Genesis to preach the Gospel farther than the life and time they perceive.

| **Bold Revelation** follows Jesus where the Spirit and the Bride say, "Come."

A Note to the Skeptic

There won't be much surprise if some theological defenses go up. I understand that. Your hermeneutics might determine a fantastic argument, and years in the classroom of theology are valuable.

But I am not asking you to dismantle your theology; I am asking you to expand your expectation.

You might be tempted to say, *"God is good, but..."* adding that His goodness is reserved for another day, or a different dispensation. But death is currently holding the flagstick marking the hole, and I believe we are called to play through.

This is **Revealed Truth.** I am protecting its right to exist, not to win an argument, but to offer an encounter. Even if your mind wrestles with the words, I invite your spirit to listen. You might just find the goodness you've been longing for.

"We would accomplish many more things

if we did not think of them as impossible."
—**Vince Lombardi** | *Legendary NFL Coach*

Personally, I would rather write to you in the beautiful pen theme of Julian Fellowes. I'd prefer a romantic novel of prose, villains you love to hate, hierarchical society, the "upstairs and downstairs" conquest played out in the luxuriant rooms of historical mansions. Maggie Smith or Judi Dench always get to say what everybody is really thinking.

But that is not the play we are running.

"Each person holds so much power within themselves that needs to be let out. Sometimes they just need a little nudge, a little direction, a little support, a little coaching, and the greatest things can happen."
—**Pete Carroll** | *Super Bowl Winning Head Coach*

Now, can we talk | Jesus?

"If I'm wrong, the life of Christ I live today,

will show me the truth and share it, tomorrow."
—**Kristen Wambach** | *Mother of four incredible sons.*

"I've been ready for this my whole life." —Rudy, Rudy (film)

Note from the Author

Have you ever sat in a Glory Moment? Coaching Church | The Trade for Intimacy

The way to enter into that revival
is through praise and worship.
No book has been written on what God is about to do.
Nobody has been this way before...
—Ruth Ward Heflin *(1939–1998)*

RUTH WARD HEFLIN WAS AN INTERNATIONALLY recognized voice who championed the doctrine of Praise and Worship as the primary pathway to revival. I once had the honor to sit in one of her three-day meetings.

It begs the question: Have you ever sat in a glory moment?
It is that "Ah-ha" vibrating deep inside of you. You know that sharing this moment—a very vulnerable moment from your life— would open doors, speak of a common struggle. But it also invites judgements maybe you might not be ready to deflect.

Like a twinkle from the future, you recognize your transformed self in God. It is His address, His threshold, a timeless entry. Why do they call it a "Pinch me" Moment?

Because *pain* is the invisible underline the words of glory sit upon.

The Piano Bench

When I transitioned into a teenager, my Mom decided that piano would bring a greater value in my life than the ballet lessons I had been taking since the age of three.

(Today, my granddaughter can wear and dance in my vintage toddler black ballet slippers, which I unpack annually and hang on my Christmas tree. Redemption has a way of circling back.)

But at the time? Piano lessons were a tough transition.

While my peers were way ahead of me, my recital pieces made me feel like "Clifford the Big Red Dog" amongst the satin sashes and pink bows of the grammar school girls. Boys, athletics, cheerleading and social pressures ticked the boxes of distraction. I never practiced the piano.

And here is another "But God" moment: Mrs. Ediger, a mint farmer's wife, and my patient piano teacher, managed to get enough basic theory in my head that God would resurrect it years later to draw me to Himself.

Dance will always move me: however, black and white keys saved me.

My hidden self-destruction was about to be wooed on the piano bench my Mom so rightfully chose to invest in. Music has the power to eradicate shame and a soothing safety to clarify value. It was a sound I hungered to hear, and redemption only He can provide.

***Brené Brown** masterfully describes it: "I believe that there is a profound difference between shame and guilt. I believe that guilt is adaptive and helpful; it's holding something we've done or failed to do up against our values and feeling psychological discomfort.*

> *I define shame as the intensely painful feeling or experience of believing that we are flawed and therefore unworthy of love and belonging—something we've experienced, done, or failed to do makes us unworthy of connection.*
>
> *I don't believe shame is helpful or productive. In fact, I think shame is much more likely to be the source of destructive, hurtful behavior than the solution or cure." | Brené Brown, Research Professor and Author*

The Song I Threw Away

Holy Spirit introduced Himself here, to a Wife and young Mom, invited once again to sit on the piano bench where she never practiced.

Up to now, neither the lack in doctrines nor pride of religion could manifest, spell, write, or announce anything close to the goodness and nature of God's Own living spirit. He touched me.

For hours, Holy Spirit and I wrote, played, moved ,and sang. He healed. My worship was loosed; my hands, arms and feet were freed to move. And the joy of dance from all those upstair-bowling-alley ballet studios was re-birthed.

During my evangelical years I attended a women's conference in Portland, Oregon. This was before my journaling days, so I rely on memory. It was a crowd of Jesus loving women and a very famous worship leader whose songs you knew from the radio.

There was a call for freedom, but still so many restrictions no one talked about.

I remember the days of radical boldness—pushing through life's hiccups and shaking in your boots. I approached the worship leader and mentioned a special song I had written. Graciously she invited me to meet with her the next afternoon.

With music in hand and jitters in my stomach, I shared it with her, singing from my secret place. When I finished, tears streamed down her face. She was so affable, making me feel important, and said she wanted to share this with her producer.

We exchanged phone numbers.

What a whirlwind. I talked with the Lord all the way home and couldn't wait to tell Don.

But then came the hidden wisdom, of the secret place.

I made a tough decision that day; I chose not to share/promote the song I wrote about having an abortion.

I didn't want people to "know" me, find popularity, or in today's language—"follow me" because of my sin, shortcomings, weakness, or fear.

Something arose in me—a gift I only wanted to give Him. This wasn't just a hymn about human life and frailties. It was about the freedoms that had occurred in my voice, body and emotions. The only words my spirit heard and sang were *Hallelujahs* to His name.

If people were to know me, it was because they saw the Glory of God in my life, not the history of my shame.

I literally threw the song in the trash and never sang it again. I have no memory of the tune or words. Only, that it was divinely special.

The Path of Hiddenness

This took me on a path of hiddenness.

It's not a stretch for me to suggest you can relate to my story. For a "cheerleader," it felt like being stripped of the title for which I had been called. No pom-poms, no uniform, no sisterhood and no "Crowd," to encourage.

For years, the behind-the-scenes servant with a leader's call. I attended a buzz-illion faith conferences secretly yearning to share the platform, sit on its stage edge, dangle my feet and have a "real" conversation about Jesus, with you!

I can't tell you how many times I'd meet an individual, have a brief conversation and they'd say, *"You were the speaker God intended for me to meet, why aren't you up on the stage speaking?"*

Why wasn't I? Little did I know what a HUGE trade I made years ago.

I raised my boys, loved and fought with my husband (who had no idea how to encourage "his" cheerleader), and—a BIG AND, I took up a conversation with God and wrote down every delicious encounter.

My crowning accomplishments?

- I am still married and have rounded the corner of our 43rd anniversary.
- I love our boys (4 adult sons and 2 daughters-in-love); they know I'm spiritually quirky, and praise God, they all live within twenty minutes of our home.
- Suzanne, my best friend since eighth grade, has seen me cheer! She sends me the best social media reels as reminders of how much she is going to enjoy when my pom-poms are public again.
- Liesel, my granddaughter. When we hang out, we both get to wear tiaras and tutus. She is my living proof that redemption has come full circle.

The Superman Cape

In this book, I'm going to talk about "Hell"—a word technically not in the Bible (Sheol/Hades), but a word well used to express where we want to send people who ruffle our feathers.

Everyone wants to hear about heaven, until someone dares to remove death as the prerequisite. We will have many conversations about spiritual things, and nope, you can't cast-it-out-of-me what Jesus has so clearly revealed. It is budding, pollinated and producing fruit.

I'll finish the abortion story from the song up above a few chapters in, Trust me, the glory is so much better than the accolades I may have set aside.

How and Why do you read this book?

HOW: Resonation! If it "feels" like the Love of God, and your Spirit dances the jig, this is How Good God is! Put your superman cape on, and may I introduce you to the King of Glory!

Why the Superman Cape? Because Kings rule kingdoms, and you will be invited to sit in His seat, next to the Father. You will understand how to "follow" Jesus and experience His dominion. Your spirit (which remembers Oneness) is without borders or boundaries.

Why? Because your current bandwidth about the Love of God is ready to expand and change.

The Playbook

Coaching Church | The Divine Strategy

I am not gonna coach you to who you are.

I'm gonna coach you to who you should be someday.

—**Doc Rivers** | *NBA Coach*

I did not begin in you; you began in me. I am not your idea; you are mine. I have strategically positioned you in order that you may abound in much fruit bearing, wherever life leads you—fruit that would ceaselessly continue this same incarnate life of union with me. From within this place, anything you desire has already been granted you by my Father. John 15:16 (Mirror Study Bible)

A FOOTBALL PLAYBOOK IS AN ESSENTIAL tool for coaches and players, serving as a comprehensive guide for understanding the strategies and tactics of the game. This document outlines the offensive, defensive, and special teams plays, as well as the roles and responsibilities of each player on the team.

Overview of a Football Playbook

You and I will experience different formations, consider divine strategies, evaluate the results, only to reveal the foundation. A foundation which has always been the same from its genesis as it will be tomorrow.

Our task: How we move the ball (of Life) to arrive at the end results of our transformation?

The Generation of Questions

Like many of you, I arrived on the scene with a "Boom" of babies questioning all the issues that caused our parents to be a generation in silence.

"Children were seen, not heard." In the 1995 film adaptation of Sense and Sensibility, Mrs. Dashwood tells her daughter Margaret, *"If you cannot think of anything appropriate to say, you will please restrict your remarks to the weather."*

But the propriety of change was loosed when Boomers arrived. Hope was in the air with our returning Bride-Grooms and Fathers from war. We carried the confidence of improved economic opportunities and the courage to lead government initiatives for change. We are a generation of first responders. Little did we know that that "first responder title" would move so close to home.

Baby Boomers questioned the quiet faith of our fathers and believed that Church had the same opportunity for economic growth. We wanted more from the gospel, and began to study the currency of heaven and the movement of the spirit.

Bouncing in at the tail end of a generation, fate's twist prepared me with a *Kairos* impact in my home and family. Notably, I was raised with three brothers and then became a parent of four sons. I was accustomed to holding my own around testosterone, but passionate in estrogen—which created the question *WHY* and the burning resolve of *HOW*.

It has been a bit of a bumpy and confusing journey that brings me here today. The complete and redemptive story is found in my debut; The UnFinished Book. I was an author, a strong female, a misinterpreted female in the local church that was still a generation behind—in silence—and found itself threatened by questions.

As if a question would implode its foundation; maybe the structure, but never the foundation.

- Jesus who came to me in my moments of surrender empowered me!
- The Jesus who revealed Himself in every spiritual growth classroom removed the dyslexia that had caused literary lack and transference of clear discernment.
- The Jesus who serves Himself personally to us through communion had a living bowl of fruit to taste of incarnate life.

My sheep know my voice; no earthly DNA could knowingly call forth the person we should be. But through intimate change, we now hunger to be that person. Jesus is our "Life Coach."

"Hunger" and "thirst" never forgets their first meal or drink...

or who invited them.

I began studying the patterns in the Playbook long before my questions ever danced their way into the local church. My early days of renewal were completely Holy Ghost-led in the privacy of my own home. You could say that was where I first learned the "Divine Team" philosophy.

The experience's shared in this book will challenge you to review the game tapes God is highlighting for our generation. (Note: *When I refer to becoming an "adult" in this process, I mean the gritty, ongoing journey of my own sanctification and transformation*).

Throughout these pages, I will lay out a timeline, inviting you to reflect on the personal and shared experiences that shape our lives. When God illuminates these plays, we gain a clear vision that guides us forward together.

Offensive Plays: The "It" Factor

A simple truth applied: If Jesus experienced it—encountered it, laid hands on it, changed it, moved it, spoke to it, prayed for it, washed it, revealed it, walked into it, translated to it, ascended to it, descended to it, subdued it, healed it, delivered it, died for it, raised it... in Him we can have communion with "it."

In football coaching, "it" often refers to the **It Factor**—an intangible, yet crucial, set of qualities that distinguishes exceptional players, teams, or even coaches themselves. It's not something you can easily quantify with statistics or Xs and Os, but rather something you "know when you see it."

Here is a breakdown of what "it" might mean in a coaching context:

For a Player:
- **Clutch Performance:** The ability to consistently make big plays in critical moments. They thrive under pressure.
- **Leadership and Composure:** Inspiring teammates and maintaining a calm demeanor in chaos.
- **Competitive Edge:** An insatiable desire to be the best and a relentless drive.
- **Intangible Instincts:** A natural feel for the game – anticipating plays and reading defenses.
- **Resilience:** The ability to bounce back from mistakes, setbacks, or injuries.
- **Effort and Heart:** Giving 110% effort, showing a passion that influences others.

For a Team:
- **Cohesion and Chemistry:** A collective synergy where they play as one unit.
- **Mental Toughness:** The ability to overcome adversity as a group.
- **Unwavering Belief:** A shared confidence in their system, even when facing a deficit.
- **Execution:** Consistently converting on third downs, or scoring in the red zone.

For a Coach:
  • **Inspiration:** Connecting with players on a deeper level to ignite their passion.
  • **Adaptability:** The foresight to adjust game plans based on changing circumstances.
  • **Presence:** Exuding confidence, and effectively leading a diverse group.
  • **Strategic Vision:** Seeing the "big picture" of the game to build sustained success.

In essence, "it" is the unseen force that propels success. In Him, we can have communion with "it."

How Good is God? The entire playbook is complete because His sacrifice secured every play call.

Defensive Plays: The Armor

TEACHINGS ARE BOUND TO CHRIST

The Bible is not completely void of teachings. However, all the teachings rest on the person Christ Jesus. Only when He has a certain experience can there be a certain doctrine or teaching. Every single doctrine or teaching is bound to His personal experience.

His incarnation is the basis of the union of God with man. His death is the basis of our dying to sin and self and the foundation of a life of holiness. His resurrection is the basis for receiving our new life. Everything we have obtained is based on what He has attained. The doctrines are absolutely based upon the person and bound to the person. This is genuine Christianity.

(*The Normal Christian Faith*, Chapter 6, by **Watchman Nee**)

Special Teams Plays: The Secret Weapons

"On the contrary, in the thick of these things our triumph remains beyond dispute. His love has placed us above the reach of any onslaught. This is my conviction; no threat whether it be in death or life; be it celestial messengers, demon powers or political principalities, nothing known to us

at this time, or even in the unknown future; no dimension of any calculation in time or space, nor any device yet to be invented, has what it takes to separate us from the love of God unveiled in our Lord, Jesus Christ." Romans 8:37-39 (Mirror Translation)

Inside the Guide

The football playbook is like a sacred text for athletes—a guide to victory and a key to the secrets of the game. Let me take you inside this vital guide:

- **Offensive Plays (The Toolbox):** These are tools crafted carefully to outwit opponents. Formations are like star constellations, each player in their perfect spot. Running plays are a dance. Passing plays are a ballet between the quarterback and receivers. Blocking schemes are the walls of a fortress.

- **Defensive Plays (The Armor):** This is the team's armor, shielding them from attacks. Strategic alignments act like the team's eyes and ears, watching the opponent closely. Blitz packages are the warriors, charging ahead boldly.

- **Special Teams Plays (The Secret Weapons):** These are the special ops—kickoff and return plays designed to gain an edge.

- **The Secret Language:** The playbook speaks a secret language of play calls and hand signals, only understood by the team—your private code for hearing God.

- **Practice & Strategy:** Practice drills are the training ground, where skills are sharpened and teamwork is built. Game strategy is the master plan, the path to victory.

Final Summary

The scoreboard is at hand.

Just as a football playbook equips athletes with strategies, formations, and roles to achieve victory, so too does our spiritual journey require intentional preparation, reflection, and execution.

We are not merely participants in life; we are players on a divine team, coached by Jesus Himself, whose teachings and presence guide every move we make.

Consider this your invitation to dive deeper, to reflect on your own life's playbook, and to embrace the lessons woven through personal and shared experiences. Whether you're on offense, defense, or part of the special teams, remember: your purpose is strategically positioned for fruitfulness.

Now is the time to re-evaluate your strategies, examine the game tapes of your life, and move forward with the clarity and courage only found through faith.

Before you go...

Consider: Do you have the "It" Factor? (Pick up your "UnFinished Book." Take action today—step into your purpose, embrace your transformation, and lead with the unique "It Factor" that God has already placed within you.)

HOW GOOD IS GOD!

THE VETERAN

The Authority of the Scar

You don't get the whistle because you bought the jacket. You get the whistle because you know the playbook *and* the pain.

A coach who has never been tackled cannot teach a player how to stand back up.

Real leadership is not about standing above the team. It is about remembering what it feels like to stand **with** them.

The clipboard gives you a **Position.** The cleats give you **Permission.**

You cannot demand what you have not delivered.

Coaches are Players First

Coaching Church | The Art of Arrival

Coaches who can outline plays on a blackboard are a dime a dozen. The ones who win get inside their players and motivate.

—Vince Lombardi

ENVISION THIS SCENARIO: At birth, you're handed a toolkit. Inside, you'll find your redemptive gifts—talents and abilities that are as much a part of you as the color of your eyes or the sound of your laugh. These aren't just any old gifts, these are tailor-made by the Big Guy upstairs.

Think of these gifts as your *Personal Grace Codes,* unlocking your potential and guiding you towards your unique purpose.

How Good is God! His goodness is defined by the absolute personalization of your gifts. They're a reflection of divine grace, a signpost pointing you towards your role in the world.

But before you can lead, you must be led. *Coaches are Players first.*

The Huddle: Defining the Role

I sat down to define exactly what we are doing here. Whether you are talking to a person or processing with "AI," the definition of a coach remains the same.

Question: *What is your definition of Coaching?*

Answer: Coaching is the art of helping someone unlock their potential, clarify their vision, and take intentional action toward their goals. It's not about telling someone what to do-it is about asking the right questions, providing perspective, and holding them accountable to their highest self.

A great coach empowers growth, challenges limiting beliefs, and inspires transformation.

Question: *What's your personal vision for how coaching could impact your life or the lives of others?*

Answer: My mantra: helping you live **Spiritually BRAVE.**

The word B.R.A.V.E Acronym:
- **B**rave Belief
- **R**adiant Resolve
- **A**ctionable Access
- **V**isible Velocity
- **E**xperience the Eternal

The "Brave Avenue"

There is a hidden depth to the word "Brave." Think of it as **BR**-ave (Brave Avenue)

The word "Avenue" comes from the French *allée*, meaning a straight path or tree-lined road. Its Latin source, *venire*, means "to come" or "arrival." In landscaping, an avenue is designed to emphasize the arrival at a grand feature.

This is the goal: To invite people onto a sacred, tree-lined path of restoration and arrival—an arrival into their truest, most aligned selves.

Writing about Coaching is like carrying a flashlight. There is always a flashlight handy, used to have a good look at any shadows that might need moving. We are not forcing change; we are helping people see what has been holding them back so they can move forward with clarity.

The Divine Team Philosophy

Do not allow current religious tradition to mold you into its pattern of reasoning. Like an inspired artist, give attention to the detail of God's desire to find expression in you. Become acquainted with perfection. To accommodate yourself to the delight and good pleasure of Him will transform your thoughts afresh from within. His grace gift inspires me to say to you that your thinking must be consistent with everything that is within you according to the measure of faith that God has apportioned to every individual. Let the revelation of redemption shape your thoughts. The parallel is clear. There are many different members in one body, yet not one competes with the other in function. Instead every individual member co-compliments the other. In Christ, the many individuals are all part of the same body and members of one another. Our gifts may differ in function, but His grace is the same. (Romans 12:2-6a Mirror Bible)

The parallel is clear: **This is the Divine Team philosophy in action.** There are many different members in one body...but one goal.

Final Summary

A coach is someone who tells you what you don't want to hear,

who has you see what you don't want to see,

so you can be who you have always known you could be.

—**Tom Landry** | *Coach of the Dallas Cowboys*

The Synthesis:

Lombardi gets you inside the player, **Romans** gets you inside Christ, and **Landry** forces you to see the true self.

Before you go...

Consider: the B.R.A.V.E Avenue? What is the charge level of the batteries in your flashlight?

The Coached | Player

Coaching Church | Defining Victory

"For me, winning isn't something that happens suddenly
on the field when the whistle blows and the crowds roar.
Winning is something that builds physically and mentally
every day that you train and every night that you dream."
—**Emmitt Smith** | *Football Hall of Fame Running back*

"A winner is someone who recognizes his God-given talents, works his
tail off to develop them into skills, and uses these skills to accomplish his
goals."
—**Larry Bird** | *NBA Legend*

"Competing at the highest level is not about winning.
It's about preparation, courage, understanding and nurturing
your people, and heart. Winning is the result."
—**Joe Torre** | *Legendary MLB Manager*

The Ultimate Definition

We have heard from the legends of the game. But what if
we handed the microphone to the Head Coach?

While directly attributing a new quote to Jesus is speculative, we can infer how His teachings align with and deepen the sentiment of these quotes, focusing on the spiritual and eternal dimensions of "winning."

What would Jesus say?

"And as for me, winning is found not in the fleeting accolades of this world, but in the faithful stewardship of the gifts entrusted to you, in the loving service rendered to your neighbor, and in the enduring pursuit of the kingdom that is within you.

For true victory belongs to the heart made pure, the spirit made humble, and the life poured out for a purpose beyond its own, building treasures where moth and rust cannot corrupt, and where eternal joy is the ultimate prize.

Therefore, walk in faith, not seeking the applause of men but the approval of your Father in Heaven. Let your light shine before others, that they may see your good works and glorify your Father above. Run the race with perseverance, fixing your eyes not on earthly crowns but on the eternal joy set before you.

How Good is God! He designed the race so that the victory is secured not by your striving, but by your faithful stewardship of what He already deposited in your heavenly origin. For in every act of love, every moment of sacrifice, and every heartbeat devoted to the will of God, you will find the true victory that never fades.

*— **Jesus** | King of Kings and Lord of Lords*

Final Summary

I am inspired only because Jesus was just as human as I am.

Father God "coached" Him!

The Coin Toss

Coaching Church | Heads or Tails?

Heads or Tails? *Matt Hasselbeck utters his infamous "We want the ball, and we're going to score" line after winning the coin toss to start overtime in a 2003 wild-card playoff game against the Packers. Instead, Al Harris intercepts a Hasselbeck pass on the sixth play and returns it 52 yards to give the Packers a victory.*

THE COIN IS TOSSED. Let's blow the whistle of truth.

For years, you have been paying rent on the best ocean-front view apartment. Your "overpriced" view affords gorgeous sunsets, watching the sun tuck itself to sleep under the blanket of the horizon.

But the real estate affords you many storms. You've lost countless hours of sleep as the wind whips the rain against your windowpane. It feels like you live just to pay rent.

The quarters are so hemmed in you feel like the Jolly Green Giant in Elf Land. Tiny bed, tiny couch, tiny kitchen, and a meager curtain to separate your ensuite. To say "studio" would conjure up the notion that there is even enough room for a little creativity.

Your giant dreams live in an inadequate space. The vision and view feed your soul, but the reality empties your pocketbook. The cramped quarters are manifesting in your bones.

The Mirror Moment

Imagine for the millionth time; you've pulled the curtain back and are standing in front of the bathroom mirror. Your rearview is depressing. Every wall space is tight, piled and stacked. The under-spaces leave no room for dust bunnies, and the reflection of the person who you are looking at is frustrated.

Your head game on auto-mode is playing pool on a table with no pockets. You've played every angle, arranged every ball, and bumped the back of your pool cue on the wall countless times.

Where is your perfect game? Losing and winning were erased from the outcome because you simply don't have the room to play.

The Spiritual Confinement

This cramped space is more than just bad real estate; it is the spiritual confinement of the Pew and Pulpit structure trying to fit a Giant IAMness into an elf-land doctrine.

Your vision—your *Rhema* Thought—is expansive, like the ocean view. But the traditional system forces it into a "tiny bed" of safe, predictable theology. The walls are tight, the floor is piled high with rules, and the lack of space is literally manifesting in your spirit, leaving you frustrated and unable to execute your perfect game.

The Coin Toss is a decision between trusting your giant, Spirit-led vision or staying in the inadequate, high-rent quarters of human striving.

How Good is God? His goodness is the promise that the view you hold is not a rental; it is your free, eternal *NOW* inheritance.

He isn't asking you to pay rent on a tiny room anymore. He's about to give you the keys to the entire house.

Before you go...

Consider: Did you call it too early? (*Like Hasselbeck, are you declaring victory while standing in a system that is about to intercept your destiny? Or are you ready to move into the mansion God actually built for you?*)

Chapter 1

The ART of Wrestling with God

Talent and Character

"Talent sets the floor, character sets the ceiling."
— **Bill Belichick** | *New England Patriots*

"So Jacob named the place Penuel (face of God), saying, 'I have seen God face-to-face, yet my life has been spared!'"
— *Genesis 32:30 (TPT)*

HOW GOOD IS GOD! He meets us not when we are polished, but when we are wrestling. His divine touch is the very force that transforms our character and seals our new *Union* (Israel).

As you embark on this unique journey through the pages of this book, imagine yourself standing at the edge of a mystical veil. Maybe you are like me, and Jesus has already dramatically redefined what you used to say "yes" to.

But this veil is more than just a metaphor; it represents the threshold between the known and the unknown, the seen and the unseen. Much like Jacob, who wrestled with God through the night in the wilderness of Genesis, you are invited to engage deeply with the ideas within these pages.

Jacob's struggle wasn't just physical; it was a transformative encounter that left him changed, forever marked by the divine touch.

The Encounter
Jacob is traveling back to Canaan when he stops to camp alone by a river. While there, he is wrestled with by a stranger until dawn.

The Wrestling
Jacob wrestles so hard that the stranger cannot overpower him at first. In the end, the stranger dislocates Jacob's hip, and Jacob asks for a blessing.

The Blessing
The stranger gives Jacob the name *Israel*, which means "he struggles with God." Jacob also names the place where they wrestled *Penuel*, which means "face of God" or "facing God."

The Meaning
The story shows how wrestling with God can lead to transformation and a deeper relationship with Him. It serves as a reminder that God meets us in our struggles and offers us divine gifts.

In the same way, this book is designed to be your wrestling ground. Each chapter will challenge you, provoke thought, and, hopefully, lead you to a personal transformation.

"Take notes on your own thoughts."

— **Myron Golden** | *Business Consultant & Author*

As you read, let yourself be open to grappling with the concepts, allowing them to shape your understanding and your journey. As you get to know the writer, you will be asked to lay your Bible aside and **go ask Jesus.**

Allow Him to breathe upon what is currently hidden in your heart and expand your "tent pegs" of knowing.

Knowing: Experiencing an awakening where the visitation never ends. You go in and out and sup with Him.

The Strategy of War

Now, let's weave in the ancient wisdom of Sun Tzu's *The Art of War.*

Sun Tzu taught that the best battles are the ones you win before they're even fought—by understanding yourself and your environment. This principle is applicable not only on the battlefield but also in our desire to know Truth by His first name. Knowing your strengths, weaknesses, and the landscape around you is crucial for success.

Think of this as akin to the evolution of infantry tactics.

I recall the movie *The Patriot*, which graphically displays Revolutionary battles. Soldiers stood shoulder to shoulder, advancing in unison in strategies called "Line Infantry." Every time I see the movie, I am baffled by the thought of men just standing there, out in the open, not taking cover.

This "Line Strategy" prioritized firepower over maneuverability. It was designed to maximize the impact of a volley by presenting a wide frontage to the enemy. It was effective, but rigid.

Line Strategy vs. Adaptive Tactics (Logos vs. Rhema)

The baffling image of soldiers standing shoulder to shoulder in Line Strategy is the perfect picture of a *Logos-driven*, traditional doctrine.

This strategy, employed by the historical Pulpit, prioritizes fixed rules and rigid structures over maneuverability and movement. It is designed to maximize firepower within a safe, predictable formation, often at the cost of personal exposure and high casualty—a costly way to live your faith.

Fast forward to modern-day American football, and you see a similar evolution. Teams now adapt quickly, changing tactics on the fly, much like an entrepreneur navigating the fast-paced shifts of the market. Each player must read the field, anticipate moves, and work in harmony with their teammates to achieve victory.

Adaptive Tactics—where a quarterback reads the defense and changes the play on the fly—is the model for *Rhema-led* faith.

This system prioritizes discernment over dogma. It trusts the living Coach (Jesus) to communicate the shift in the field, allowing the player to operate with grace and velocity, ensuring the structure supports the win rather than confining the players.

A.R.T.

Your wrestling (A.R.T.) is the process of choosing to trade the safety of the fixed Line Strategy for the victorious chaos of Adaptive Tactics.

Active

Recovery

Therapy

Your hip may be out of joint for a season (the trauma/struggle), but that is simply the *Active Recovery Therapy* required to gain the new name (Israel).

Final Summary

As you read, I encourage you to blend these insights—spiritual wrestling, strategic wisdom, and adaptive tactics—into your own life and the lives you have the privilege to influence.

Each page is an opportunity to step beyond the veil and embrace a new perspective, much like how a quarterback reads the defense or a general surveys the battlefield.

May you find not just knowledge, but inspiration, and the courage to act.

So, dear reader, step beyond that veil.

Wrestle with the ideas. Strategize your path. And transform your reality.

Let's begin this extraordinary journey together.

Your invitation: How Good is God?

PLAY SHEET | PROPHET

Prophet Edition
Redemptive Gifts Summary

THIS CHAPTER IS A HEAVYWEIGHT PLAY designed to move you from the sidelines of your talent to the "Wrestling Mat" of your Character.

It is a call to stop relying on the rigid *Line Strategy* of rules and to embrace the *Adaptive Tactics* of a face-to-face encounter with the Divine.

The DNA Wristband Audible Chapter Play Call

1. The Green Dot Helmet (*Individual Redemptive Gift*): **Prophet**

The Green Dot Helmet: *in American Football, is a helmet equipped with a radio receiver that allows a designated player to hear play-calls and tactical adjustments directly from the coaching staff on the sidelines.*

The Setup: The frequency for this play is set to the **Prophet**. This is your gift of "Design and Purpose." You are hardwired to recognize when a *Line Strategy*—a life built on fixed rules and predictable structures—is no longer enough to secure the win.

The Prophet in you isn't content with just having Talent (your floor); it demands an encounter that sets your Character (your ceiling). You are being called to step beyond the veil of the "seen" and wrestle with the Truth until your name is changed.

2. The Coaches' Booth (*Legacy Anchor): The Shack* by William Paul Young

The Coaches' Booth: *a high-vantage press box where assistant coaches and coordinators observe the entire field to analyze defensive schemes, track personnel groupings, and relay strategic adjustments down to the sidelines via headsets.)*

The Connection: In the "Booths" of your spiritual legacy, *The Shack* (Prophet/Design) represents the deep, mystical meeting point where your personal "limp" and your divine purpose collide.

You apply this by realizing that God is not waiting for you to be "polished" or "perfected" before He meets you; He meets you in the middle of your struggle. This anchor reminds you that the ART of wrestling is about trading the safety of your religious dogma for the "victorious chaos" of a living relationship with the Coach.

3. The Play-Call from God

Child, check your helmet—the field has shifted.
I see you standing shoulder-to-shoulder in a 'Line Strategy,' exposed and taking hits from a defense you weren't meant to face alone. I am calling an audible: Talent sets your floor,

but our Character sets your ceiling! I didn't bring you to this river to break you; I brought you here to seal your Sonship. I watched My Son, Jesus, navigate the field with grace and velocity, always reading the Father's defense and changing the play on the fly. That is the C♡♡Lness of our Oneness.

When you lay aside your rulebook and ask Me for a blessing, you are undergoing Active Recovery Therapy. You are trading the casualty-heavy life of tradition for the winning maneuverability of My Spirit.
Don't be afraid of the limp you carry; it is the mark of a King who has seen My face. Your DNA is hardwired to be 'Israel'—the one who prevails. Be Spiritually BRAVE enough to wrestle through the night, knowing that My touch is what transforms your reality.
I am so good that I meet you in your unpolished state just to show you who you really are. Run the play, Child. The wrestling ground is where you find your crown."

4. The Audible *The Timeline of Now*
Audible: A real-time play change called by the quarterback at the line of scrimmage after observing the defense, allowing the offense to switch from a failing strategy to one better suited for the immediate situation.

The Move: The enemy wants you to stay "confined" by the structures and rules of your past. The Audible is this: The veil is open!

Right now, on the timeline of today, I am calling for Adaptive Tactics. I am expanding your tent pegs of knowing. Stop taking cover behind old doctrines and step into the open field of My presence. You are not just a player; you are a world-changer.

How Good is God!

Reformation Data: The Architecture of the Wrestle

To understand the "field" you are playing on, consider how to apply the evolution of tactics to your own growth:

- **The Floor vs. The Ceiling:** In "Redemptive Leadership," Talent (IQ, skill, giftings) gets you into the stadium. However, Character (integrity, resilience, face-to-face history with God) is what determines how much of the "kingdom Domain" you can actually govern. *Apply this:* invest more in your "Quiet Place" history than in your public performance.
- **Line Strategy Casualties:** Historically, "Line Infantry" soldiers stood in the open to maximize firepower, resulting in high casualty rates. When you live a "Logos-only" faith without Rhema discernment, you suffer high emotional and spiritual "casualties." *Apply this:* Switch to Adaptive Tactics to reduce your stress and increases your "Wins" because you are moving with the Coach.
- **The Penuel Principle:** Jacob named the place Penuel because he saw God "face-to-face." Clinical data on "Transformational Growth" suggests that a single experiential encounter (knowing) has more impact on behavior than 1,000 hours of cognitive learning (studying). *Apply this:* Choose to "sup with Him" until the visitation never ends.

Section I

Gates of Hell

HOW GOOD IS GOD!

THE OPEN DOOR

"So you are no longer a slave, but God's child; and since you are his child, God has made you also an heir." — Galatians 4:7 (NIV)

The striving stops at the threshold.

We often knock like strangers, hoping to be let in.

But the Father does not keep guests waiting. He keeps sons close.

The door is not a barrier to your worth. It is the entrance to your rest.

You do not need a key. You are the heir. Welcome home.

Chapter 2

Sonship Authority

The Inherent Truth That Turns the Gates Into a Door

"The only sign we have in the locker room is from The Art of War: 'Every battle is won before it is fought.'"
—Bill Belichick | Legendary NFL Coach

HERE IS AN ACRONYM FOR "HELL" that incorporates motivational leadership and enduring truth—the kind of thing a Head Coach might scribble on the locker room whiteboard:

H.E.L.L. Harness Eternal Lessons Liberally
Let's break the game film down:
- **Harness:** Motivational and action-oriented. It implies taking control and utilizing something powerful. A coach might say, *"Harness that potential!"*
- **Eternal Lessons:** Thought-leader and scripture-considering. This points to enduring truths and wisdom.
- **Liberally:** Practical application. It suggests an abundant and generous application of these lessons. A coach might yell, *"Apply yourselves liberally to the task!"*

The Gates Are Already a Door

The world often teaches us that power must be earned through striving, and that spiritual battles are fought by sheer human effort. This chapter rewrites that narrative.

It's time to live Spiritually BRAVE and recognize that the authority you need isn't a future reward; it is you being One with Inherent Truth right now.

The enemy's masterpiece is the illusion that the gates of limitation, fear, and condemnation (the "I-am-not-tree") are solid, unmovable barriers. This deception is merely a falling away in our minds from our true identity as image and likeness bearers of Elohim.

Just as Eve was deceived to believe a lie about herself, we, like sheep, have gone astray [Isa 53:6].

But consider this profound truth: The Story was first lived before the text was ever written.

Jesus is God's mind made up about you! Before the foundation of the world, God lavished every blessing Heaven has upon you in Christ. He always knew in His love that He would present you again face-to-face before Him in blameless innocence. [Mirror Translation, cf. Ephesians 1:3-4]

Your spiritual DNA is not a record of your failures; it is the Love-Code of the Father's eternal plan. The mandate to "subdue the earth" (Genesis 1:28) was simply the natural expression of Adam and Eve's perfect, unfallen Sonship Authority—the outflow of their established Oneness with the Creator.

This means that for you, the gates of any challenge—sickness, scarcity, or fear—do not need to be battered down; they need to be recognized as already having been redefined.

You are not fighting *for* victory; you are acting *from* the finished victory of Christ.

The Deception of Distance

When you stand in Oneness with Inherent Truth, you realize the Gates of Hell are not a final barrier but merely a fallen boundary. You carry the master key—the revelation of your permanent, blameless Oneness in Christ. This makes the gate function as a door, ready for you to walk through into the authority and supernatural wisdom that rewrites lives.

The battle for your limits was already won in His heart.

God found us in Christ before he lost us in Adam. We are presented in blameless innocence before him.

Your in-Christness is not the result of a lucky draw. Calvinism lied to you. Neither is it the result of your "choice" to follow Jesus. Something doesn't become true by popular vote. Or by our beliefs. If it wasn't true to begin with, we're wasting our time trying to "believe" it true.

Faith happens to you when you encounter the good announcement. *"Of God's doing are we IN CHRIST..."* (1 Corinthians 1:30)

For "evangelical theology" to miss the meaning of mankind's inclusion IN CHRIST before they knew it or believed it, is to completely miss the point of the death, descent into hell, resurrection and ascension of Jesus. This would make Jesus irrelevant and reduce the salvation of the human race to their own fate managed by institutionalized religion.

By dying our death as fully God and fully man, once and for all, death became the doorway, whereby Jesus would enter into our hell and deepest darkness and sense of lostness and loneliness as a result of the lies we believed about ourselves - to triumphantly lead us out as his trophies and relocate us face to face with the Father of the universe.

Ephesians 1:3,4 and commentary portions, du Toit, Francois. Mirror Study Bible

And the Gates of Hell were wide open, until TRUTH removed who built the gate all together!

Psalm 24: The King is Coming

Jesus has redefined what I used to say yes to.

"Seated in heavenly places." Dimensions: the kingdom within you, the kingdom without you, creation, time, and the entirety of the Kings domain.
"The earth is the Lord's" is found in Psalm 24:1-7 TPT.

Yahweh claims the world as his.
Everything and everyone belong to him!
He's the one who pushed back oceans
to let the dry ground appear,
planting firm foundations for the earth.
Who Comes before the King? Who, then, is allowed to ascend
the mountain of Yahweh? And who has the privilege of
entering into God's Holy Place?
Those who are clean—whose works and ways are pure,
whose hearts are true and sealed by the truth,
those who never deceive, whose words are sure.
They will receive Yahweh's blessing
and righteousness given by the Savior-God.
They will stand before God,
for they seek the pleasure of God's face, the God of Jacob.
Selah
The King is (has come) Coming! So wake up, you living
gateways!
Lift up your heads, you doorways of eternity!
Welcome the King of Glory,
for he is about to come through you.

The Immovable Kingdom

Jesus gives eyes to see, ears to hear. He commands us to follow, to be seated in authority and gives us the keys.

We are fully associated in this immovable kingdom; an authority that cannot be challenged or contradicted. Our participation echoes grace [and not law and fear-inspired obedience] as we accommodate ourselves to God's delight, yielding in awe to his firm embrace. His zeal for us burns like fire. (Hebrews 12:28-29 Mirror)

But to each one of us grace was given according to the measure of Christ's gift. Therefore it says,
"WHEN HE ASCENDED ON HIGH,
HE LED CAPTIVE THE CAPTIVES,
AND HE GAVE GIFTS TO PEOPLE." (Psalms 68:18)

Now this expression, "He ascended," what does it mean except that He also had descended into the lower parts of the earth?
Ephesians 4:8, 9 NASB

Love has no bounds or borders. Love will allow you to choose the illusion of distance, fear, anger and all manner of hate—Until the teeth of gnashing have been ground to the gums and the weeping of control, surrenders, to erase the illusion.

Sheol is cradled in an all-consuming fire of His love.

HOW GOOD IS GOD?
This is my conviction; no threat whether it be in death or life; be it celestial messengers, demon powers or political principalities, nothing known to us at this time, or even in the unknown future; no dimension of any calculation in time or space, nor any device yet to be invented, has what it takes to separate us from the love of God unveiled in our Lord, Jesus Christ. Romans 8:38-39 (Mirror)

Herein lies the secret of the power of the Gospel; there is no good news in it until the righteousness of God is revealed.

Quoted from Romans 1:17 du Toit, Francois. Mirror Study Bible

The Strategy of Illumination

If Sun Tzu were contemplating the "Gates of Hell" and the profound wisdom presented here, I believe he would offer this:

"The true battle for the Gates of Hell is fought not with steel, but with illumination. For how can one defend a gate that has ceased to exist, its very foundation dissolved by the radiant truth of an already-won victory? The illusion of separation, like a formidable wall, crumbles when the light of an inherent belonging is fully embraced, revealing the open expanse of the King's domain."

Activation

Turning the Gate into a Door

Having shared foundational truths—that the Gates of Hell have been accessed, and are accessible with a key, and ultimately vanquished by God's inherent victory in Christ— let's now allow the questions of Jesus to open a personal conversation with Him.

These are not questions to be answered intellectually, but invitations to experience the living truth that He alone reveals.

A Direct Conversation with Jesus

1. "Who do you say that I am?" (Matthew 16:15) This is the most pivotal question in your faith journey. It is not an invitation to affirm a theological position but to receive a personal revelation of His identity. Take a moment, find a quiet space, and simply ask Him, *"Jesus, who are You to me?"* Be still and listen for His voice, His Spirit, or a stirring in your heart.

2. "Why are you so afraid? Do you still have no faith?" (Mark 4:40) The fears that bind us are real, but they often stem from believing a lie. The chapter reveals that Jesus has already won. Now, bring your specific fears to Him and ask, *"Jesus, why am I so afraid? Help me see the truth You have already revealed about this."* Listen for His peace to vanquish the fear and for His truth to replace the lie.

3. "What do you want me to do for you?" (Matthew 20:32) This is Jesus' direct question to those who are desperate for a change. It is an invitation to bring the deepest longings of your heart to Him. What is it that you truly need? Find the courage to ask Him directly, "Jesus, here is what my heart truly desires..." He stands ready to respond.

Reflect and Respond: Take a moment to record what you received in this time of conversation with Jesus. What did you hear? What did you feel? How did His truth manifest for you, personally?

____

____

____

____

Next Step

Over the next few days, choose one of these questions and carry it with you. As life unfolds, continue to speak to Jesus and listen for His response. Practice living as a disciple who is in constant conversation with their Teacher and Lord.

Prayer and Contemplation

Father, thank you for the truth that is Jesus. Today, I choose to live from the power of a personal encounter with You, not just from what I have been taught. Open my ears to hear and my heart to respond. In Jesus' name, amen.

PLAY SHEET | RULER

Ruler Edition
Redemptive Gifts Summary

THIS CHAPTER IS THE ULTIMATE "Game Film" session on the reality of your identity.

It's a heavyweight play designed to shift you from a defensive posture—trying to survive the "Gates of Hell"—into the offensive, legislative authority of a Son who realizes the battle was won before the first whistle ever blew.

The DNA Wristband Audible: Chapter Play-Call

1. **The Green Dot Helmet** (Individual Redemptive Gift): **Ruler**

The frequency for this play is set to the Ruler. This is your gift of the "Architect of Authority" and the "Steward of Systems." You are hardwired to understand the legalities of the kingdom.

While others might see a "Gate of Hell" as an immovable barrier of sickness, scarcity, or fear, the Ruler in you is designed to look at the Deed of Ownership. You have the inherent capacity to realize that the 'I-am-not' tree—the illusion of the Tree of Knowledge that tells you that you are separate, lacking, or 'not enough'—is a fraudulent claim. You are being called to apply your Sonship Authority to recognize that every "Gate" is legally obligated to function as a "Door" because you are One with the Inherent Truth.

2. The Coaches' Booth (*Legacy Anchor*): *More Than a Carpenter* by Josh McDowell

In the "Booths" of your spiritual legacy, *More Than a Carpenter* (Ruler/Architecture) represents the investigation into the solid, structural reality of who Jesus is.

You apply this by moving beyond "sentimental" faith into a "Structural" confidence. Just as this anchor book dismantled lies about Jesus, you are applying it to dismantle the lies about *yourself*. It reminds you that the "Fall" was simply a "falling away" in your mind, not a change in your DNA. This anchor proves that your blameless innocence is a historical and eternal fact, not a "lucky draw" or a popular vote.

3. The Play-Call from God

"Child, tune into the headset. I see you standing at the 'Gates of Hell,' weary from trying to batter them down with your own effort.

I am calling an audible:

Harness Eternal Lessons Liberally! *I didn't wait for you to 'make the team' before I blessed you; I associated you in Christ before the foundation of the world.*

I watched My Son, Jesus, descend into the lower parts of the earth to lead your captivity captive, so that you would never have to live in the illusion of distance again. That is the C♡♡Lness of our Oneness.

When you stand in the 'Inherent Truth' of your identity, those gates cease to be a final barrier and become a Living Gateway. Stop believing the lie that you are a sheep gone astray. Your DNA is a Love-Code that I meticulously authored. Be Spiritually BRAVE enough to lift up your head and welcome the King of Glory—not as a visitor, but as the One who is about to come through you.

I am so good that I found you in Christ before I ever lost you in Adam. You are flawless, free, and fully authorized. Run the play, Child. The door is wide open."

4.   The Audible *The Timeline of Now*

The enemy wants you to remain in a "Locker Room" of religious striving, hoping to one day earn the key. The Audible is this: **You ARE the Key!**

Right now, on the timeline of today, I am removing the "I-am-not" beliefs from your mind. I am releasing the supernatural wisdom that rewrites your life. The gate is already a door. Step through into the authority of My delight. **How Good is God!**

Reformation Data: The Architecture of Your Authority

To understand the "field" you are playing on, consider how to apply these "Ruler" principles to your own territory:

- **Harnessing Eternal Lessons:** In *"The Art of War,"* the battle is won before it is fought. *Apply this:* settle your identity in the "Quiet Place" before you face the challenge. When you enter a room already persuaded of your Oneness with God, the "Gates" of opposition lose their structural integrity.

- **The Living Gateway:** Psalm 24:7 commands, *"Lift up your heads, you gates!"* *Apply this:* Realize that *you* are the gateway. When you "lift your head"—changing your mindset from a victim to a Son—the environment around you is forced to realign with the King of Glory who lives in you.
- **Redefining the "Fall":** If "evangelical theology" has made you feel irrelevant or managed by institutional religion, apply the Higher Law. 1 Corinthians 1:30 states that "of God's doing are we IN CHRIST." *Apply this:* Refuse to let your "performance" or "beliefs" be the basis of your truth. The Truth is a Person, and He has already included you.

HOW GOOD IS GOD!

THE END OF DISTANCE

"Nevertheless when one turns to the Lord, the veil is taken away. Now the Lord is the Spirit; and where the Spirit of the Lord is, there is liberty." — 2 Corinthians 3:16-17 (NKJV)

The chasm is closed. The veil is lifted.

We are not shouting across a void. We are breathing the same air.

Like a holy lacing, the Spirit draws us in, weaving our weakness into His strength, until the gap between "God" and "Me" disappears.

Rest in the Union. There is nothing left to separate you. There is only One.

Chapter 3

He that Comes Face to Face

The Corset & The Chasm: A Journey of Persuasion

"There's no traffic past the extra mile."

—Paula Abdul | American singer & Choreographer

THE MIRROR TRANSLATION by Francois Du Toit, which aims to convey a deeper, often more theological and experiential understanding of the text. His commentary from John 6 has become an internalized narration of new life communion for me—a written perspective that answered so many *why's* and *impossibilities.*

It's true, there isn't much traffic in the lower realms of the earth. "Jesus, an extra mile kind of guy, clearly says; taking you or I there, births 'Us' into newness of life in His resurrection.

How Good is God! His goodness is measured not by how much He can impress us, but by how completely He persuades us about our own inherent, blameless identity."

"Jesus said, I am the bread of life. He that comes face to face with me shall never hunger and he who finds his faith resting

in me shall never thirst. But even though you have seen me, you are not persuaded.
(You might be happy with the healings and be entertained by the signs, but still you fail to understand who I am. I'm not here to impress you with me.
I'm here to persuade you about you.
Your sonship is what I am all about.
And the only way that I can persuade you about you is to take you with me into your death and darkness and overcome your fear and hell and birth you again into newness of life in my resurrection.)" (John 6:36, Mirror Commentary)

The Rescuing Mission

Everyone whom the Father has given me <u>will</u> come face to face with me. And here, mirrored in me they will see that I am not the Judge. I will not cast anyone out. For I have stepped down out of Heaven, not to make a name for myself. I did not come to become a mere historic hero. I have come <u>to communicate the resolve of him</u> who sent me. (I am here to demonstrate to you how persuaded my Father is about you.) My Sender's desire is for me to rescue every single individual - this is his gift to me - that I will lose no detail of their original identity mirrored in me. My rescuing mission will conclude in their joint-resurrection.
This is the completeness of time. John 6: 36-39 Mirror Translation —Francois du Toit

The Witness of Scripture

Written in pages of *the UnFinished Book,* you find me wrestling with the traditions of man and the culturally related doctrines of Jesus walking the earth. Put a set of kingdom keys in my hand and a love relationship with a resurrected King and the story begins to change.

Dripped from pen in translation: It is impossible to experience the cross, the corridors of the tomb and the Oneness of our resurrection without the imprint of others in the sound, the echo.

The epitome of **"Play for the man next to you"** reverberated; this is a team effort on the athletic fields of our IAM life.

You scrutinize the Scriptures tirelessly, assuming that in them you embrace the life of the ages - yet I am what the Scriptures are all about. Still you refuse to resort to me as the very source of the life you seek. (I echo the life of the ages within you.) I am not anchoring my belief in people's opinion. But what I observe about you, is that God's love does not resonate within you. (You're so obsessed with the rule book that all you see in it is a god of judgment and wrath and miss out on God's love.) Here I am representing my Father and you have a problem with that; yet someone completely unknown to anyone would come in his own name and you will give him your full support. How is it possible for you to even venture into the dimensions of faith, if you already have your minds made up to go with popular opinion within your own ranks, while you show no desire to esteem him who proceeds directly from God? No, I am not the one to accuse you before the Father - you stand condemned before your trusted friend Moses. Had you discerned my Father's voice in Moses you would have been persuaded about me in his writings. If you already doubt his words to begin with, my conversation will be irrelevant to you.
(John 5:39-47 Mirror)

The "Peak" District

Three curiosities that compelled my lower realms of the earth journey.

While standing on the boundary of heaven and earth (see The UnFinished Book, Chapter Six: "Earth Invading Heaven"), I had an encounter—a pinpoint prophetic word delivered the same day I would be teaching about heaven.

What did while "standing on the edge" look like?

You would need to be a Jane Austen fan to get this pun: Let's all go to the "Peak" District.

In the 2005 movie *Pride and Prejudice* with Keira Knightley, there is a famous scene where Elizabeth Bennet stands on a cliff in England (Stanage Edge). The wind is blowing her hair and clothes as she gazes mystically at the horizon, pondering the ebb and difficult flows of life.

Now, in my continuing divine education of "While standing on the boundary of heaven and earth," I find myself firmly situated on this heavenly-historical cliff with God, on the edge.

The Corset and The Chasm

1. **The Edge:** I stood on the cliff.
2. **The Lacing:** The Spirit of God reaches across the chasm, as if lacing a corset. In the process of cinching it, Holy Spirit pulls the two "realms" (Heaven and Hell, God and Man) together.
3. **The Story Teller:** The first storyteller in the encounter was God; invisibly, He turned the page. Now the story "show-er" is Jesus.

Bookmarked between quotations from John 6 commentary above: *"And the only way that I can persuade you about you is to take you with me into your death and darkness..."*

The author concedes, *I needed persuading!*

Reader, and where is your "persuasion?" (Another Jane Austen pun—couldn't help myself.)

Periscope Down. (More elaborated in coming chapters about descending to the Gates of Hell.)

"It's not the will to win that matters—everyone has that. It's the will to prepare to win that matters."

—Paul Bear Bryant | Legendary Alabama Football Coach

Activation

He that comes Face to Face

a Corset and a Chasm

This chapter takes us to the "extra mile," where the chasm between Heaven and earth is cinched like a corset, allowing for a divine "out of the box", face-to-face encounter with our King. It's a lesson in shifting from a transactional faith to a transformational one. As we consider Jesus's mission to persuade us about our own sonship, let's step into this sacred space and have a direct conversation with Him.

A Direct Conversation with Jesus

1. **"Why do you not understand my language?"** *(John 8:43)* In the midst of a crowd, Jesus asked this question, pointing to the chasm between His spiritual reality and the carnal mind. This echoes the "Corset and a Chasm" metaphor, where you found a new, internalized narration of a God who bridges the gap. Ask Jesus: *"Where in my life have I failed to understand your language, so I can enter into a deeper conversation with you?"* Listen for Him to identify the blockages and incongruent flow of "electricity" in your mind that has kept you from a deeper spiritual awakening.

2. "Are you ready for the baptism I am to undergo?" *(Mark 10:38)* This question, posed to the ambitious disciples, is a profound challenge to our will to prepare. It's an invitation to join Him on the "extra mile," past the earthly traffic, to a place of greater purpose. Reflect on Paul Bear Bryant's quote on preparation. Ask Jesus: *"Where do you want me to go past the extra mile with you, where I can show my will to prepare, as I navigate my own death and darkness to enter newness of life with you?"* Take a moment to listen for His answer.

3. "Who are my mother and my brothers?" *(Matthew 12:48)* Jesus asked this question while pointing to His disciples, redefining family and belonging not by blood, but by a shared life of obedience to His will. This speaks directly to our "IAMness" and the profound truth of sonship that Jesus came to persuade us about. Ask Jesus: *"What am I willing to let go of in order to be a part of your family and show my desire to be a member of the body of Christ?"* Be still and listen to what He says about your divine design.

Reflect and Respond

In your journal, write down what you heard from Jesus in this conversation. What did you learn about your own identity? What is one step you can take today to move past the extra mile in your faith journey?

____

____

____

____

Next Step

This week, pay attention to the "traffic" in your life—the distractions, the worries, the old doctrines that can keep you from a face-to-face encounter. Consciously take a step past it, remembering that there is no traffic on the extra mile with Jesus.

Prayer and Contemplation

Lord, thank you for being a God who is willing to cross any chasm to meet me face-to-face. Thank you for not being here to impress me, but to persuade me about my identity in You. Give me the courage to prepare my heart to go the extra mile, to know You more intimately, and to live in the fullness of my sonship. Amen.

PLAY SHEET | PROPHET

Prophet Edition
Redemptive Gifts Summary

THIS CHAPTER IS A DEEP-FIELD DIVE into the Reclamation of Identity, where the distant land masses of Heaven and Hell are cinched together to prove that our Sonship is the only score that matters.

It is a journey of being fully persuaded by the Coach that you belong in the game.

The DNA Wristband Audible: Chapter Play-Call

   1. The Green Dot Helmet (Individual Redemptive Gift): **Prophet**

The frequency for this play is set to the Prophet. This is your gift of "Design and Persuasion." You are hardwired to look past the "traffic" of popular opinion and the heavy rule-books of judgment to find your original Design mirrored in Christ.

The Prophet in you isn't satisfied with just being "impressed" by signs or miracles; you have a deep, soul-level need to be persuaded by the Truth of your blameless identity. We are being called to stop searching the "text" for a god of wrath and to start looking into the Face of the One who echoes your true life back to you.

2. The Coaches' Booth (*Legacy Anchor*): *The Shack* by William Paul Young

In the "Booths" of your spiritual legacy, *The Shack* (Prophet/Design) represents that moment where the chasm between your pain and God's love is cinched together.

You apply this by realizing that Jesus is not a "historic hero" on a pedestal, but a Friend who meets you in your deepest darkness. This anchor reminds you that the "corset" of the Spirit is pulling your earthly struggles into His heavenly resurrection. Just as the character Mackenzie had to be persuaded of Papa's goodness, you are invited to let go of the "rule-book" and step into a face-to-face encounter that transcends religious logic.

3. The Play-Call from God

"Child, tune into the frequency of the 'Extra Mile.' I see you standing on the edge of the chasm, feeling the wind of your questions blowing against your heart.

I am calling an audible: I AM NOT HERE TO IMPRESS YOU, I AM HERE TO PERSUADE YOU ABOUT YOU!

I didn't step down out of Heaven to make a name for Myself; I came to show you how persuaded I am about your original identity.

I watched My Son, Jesus, enter into your 'hell' and your sense of lostness just to lead you out as My trophy. That is the C♡♡Lness of our Oneness. When you feel the

'Corset' of My Spirit pulling the realms together, don't resist the tension—it's the sound of the chasm closing.

Stop letting the 'traffic' of human opinion and 'Pew history' tell you who you are. Your DNA is a mirror of My own. Be Spiritually BRAVE enough to go the extra mile with Me, past the noise of the world, to the place where we can be face-to-face.

I am so good that I have rescued every detail of your design, and I will lose nothing. Run the play, Child. We are birthed into newness together."

4. The Audible *The Timeline of Now*

The enemy wants you to remain "unpersuaded," stuck in the traffic of doubt and religious duty. The Audible is this: *Periscope down into the Truth!*

Right now, on the timeline of today, I am cinching the gap between your "hell logic" and My "heavenly reality." The chasm is closed. The persuasion is complete. Your Sonship is the final word.

How Good is God!

Redemptive Stats: The Logic of Your Persuasion

To understand the "field" you are playing on, consider how to apply the "Extra Mile" strategy to your own life:

• **The Will to Prepare:** Coach Paul "Bear" Bryant said it's the will to prepare to win that matters. *Apply this:* Choose the "extra mile" of spiritual discipline—not to earn points, but to remove the distractions that keep you from seeing His face. Preparation is the bridge across the chasm.

• **The "Moses" Block:** Jesus told the crowd that if they really believed Moses, they would believe Him. *Apply this:* Examine your own "internalized narration." If your view of God is still anchored in judgment (the old rule-book), ask the Lord to "cinch the corset" and show you the Love that resonates within the Living Word.

• **The Extra Mile Margin:** There is no traffic on the extra mile. *Apply this:* Realize that most people are satisfied with "healings and signs" (the crowd). When you choose the extra mile of intimacy and persuasion, you find a level of authority and peace that is unoccupied by the noise of the world.

Chapter 4

Mothers and Daughters

"Fight, Flight, or Freeze"

She has played every position; Her defensive fortitude was harnessed learning to look through the eyes of her opponent.

She offended herself, protecting and creating opportunities for the family coming from behind her.

The ball is more valuable when transferred from her possession.

A mother's love is the unshakeable foundation.

It's the silent strength that picks you up when you're down, instills the belief that you can always do more, and sends you out into the world knowing you've got a champion in your corner.

Without that, no trophy, no victory, means a thing."
—MOM!

MY STORY BEGINS WITH A PHONE CALL from Ema. Her voice was filled with heavy concern as she relayed a recent conversation with her sister's son Kevin.

Sara, Kevin's sister, had just been diagnosed with stage four breast cancer. The family was in shock, blindsided, and life—altered into a traumatic event. They were in "fight, flight, or freeze."

Ema conveyed on our call the torment in Kevin's voice as he described his sister Sara's behavior in times of trouble. Her past "freeze" behavior consisted of locking herself away from family and all support systems. Sara's family, unable to battle against the isolation dynamic, was left barred-out with a diagnosis of despair and hopelessness.

The purpose of Ema's phone call she asked me to pray for them.

(*Note: Names have been changed to honor the privacy of friends and family.*)

Before the phone call ended Holy Spirit had spoken to my heart the course of my prayers. *God still uses party-lines!*

(The Party Line) A phone party line was an early telephone system where multiple households shared a single circuit. All connected parties could hear rings for others and, if they picked up, listen in on any ongoing conversation.

My heart-ears recorded another assignment to follow my Lord's footsteps into the lower realms of the earth.

The Panoramic View: How I Hear

Just the other day, Ema asked how I hear the Lord speaking. *Is it in words like we talk?*

I responded, in my experience conversations are more "*felt*" in a phraseology. You hear the heartbeat of the Father as if looking at a panoramic photo. Your "hearing or audible feeling" scans over the timeline of the panoramic photo, observing the visual scene. Your spirit "Sees":

- *Range:* The scope and extent of the viewed location (the prayer request) or adding the pictures to create a question.
- *Panoramic Experience:* The entirety of view, specifically looking for what might be blocking the desired outcome. (God's view)
- *Answer:* The outcome frames the picture in your understanding. (The overcoming strategy, prayer model, Courts of Heaven, or assignment.)

The "picture in phraseology" we hear/see/sense may be formed through infinite modalities. Nature, scripture, memory, science, music, sound, logic, love, prior life experience and all matters in the libraries of the unseen.

It is important to park logic and reason, until you discuss what you perceived with the Lord.

The scripture where God asks Jeremiah what he saw is found in Jeremiah 1:11-13

"The word of the Lord came to me: 'What do you see, Jeremiah?' 'I see the branch of an almond tree,' I replied." "The word of the Lord came to me again: 'What do you see?' 'I see a boiling pot, tilting away from the north,' I replied."

Truth, trust and confidence in relationship is the battle won before fought.

The Stairs to the Heart

I have attended and officiated my share of funerals and memorial services over the course of life. It's an honor as a Pastor to capture the life of the deceased in a way that ascends their best self into the arms of the Father for the loved ones in attendance.

The stairs to the heart ascend in different ways. Crisis and crossroads divinely open a door to the heart of the individuals who have been touched by the life of the deceased, allowing the infinite love of Trinity to flow hope.

Sometimes the pools of the heart are clear and have a consistent flow from the headwaters of Heaven. Hope floats with untethered buoyancy caressing every shore of life.

Other times, the heart that has suffered fractures after years of starvation offers only a sliver of entry to its murky waters. Yet, when stirred or refreshed, hope again floats in the re-recognition that a Life Preserver ring has always been present.

When *TRUTH* erased the separation illusions in my own thinking, spiritual eyes developed through seasons of practicing His ascended presence. I usually witness the deceased attend their own service. Those who have included themselves in the Cloud of His Witnesses continue to cheer our lives from the unseen realm—more than we know.

Tears of disconnection no longer fall from my eyes since my heart doesn't feel distant from them.

However, that same Truth also discerns when a person has still not chosen to include themselves in His love. **Yes, they are in hell.**

Curiosity is a king, searching for truths, hidden for them to find.
"It is the glory of God to conceal a matter,
But the glory of kings is to search out a matter." Proverbs 25:2.

I do not look or ask in personal curiosity. With the same spiritual etiquette, I do not abuse the privilege it has been to have my sight restored. Spiritual sightedness is a Holy gift.

The Assignment

A divine prayer assignment also has divine privilege to outwork it. Not hierarchical by any means, it's the willingness to say "yes" before we address the logic.

I've learned more in the *doing*, than all the hours of acquiring knowledge.

Holy Spirit's conversation—the "panoramic spiritual photo" encountered in response to being asked to pray for Kevin's sister Sara—created a queue of questions for active prayer:

• *Who* is the best person in Sara's life to have a good sit-down talk with her about a behavior? ("Freeze/isolation behavior" isn't loving to Sara or those who love her?)

• *Who* could touch Sara in the most nurturing way to bring healing and restoration?

• *What* is the true root of the disease? At the breast or heart —the Cancer of the isolation behavior?

I spiritually discerned that Ema's sister—Sara's Mom, who had passed away years before—was not seated in the Cloud of Witnesses. *Yes, she is in hell.*

Heaven's prayer-answer communicated *"Mom" needs to be there!*

My assignment took me into Sheol to preach the gospel of love. (Psalms 68:18, Ephesians 4:8)

I can hear you ask me: *What does that look like? Sheol or the Preaching?* Preaching is not a matter of mere words. Use your imagination from the story of Rich man and Lazarus found in Luke 16:19-31

"And he cried out, Father Abraham, have mercy on me and send Lazarus to dip the tip of his finger in water to cool my tongue, for I am sinking into this flame!"

If you found yourself sinking into this 'flame' (Sheol) and a family member shows up to speak with you, "moving about in the flame unbound and unharmed," obviously, the love of God has sent them there.

LOVE would need no words.

The easiest street ministry I have encountered to date is on the streets of Sheol!

Hugs all around! Tears of great joy and humble, humble gratitude. The words that I do remember saying, "Your daughter needs you."

This same scene I have witnessed every time the divine privilege has invited me to Sheol on behalf of LOVE. And yes, I will reiterate every-time, *I call that a 100% altar call.*

The Staircase

For curious minds: This is a fascinating, repeated occurrence after LOVE has preached the gospel.

LOVE opens everyone's spiritual eyes. A brightly lit, beautiful, wide marble staircase appears, ascending into Heaven, just as is written in our hearts. All struggle, weeping and gnashing of teeth evaporated in the baptism of His death.

Jesus is always there, and many times relatives are waiting at the top of the stairs, arms wide open! Time is irrelevant, just love!

Sara's Mother stepped into the eternity God the Father had so meticulously prepared for her.

(For the curious ones: a thought provoking manifestation to make note of: an inner spirit knowing to never step foot or toe on this divine staircase. It is "Not a door for the living-on-earth." End of encounter.)

The Result

> "Most of the mistakes in thinking
>
> are inadequacies of perception rather than mistakes of logic."

—**Edward de Bono** | Authority on Creative Thinking

OUR HURRAY: "Jesus is the King of Kings", seated at the right hand of the Father, risen and rockin' it, in the school of "Follow me."

How Good is God? Two weeks later, Ema received a phone call from a very heart-touched Kevin and in turn, Ema called me.

A miracle had occurred. Sara's behavior radically changed. She opened the "Freeze" door from self-protection and controlled isolation and allowed her family to support and love on her.

We will only know when eternity gathers us at the table of the Lord how Mom and daughter had a life-altering conversation. Did she visit her in a dream? Did the angels repeat a series of comforting memories? Audible thoughts to the heart? Maybe a vision?

But the conversation did occur from the Cloud of Witnesses.

Four years later, this is Sara's testimony: she is cancer-free and living a happy, full life.

This is my conviction; no threat whether it be in death or life; be it celestial messengers, demon powers or political principalities, nothing known to us at this time, or even in the unknown future; no dimension of any calculation in time or space, nor any device yet to be invented, has what it takes to separate us from the love of God unveiled in our Lord, Jesus Christ. (Romans 8:38,39 Mirror)

Activation

Mothers and Daughters

"Fight, Flight, or Freeze."

Having explored the story of Sara and the courage required to overcome deep-seated patterns, let's now allow the questions of Jesus to open a personal conversation with Him.

His heart is always in a state of healing, and sometimes the way He brings that healing to us and through us requires us to step outside the confines of time.

A Direct Conversation with Jesus

1. **"Do you want to get well?"** (*John 5:6*) Jesus asks this of a man who had been paralyzed for 38 years. His condition was chronic, just as some generational patterns can feel. Bring a pattern, behavior, or deep-seated wound that you carry to Jesus and simply ask: "Jesus, do I truly want to get well from this?" Be honest. Then, listen for His response. The TRUTH is, God has already provided healing. Ponder outside the box of time—what does healing look like to God, who exists beyond our earthly timeline?

2. "What is your name?" (*Mark 5:9*) In the chapter, we see how our response to life's traumas can form an identity: "fight, flight, or freeze." Jesus asked this question to a person who had lost their true identity to torment. In a quiet moment, bring your own core self to Him and ask: "*Jesus, what is my true name? Who do you say that I am, beyond my coping mechanisms?*" Listen for His voice to declare your original, whole identity.

3. "Do you love me?" (*John 21:16*) The story of Sara and her mother shows us that love is the language of restoration, healing where words cannot. This is a simple, direct question from Jesus that cuts to the core of everything. Bring your whole heart—the wounds, the triumphs, and the questions—to Him and simply ask: *"Jesus, do you love me?"* Sit in the answer. His love is the healing touch that needs no words.

Reflect and Respond

Take a moment to record what you received in this time of conversation with Jesus. What did you hear? What did you feel? How did His truth manifest for you, personally? Let this be a record of your direct experience of His living presence.

____

____

____

____

Next Step

Over the next few days, carry the question that resonated with you the most. Practice listening for Jesus' voice and responding to His truth. Let your newfound spiritual ears guide your every step.

Prayer and Contemplation

Father, thank you for the truth that is Jesus. Thank you for the way you speak to me personally, in ways that I can understand and experience. I open my heart to your love, your identity, and your healing, trusting that it will unfold in your perfect, timeless way. In Jesus' name, amen.

PLAY SHEET | MERCY

Mercy Edition
Redemptive Gifts Summary
THIS CHAPTER IS A DEEP-FIELD RESCUE MISSION that proves the **Mercy** of God has no "out-of-bounds" lines.

It is a revelation that the patterns of your past—the "fight, flight, or freeze" responses—can be melted by a Love that reaches through time to restore your original design.

The DNA Wristband Audible: Chapter Play-Call

1. **The Green Dot Helmet (**Individual Redemptive Gift): **Mercy**

The frequency for this play is set to Mercy. This is your gift of the "Internal Healer" and the "Atmosphere Shifter." You are hardwired to look past the "cracked pools" of a person's behavior and see the "headwaters of Heaven" trying to flow through.

When you encounter someone (or a part of yourself) stuck in "freeze" or isolation, your Mercy gift is designed to go beyond logic. You are being called to be Spiritually BRAVE enough to look into the "unseen realm" of a relationship and offer the "Life Preserver" of hope. Your authority isn't in your words, but in your willingness to let Love be the primary sermon.

2. The Coaches' Booth (*Legacy Anchor*): *The Five Love Languages* by Gary Chapman

In the "Booths" of your spiritual legacy, *The Five Love Languages* (Mercy/Healing) serves as your ultimate guide to the Healing of the Heart.

You apply this by realizing that communication is the bridge across every chasm—even the chasm of death. This anchor reminds you that Love has many "dialects." Sometimes the most powerful language you can speak to a "frozen" heart is the language of a "panoramic prayer"—seeing the whole story through God's eyes and inviting the "Cloud of Witnesses" to join the conversation. It proves that there is no boundary, doctrinal or otherwise, that can stop the flow of a heart-to-heart restoration.

3. The Play-Call from God

"Child, check your helmet—the atmosphere is thinning. I see you looking at the 'panoramic photo' of your family's pain, wondering if the isolation and the 'freeze' are a final score.

I am calling an audible: *Love would need no words!*

I didn't just save you for a trophy case; I saved you to be a part of the Restoration of All Things.

I have given you 'Spiritual Sightedness' so you can see the 'Marble Staircase' I've prepared for your lineage. That is the C♡♡Lness of our Oneness.

When you feel the weight of a generational 'freeze,' don't address it with logic—address it with the fire of My love. I want you to know that the 'umbilical connection' of My breath in you is stronger than any cancer of the heart. Stop believing the lie that you are stuck in a 'fight or flight' cycle. Your DNA is a Love-Code that cannot be separated from Me by anything in the known or unknown future. Be Spiritually BRAVE enough to trust the 'felt phraseology' of My Spirit.

I am so good that I use your 'doing'—your simple 'yes' to pray and love—to relocate souls from the darkness into My light. The door is open, the teeth of control have been ground down, and I am meeting you at the top of the stairs. Run the play, Child. Love is the only thing that remains."

4. The Audible *The Timeline of Now*

The enemy wants you to remain "paralyzed" by the chronic patterns of your history. The Audible is this: The "Freeze" is over!

Right now, on the timeline of today, I am removing the "inadequacies of perception" from your mind. I am releasing a "100% Altar Call" for your family line. The chasm is closed. The witnesses are cheering. The healing is here. *How Good is God!*

REFORMATION DATA: THE ANATOMY OF YOUR RESCUE

To understand the "field" you are playing on, consider how to apply these "Mercy" principles to your own life:

• ***Panoramic Sight:*** Before you react to a "frozen" family member, ask the Lord for a "panoramic photo" of their soul. *Apply this:* Scan the timeline of their life—their range, scope, and obstacles. When you "see" from God's perspective, your prayer shifts from a "request" to a "Holy Assignment" that brings restoration.

• ***The "Doing" Over the "Knowledge":*** *Apply this:* Practice the "doing" of spiritual intercession. Don't wait until you understand the "logic" of Sheol or the "how-to" of the heavens. Say "yes" to the nudge, step onto the "streets" of the situation, and let the "free electrons" of God's goodness neutralize the inflammation of your trauma.

• ***Truth as the Life Preserver:*** In the midst of crisis, "Hope floats with untethered buoyancy." *Apply this:* Choose to believe that the Life Preserver has always been present. By speaking the Truth of a person's "Heavenly Origin" (who God says they are), you are providing the "sliver of entry" for the murky waters of their heart to be refreshed by the headwaters of Heaven.

Chapter 5

First Loves: a 4-Minute Mile

"He smiles at me, and I am suddenly seventeen again—the year I realize that love doesn't follow the rules, the year I understood that nothing is worth having so much as something unattainable."
—Jodi Picoult, 'My Sister's Keeper.'

THAT YEAR LIVES IN EVERY CREVICE AND SPIRIT conversation of my heaven and earth. Little do we know when caught in the raptures of first love, that a veiled novel is being written across our lives. There are countless pages with the corner flap notched, thoughts marked over with a highlighter pen, and when life really needs to talk to you; your "first" (reminding you of *His* first love) has intuitive powers that visit you.

That is love attained in the unattainable.

My sophomore year in high school was larger than life. Still wet behind the ears with a youthful glee, life dilemmas were solved in one BFF sleepover. With two elder brothers marking the academic halls ahead of me, and my second eldest brother making his grade athletically in his senior year, the "family name" had a little voting clout in our small hall of fame. It awarded me the title of "Queen"—head cheerleader.

Like it was yesterday, I can see the sassy red and white pleats of our short uniform skirt, underlaid by a white, long sleeve sweater with large red stripes across the breast, covered by and looped-stitch emblems of mascot: the Central Panthers. My sweater emblem had a little gold crown on it. Whether wearing the football or basketball uniform at least two times a week, my head was held high, over the souls of those red and white saddle shoes.

Funny how memories embed in your brain.

It was the 1980s. When Farrah Fawcett changed the way women wore their hair, I always claimed she copied me: feathered bangs and shaggy blonde layers upon layers past my shoulders.

Our basketball team began its ascension towards State Champs and Friday pep rallies mandatorily excused the student body for one free afternoon period. Herkie Jumps, splits, high-kicks and *who had a car* were the only fuel one needed to burn the oil of youth.

My first love. I don't remember the first time we met; what stands out in my youthful kindled thoughts are the moments I couldn't live without him. The sneak-peeks around the senior hall corner to catch a glimpse. Do you remember the "Good Old Days" when you purposely timed your footsteps just to get a look? *Oh-oh*, late to Home Ec class, again. Youthful fervor, just to be noticed, heart palpitations dancing across any common sense. We all need a pin-prick reminder of when love led the way, pushing distractions and rules aside, all with the intent of being in the same room with one another.

You might ask where did he come from. Surely, in a school of fewer than six hundred students, we had passed each other in the hall. Maybe *where* I came from is a better question.

With that, I don't think he would mind if I told you some secrets. I taught Randy how to kiss—and I mean *kiss*. Girls have a little more opportunity to gain experience in this area. My concerned folks would flash the front porch light to interrupt our very long goodbyes from the gravel driveway, signaling it was time to come inside.

I learned how to say "no" to negative friend influences, even at the peer expense Randy was struggling with. I think this is what ultimately broke up our six-month (a lifetime in high school): peer pressure.

The best secret—that none of those peers could have known—is our love was pure, innocent and looking back today, divinely holy. My heart always wanted to get back together, but Randy moved on with a faster crowd.

Years—many years—later, I called him from San Diego, during one of those "BFF had too much to drink" binges. He was very gracious; I'm sure I made him laugh. Our conversation was like two best friends where trust had never waned, and that pure love could bask in the light of youth one more time. Your window of time together is sacred; purity kept it that way.

Beloved, love always includes others, since love springs from God; its source is found in the fellowship of the Father, Spirit and Son. Everyone who encounters love immediately knows that they too are born of the same source! It is not possible to fully participate in love without discovering God. To love is to know God; to know God is to love. Not to love, is not to know God. There is nothing in love that distracts from who God is. Love is who God is - they are inseparable. John 4:7,8 MTB

INSEPARABLE OR NEW GROUND?

An article from the *Harvard Business Review* by Bill Taylor

discusses the passing of Roger Bannister, the first human being to run a four-minute mile. The article is titled: *"What Breaking the 4-minute mile taught us about the limits of conventional thinking."*

In part, Taylor says: *"As it turns out, when he [Bannister] broke through a previously impenetrable track-and-field barrier, he taught all of us what it takes to break new ground."*

[Notes from Journal and Drawings] For some time, Jesus had been sharing the landscape of the garden of my heart. He made it easy on my understanding, illuminating my spirit to perceive plants, trees, garden walls, trellising, fountains and quiet places to sit. There are so many different "Spiritual Universities" we attend in the restorational growth of sonship and discovery beyond the veil. Many times, if Jesus and I left the confines of the garden a familiar knowing, He would be teaching me principles in the path scripture declares He walked.

First spiritual sense developed was *"spiritual sight."* It is the first marker of development, experience and wisdom: learning to close my eyes to perceive *first*, then see. It is a tool that continues to guide me into all the truth He leads me to—to change, to know, to be intimate with. Truth is sandwiched nicely between Way and Life.

If we were to attach a photograph to said "garden" encounter, you would imagine Jesus opening a weathered iron garden gate (*Gate of Present Tense*) supported by an ancient stone wall (*External Wall*). The wall about four foot in height, merely the culmination of "stones" removed from the soil—stones picked, stacked, and piled, making a nice geography of a garden.

I walk through the gate and He closes it behind us. Today, from our dirt road path, I could see the incline of a summer-dried, slow-rolling field. About a hundred yards or halfway up the field was another stone wall jetting midway, visually splitting the field in half. The grasses were spent; a lonely juniper tree curled an almost silhouette as the distance was framed by ungoverned land.

Jesus and I veered off the road into the field. Presuppose the soles of your feet as being an intuitive and knowing receiver, as the divine parable begins to flood your body. Jesus remains close on my left as He experientially instructs our day journey. My mouth flooded with a taste cognitive to a scribe dipping pen into ink. I was familiar with the text.

This is the field of Judas's death.

Acts 1: Jesus had just ascended into heaven and the Apostles returned from the Mt of Olives. We pick up the scripture in verse 12-20

"Then the apostles returned to Jerusalem from the hill called the Mount of Olives, a Sabbath day's walk from the city… In those days Peter stood up among the believers (a group numbering about a hundred and twenty) and said, "Brothers and sisters, the Scripture had to be fulfilled in which the Holy Spirit spoke long ago through David concerning Judas… (With the payment he received for his wickedness, Judas bought a field; there he fell headlong, his body burst open and all his intestines spilled out. Everyone in Jerusalem heard about this, so they called that field in their language Akeldama, that is, Field of Blood.)

"For," said Peter, "it is written in the Book of Psalms: 'May his place be deserted; let there be no one to dwell in it,' and, 'May another take his place of leadership.'"

This refers to Psalm 69:22-28:
"May their table become a snare… May their eyes be darkened so they cannot see… Pour out Your wrath upon them… May they be blotted out of the Book of Life and not listed with the righteous."

How Good is God?

The first person (captive) Jesus went to find, see, retrieve, in the lower realms of the earth, **was Judas…**

A worthy *Selah!*

Your heart says *YES!* As you high-five Your Lord!

BACK TO MY LOVE STORY

"The future for me is already a thing of the past /

You were my first love and you will be my last."

- Bob Dylan, 'Bye & Bye.'

We were inseparable high school BFFs, she knew all my secrets. She knew my loves, the emotional tears, that we skipped school together (and never got caught), and that my Mom sewed every dress worn to that special dance. At times one shakes their head how the Lord stays on the party-line of relationships.

Growing pains separated us as we passed the tassel right to left on the mortarboard of high school days. Years passed, and this will make you gasp—at least it did for me. We reconnected during an office visit to my gynecologist; she worked as an office administrator for my doctor. OMG! I guess secrets of youth, still whisper from the love of friendships.

A few months later, after that embarrassing office visit, I received a very honoring Facebook direct message from her. She said, *"Kristy, I thought you should know: Randy committed suicide last week."*

She was right. I did want to know. To this day, I respect her for informing me. She could tell you first-hand about my first love. I know God will bring a harvest from her loving seed.

COACH'S NOTE: THE REALITY OF THE BARRIER
Statistics I pray this book will assist in changing.

When we talk about "breaking the four-minute mile" in the spirit, we must understand the density of the barrier we are up against. Suicide is a silent epidemic, a "Field of Blood" that claims too many. Based on recent data (2023-2024), the reality is stark:

• *The Scale:* In the U.S. alone, approximately *49,316 people* died by suicide in 2023. It is the 11th leading cause of death.

• *The Gender Gap:* Males account for nearly *80%* of suicides, despite being 50% of the population.

• The Youth: It is the second leading cause of death for individuals aged 10-34.

• *The Global Picture:* Worldwide, more than *720,000 people* die by suicide every year.

Why do I share this? Because just as Roger Bannister broke a psychological barrier for humanity, we are called to break a spiritual barrier for those we love.

As stated in the introduction: What if Revelation was the ball?

| Revelation is meant to humbly heal the Mom, whose son committed suicide.

In honor of Randy's family: love is brave, love is pure, love is gracious and long-suffering.

Jesus lovingly showed me Judas's field that day to prepare me for this conversation with you. I know your heart is already perceiving the sound of an All-Consuming Fire!

That day in the courts of heaven Jesus handed me a special *Gold Key*. I was to take that golden key and unlock the chains that held my "first love" there.

With a recorded mandate in hand, I found myself stepping through a double-pane glass French door, closing it behind me. Walking down a path, noticing the difference from other encounters to the lower realms of the earth, it looked like a pit. There are storm clouds with lightnings held inside of them above, and people standing in a field. Reminded me of the field Jesus showed me where Judas took his own life. *Akeldama.*

There are many here, in this part of Sheol. They do not even seem to see me walking by. As per Psalm 69: their eyes are darkened so they cannot see.

I see Randy.

He is a slight man sitting on a rock, bent over, completely by himself, with chains around his ankles. I walk towards him and see myself carrying a light from heaven, with my mandate papers in my hand. These papers restore his name to being listed with the righteous.

I put my hand on his shoulder. Randy looks up at me. His teeth seem to be knocked out; he doesn't seem to know who I am.

I say, "Randy it's Kristy."

He repeats my name back, "Kristy?"

And I begin to tell him our story of first love, and that is why I am here—to restore him. To share with him about Jesus.

"I have a key to unlock your chains, given to me from Him for you."

Randy still seems to have no thought; so I unlock his chains. They fall to the ground and melt into the ground of this field. The lightnings held in the clouds burst and he stands up, transformed as the young man I remember from high school. The same light that is on me is now on him.

Randy hugs me and says: *I knew that you would come. I always knew you would come. I just couldn't remember what I knew.*

I said, "The voice of the blood of this field can no longer hold you. You are forgiven, my dear friend."

Together we walked back through that barren and blind field, stepping back through the double doors. Jesus is standing on the other side. He gives Randy a huge hug, heart to heart. Then, Jesus reaches into a resource unseen and pulls a crown, placing it on his head.

He says: *"Randy, you have overcome. Love—the love you two shared has completed this path to your overcoming."*

I grasp his hand just for a moment. Randy thanks me with that cute smile that can melt butter (or at least the heart of this cheerleader) and says again, "I knew you would come."

Jesus and Randy walked into the light.

DEFENSIVE PLAYS

TEACHINGS ARE BOUND TO CHRIST

"The Bible is not completely void of teachings. However, all the teachings rest on the person Christ Jesus. Only when He has a certain experience can there be a certain doctrine or teaching... Everything we have obtained is based on what He has attained. The doctrines are absolutely based upon the person and bound to the person. This is genuine Christianity."
— The Normal Christian Faith, Chapter 6, by Watchman Nee

The proceedings of the heavenly court case or the "how-to" are hidden in my journal. If you or a family member have been traumatically touched by suicide, it is a conversation or teaching I am more than honored to share.

No other time in life has the brain of understanding been so washed with the purity of innocence and the heart of that moment. That moment has meant more to me in a collection of moments than when I lived in them.

ACTIVATION

First Love's: a 4 Minute Mile

This chapter takes us on a journey through the profound truths hidden in our first loves and the courage to face impossible barriers.

Now, let's allow the questions of Jesus to open a personal conversation with Him, inviting you to run past the limits of your own conventional thinking and into the divine reality of His love and victory.

A Direct Conversation with Jesus

1. **"Woman, why are you crying?"** (John 20:13) Jesus asks this of Mary Magdalene at the tomb. His question does not dismiss her grief, but rather invites her to bring it fully into His presence. Bring your own tears—for a love lost, a hope unfulfilled, or a story left unfinished—to Jesus.

   • **Ask Him:** *"Jesus, why am I crying?"*

   • **Action:** Be still and allow Him to meet you in the sacred space of your grief, just as He did for Mary.

2. **"Why do you look for the living among the dead?"** (Luke 24:5) This powerful question was asked of those searching for Jesus in the tomb. This chapter reveals that even in the face of loss as profound as suicide, there is a living truth. Take a moment to bring a moment of despair or hopelessness to Him.

   • **Ask Him:** *"Jesus, where am I looking for the living among the dead?"*

   • **Action:** Listen for His truth to point you toward life and resurrection, even in the fields of sorrow.

3. **"Have you never read?"** (Matthew 21:16) Jesus often used this question to challenge the conventional thinking of His day, revealing a deeper truth already written. This is the heart of breaking the "four-minute mile." In light of the author's story:

- **Ask Him:** *"Jesus, what truth have I never read about my own life? What barriers have I accepted as impossible, but are a part of Your already-won victory?"*
- **Action:** Listen for Him to illuminate a hidden truth for you to find.

Reflect and Respond Take a moment to record what you received in this time of conversation with Jesus. What did you hear? What did you feel? Let this be a record of your direct experience of His living presence.

____

____

____

____

Next Step Over the next few days, carry the question that resonated with you the most. As you go about your day, practice listening for Jesus' voice and responding to His truth. Let your newfound spiritual ears guide your every step.

Prayer and Contemplation *Father, thank you for the truth that is Jesus. Thank you for the way you speak to me personally, in ways that I can understand and experience. I open my heart to your love and healing, trusting that it will unfold in your perfect, timeless way. In Jesus' name, amen.*

PLAY SHEET | GIVER

Giver Edition
Redemptive Gifts Summary
FIRST LOVES: A FOUR-MINUTE MILE

This chapter is a breathtaking pursuit of the one who was lost, proving that *Love never clocks out and never accepts a "limit" like the four-minute mile.*

It is a call for you to break the psychological and spiritual barriers of death and realize that no territory in your history is out of reach for the Resurrection.

THE DNA WRISTBAND AUDIBLE: CHAPTER PLAY-CALL

1. **The Green Dot Helmet** (Individual Redemptive Gift): **Giver** The frequency for this play is set to the Giver. This is your gift of "Restoration and Generational Territory." You are hardwired to believe in the "impossible" return on a life or a dream that seems to have been lost to the "Field of Blood." The Giver in you doesn't see a "final whistle" in a tragedy; you see a territory that needs a "Gold Key" of reclamation. You are being called to stop looking at the "unexplainables" of your past as a dead-end and to start applying your mandate to restore the crowns and the "IAMness" of those you love.

2. **The Coaches' Booth** *Legacy Anchor: Heaven is for Real* by Todd Burpo In the "Booths" of your spiritual legacy, *Heaven is for Real* (Giver/Abundance) represents the breaking of the "Conventional Thinking" that Heaven is a distant, silent place. You apply this by realizing that the "unseen realm" is more tangible and active than you have been taught. This anchor reminds you that the "*Cloud of Witnesses*" is standing by, and that the resources of God are available to bridge the gap between your grief and His glory. Just as the world's psychological barrier was broken by the four-minute mile, your barrier is broken by the reality that Heaven is active in your family story right now.

3. **The Play-Call from God**

"Child, check your helmet—I am speaking to the 'first love' I have for you. I see you looking at the notched pages of your life, wondering if the stories that ended in sorrow are truly finished.

I am calling an audible: The future for Me is already a thing of the past! I haven't forgotten the 'youthful fervor' or the purity of the love I placed in your heart.

I watched My Son, Jesus, run the ultimate 'Four-Minute Mile' into the deepest pits of the earth to find the one the world had written off. That is the C♡♡Lness of our Oneness.

When you feel the 'palpitations' of grief or the 'death notice' of a dream, I want you to remember that I have given you a Gold Key. I have authorized you to walk through the 'French doors' of revelation and unlock the chains of the past.

Stop believing the 'death doctrines' that leave you without hope. Your DNA is hardwired for the Restoration of All Things. Be Spiritually BRAVE enough to take My light into the darkened fields of your history. I am so good that I have saved the best wine for the first, last, and everlasting days. You are not a victim of 'lost time'; you are a King's Champion who is restoring the righteous name of your lineage. Run the play, Child. Love is inseparable from who I AM."

4. The Audible The Timeline of Now

The enemy wants you to remain "darkened" by the statistics and the despair of a world that says *'it's over.'* The Audible is this: The barrier is broken! Right now, on the timeline of today, I am removing the "psychological limits" from your mind. I am releasing the power to see the living among the dead. The chains are melting. The crown is being restored. How Good is God!

REFORMATION DATA: THE ARCHITECTURE OF YOUR BREAKTHROUGH

To understand the "field" you are playing on, consider how to apply the "Bannister Principle" to your own life:

• **Breaking the Psychological Barrier:** Roger Bannister's sub-four-minute mile (3:59.4) proved that the "limit" was in the mind, not the lungs. You apply this by identifying the "death doctrine" or "unfulfilled hope" that has been a barrier in your family. By choosing to believe in the Resurrection of the Story, you break the barrier for everyone coming behind you.

• **The "Judas" Precedent:** Jesus went to the "Field of Blood" (*Akeldama*) first. You apply this by realizing that there is no "pit" deep enough to outrun His presence. When you pray for a "lost" cause, you aren't trying to persuade God to care; you are joining Him in a rescue mission He has already initiated.

• **The Gold Key Mandate:** You apply the Giver's Authority by recognizing your "Mandate Papers." These are the scriptures and prophetic words that declare the "Restoration of All Things." When you carry the light of heaven into a situation of "suicide, addiction, or loss," you are legally authorized to unlock the ankle-chains of the past and restore the "Righteous" status of your lineage.

Chapter 6

The Anatomy of Anger:

A Soul's Final Right

— 1 Corinthians 15:26 (KJV)
"The last enemy that shall be destroyed is death."
And said again from the (MSB)
Resurrection life will finally triumph over every definition of
death. —Apostle Paul.

The angriest person I have ever observed in Sheol

LIFE ISN'T FAIR! The times your heartbreaks and manages to recover is astounding.

There is a statement I have heard over the years; when a loved one passes away—whether a child before the parent, or when trauma or accident interrupts life. Well-meaning people with marbles in their mouth will say: *"God is calling them home or God needed them."*

I agree when sickness or disease has ravaged a body for years, it feels merciful to release them of horrendous pain. But it never agreed with me when a life was cut short or "taken" before love and destiny had run its course. God is not selfish. He is not in need of us to be in Heaven with Him. There is too much lack of understanding—too much grey area between black and white.

Death and decay is truly the last key we need to figure out how to possess.

My ninety-two-year-old Mom asks me all the time, *"When we are in Heaven will we live together? Will we be together?*

I have always answered her with yes, but the daily requirements that fill our life on earth today are different there. There is no need for sleep to restore the body, though resting and napping are a delight. Food is for community and joy. Energy is sourced divinely through Him. Houses and Mansions, in all the different forms they take on, are for learning, not keeping your stuff or family protected from the elements.

Yes, there are elements we enjoy and storehouses of weather.

But we LIVE in learning, growing in relationship with His omniscience, discovering, creating unformed worlds and galaxies, and governing the heavenly "jobs" we are passionate about.

I struggle to find a better word than "Jobs." Assignment? Vocation? Field? Activity? No sitting on clouds playing harps—unless you are passionate about playing a harp, in which case the setting will be much grander and filled with an atmosphere of *Shekinah* and worship.

Maybe I should explain it to her, Mom, this way: families have stories that continue to be shared from one generation to the next. Time and heavenly distance is irrelevant. Your family, within the Cloud of Witnesses, continue to encourage you and work towards fulfillment of that family story.

What happens if a person is not amongst the cloud of witnesses? You mean they are in "hell?" Sadly, their part of the story is hindered.

THE RIGHT TO SEPARATE

During the three days in which Jesus' body is recorded as "inside" the tomb, He took a little trip into the lower realms of the earth.

1. Psalm 68:18 is what Jesus read and learned about Himself.

2. Ephesians 4:8 is what we digest as a "Living text" about Ourselves in Oneness.

He led captivity captive. Grace was given to embellish the portion of Himself He gave as ministry gifts, and recovered the keys of the kingdom.

As I mentioned, the family story is hindered if the person is still captive; the gift is not ministering. The gift is as trapped as the individual holding onto their *"Right to..."* separate themselves from knowing the love of God.

1. The Right to be angry.
2. The Right to withhold forgiveness.
3. The Right to be in judgment.

"But to each one of us grace has been given as Christ apportioned it. This is why it says: 'When he ascended on high, he took many captives and gave gifts to his people.' "(What does 'he ascended' mean except that he also descended to the lower, earthly regions? He who descended is the very one who ascended higher than all the heavens, in order to fill the whole universe.)" — Ephesians 4:7-10 (NIV)

In the timeless process of filling all things, He received gifts from men, "even the rebellious" (Psalm 68:18).

Is a person in heaven rebellious? No. But mothers today still beat the drum of life with the "rib" of humanity. We have always known our identity as one that protects vital organs (the heart), facilitates breathing (the womb of the breath of Life), and provides attachment points for the muscles (strength throughout life).

We Mothers are truly amazing.

KATHERINE'S STORY

Imagine a woman whose life was shortened by tragic health circumstances. In this story, she is named, Katherine.

She has always been strong, passionate about her beliefs, loving, adventurous and giving of her time.

Katherine's strength is beyond words as she courageously fought illness and its treatment's side effects right along with the beautiful grace of raising and loving her family.

That curtailed-timing moment, left her family devastated by the shortness of her life.

By this time I had already experienced Sheol and the grace given me from the Lord's gifts. I knew it was a recurring gift —"grace-encounter-offering." I would be asked to implement it, and I would also do the asking, bidding of the heart. It is walking in His footsteps to constantly give back to the beloved. *(God's Continual Filling All Things)*

Katherine was quickly gone—a devastating phone call where surprise and grief collide. Her growing family, a devoted husband of many years, and a host of friends and co-workers now missing her constant love and support.

Over the course of our friendship, I had heard countless times of Katherine's difficult mother. Katherine freely shared the stories of her family outings, which filled the frames of her woodland home and littered her phone photo files. Her children, now having children, have become family to me. Daughters living; heavenly mothers from a divine realm continuing to share the family story.

As with all "Prayer" requests from heaven, they're asked and responded to in the time it takes the heart to beat, pushing a deep knowing in your heart. Moms need daughters and daughters need Moms to encourage them through all transitions in life.

This book is devoted to removing the death barrier as a fortress or wall. Death has been defeated, including the limitations that have created mindsets and chasms in our beliefs.

It is odd how you know things in the spirit. No one ever assumed a "word of knowledge" should span the timeline and reach back into the unseen realm. As with other "lower realms" of the earth and the encounters I have experienced, the magnitude of our Oneness in Him, is incomprehensible.

In this case, love reached like an audio-satellite-stream: from Heaven, to Earth, to Sheol ,and back to Heaven. I knew that I knew: My recently deceased friend's intense mother was not there to welcome her daughter to her heavenly abode.

Yes, Katherine's difficult mother was in hell.

COACH'S CLIPBOARD: THE WORLD ON "HELL"

Think of all the ways "going to hell" is portrayed in our culture. We say in the heat of the moment, in western slang, *at the end of a gun-barrel threat,* or *in impatient frustration at a traffic light.* We never hesitate to verbally send a person there.

- "Go to Heaven for the climate, Hell for the company."—Mark Twain
- "I'd walk through hell in a gasoline suit to play baseball."—Pete Rose
- "You may all go to Hell, and I will go to Texas." —Davy Crockett
- "The safest road to hell is the gradual one - the gentle slope, soft underfoot, without sudden turnings, without milestones, without signposts." —C.S. Lewis
- "It is easy to go down into Hell; night and day, the gates of dark Death stand wide; but to climb back again, to retrace one's steps to the upper air- there's the rub, the task." Virgil
- "The hottest place in Hell is reserved for those who remain neutral in times of great moral conflict. "—unknown
- "I hold it to be the inalienable right of anybody to go to hell in his own way." —Robert Frost

- "I am afraid that the schools will prove the very gates of hell, unless they diligently labor in explaining the Holy Scriptures and engraving them in the heart of the youth."—Martin Luther
- "I'm going to let God be the judge of who goes to Heaven and hell." —Joel Osteen
- "If I'm going to Hell, I'm going there playing the piano."—Jerry Lee Lewis.
- And my favorite, found on my husband Don's coffee cup (Marine Corp, Vietnam Era):
- "Marines don't die. We just go to hell and regroup." — Christopher Hopper, Gods and Men.

THE GATES SHALL NOT PREVAIL

In all our sayings and issues that we account as odds against God, man has not contemplated the frivolities of lying in bed with his "rights" clamped tight in his fists when his body is no longer able to make amends for them.

Or, consider the measure of "saving" time. Some say, *"By the time you fall off a horse,"* a heart prayer is heard by God from the "hellion" who never spoke it aloud. Grace records it as a moving miracle and the changing of his eternal address.

"The rich man shouted. "Father Abraham, have some pity! Send Lazarus over here to dip the tip of his finger in water and cool my tongue. I am in anguish in these flames." Luke 16:24 NLT

Once the door is opened in the spirit of your understanding, and you have journeyed to learn with the Master, the key remains in your hand. Not that one would want to snoop around—it's odd to say, but it is a holy place. Maybe *sacred* is a better term.

God gives man the sacred right to hold odds against Him, against others, and against life for eternity. Or at least until someone, family or friend, is called to ask that entitled individual...*how is it working out for you?*

Truly, to preach the Gospel of good news.

Matthew 16:18 Jesus says to Simon Peter, *"and on this rock I will build my church, and the gates of hell shall not prevail against it."*

I SUGGEST THIS MEANS WE ENCOUNTER THE GATES IN ORDER TO PREVAIL AGAINST THEM!

And The Passion Translation brilliantly tells us more about our gifts. Jesus replied: *"You are favored and privileged Simeon, son of Jonah! For you didn't discover this on your own, but my Father in heaven has supernaturally revealed it to you. I give you the name Peter, a stone. And this rock will be the bedrock foundation on which I will build my church— my legislative assembly, and the power of death will not be able to overpower it! I will give you the keys of Heaven's kingdom realm to forbid on earth that which is forbidden in heaven, and to release on earth that which is released in heaven."*

How about we forbid the gates of hell?

Sheol, in my experience, has different areas or landscapes. What is held against God, held against our brother, or held against life seems to have shaped the topography of the spiritual land.

THE QUARRY

The assignment for Katherine: I love my friend. My heart is broken personally and for her family that I deeply care for. If Katherine's "Mom" has been a pickle throughout her life, it's time to get the pickle out of the pickle barrel of death.

Love is, that powerful.

A note about Sheol: the desire and access is *for the beloved*. Curiosity, or looking to get "creeped out" like it is a horror movie, just doesn't come to mind. One doesn't snoop through another's transgressions. *Love is always the reason to descend.*

We step into His omnipresence, and as His kids, we continue to learn how to function spiritually wherever we are called to shine. There is an inner ear or equilibrium one develops, Sheol "feels" down, lower, under, beneath—though with practice, its as easy as tuning into your mind's eye. With His agreement assigned to me, my spirit stepped in. Waiting for my senses to "ping" the location, room, environment. Remember, we bring the light.

My family would go camping every year during the hottest of summer months. At four thousand feet elevation in the Pacific Northwest mountains, the dust is light, the forest roads high and winding. Mid-week, my husband Don, our boys and many of their cousins would hop into their 4x4s and drive up into the back country to a broken ridge rock quarry to shoot. They'd arrive back at camp overheated, dusty, just as dusk was lining the forest surroundings.

That is where I found Katherine's mother in Sheol

It was a hot, dusty and dimly lit rock quarry. Katherine's mother—for the story purpose, her name is Marge—was unrecognizable. She was hunched over, and just as hard, craggy and slumped as the rock environment she was within would suggest.

It was as back country as you could get. No one else in sight, just Marge. Alone, separated, and so crippled over from her anger. She didn't notice me. Her bitterness was playing a single 45 vinyl record on a player, stuck on repeat. The arm and diamond needle never lifted, and neither did her obsession of holding onto her negative rights.

I said her name firmly: *"Marge, Katherine needs you."* She didn't straighten up; painfully, she lifted her chin and cold eyes.

Again I said; "Marge, Katherine is here in Heaven and she needs you."

The look upon her face softened. The softness brought memory, and the library of her life recognized me.
Love is that powerful!

The right to be angry and live in the refuse of trauma has living soul memory, but bitterness couldn't wipe away the umbilical connection of Mother and Daughter. In the womb, the breath of life has an eternal spark. Love is a vibration that resets the B-17 button on the juke box of life.

I laid my right hand on her hunched-over left shoulder and said for the third time: *"Marge, Katherine is here in Heaven and she needs you."*

Within a miracle instance of Marge's recall, discerning Katherine's life expectancy and timeline shouted volumes. Memory of her loving family (despite her disagreeable nature) reached from earth to Heaven, reached even hell.

The broken "Story" link which Marge's anger separated, could now be soldered together.
Love is that powerful.

Marge's nanosecond recall ignited a mother's story that she needed to hear. The fight to be humanly "right" was dramatically humbled by her divine *inalienable* rights within the love of God. The work of Christ illuminated her daughter's need; no longer was it about her. The love of God removed the distance, solitude and aridness of heart that anger created.
Love is that powerful.

In the next moments, I was standing at the base before the staircase to Heaven, looking up, watching. Jesus and Katherine standing at the top, arms wide open, beaming with joy as Marge was ascending.

She was altered by the Giver of Life Himself—filled with light, softened, returned youth, and no memory of ever having wasted a single moment beyond the gates of hell.
The Good News of the Gospel was preached.

Activation

The Anatomy of Anger: A Soul's Final Right

This story invites us to confront the deep-seated anger and bitterness that can separate a soul, even beyond this life.

It reveals that the power of love, empowered by Christ's victory over the grave, can overcome even the most hardened heart. Now, let's allow the questions of Jesus to cut through the noise and open a conversation with your heart. The gates of hell shall not prevail against us—because we are called to prevail against them.

A Direct Conversation with Jesus

1. **"Why do you see the speck in your brother's eye, but do not consider the plank in your own eye?" (Matthew 7:3)** The story of Marge's anger is powerful, but it's a mirror for us all. The human tendency to focus on another's brokenness keeps us from seeing our own. Before you intercede for another, first bring a moment of anger, judgment, or unforgiveness you have held to Jesus.

   • **Ask Him***: "Jesus, what plank is in my own eye? Where have I been holding on to my 'right to be angry?'"*

   • **Action:** Listen for His compassionate truth to reveal and heal that area of your heart.

2. **"Is it not lawful for me to do what I wish with my own things? Or is your eye evil because I am good?" (Matthew 20:15)** This is a challenging question that confronts our bitterness when God shows undeserved grace. Marge's story shows a radical act of grace that transcends our human sense of fairness. Consider someone you believe is unworthy of God's grace.

   • **Ask Him:** *"Jesus, is my eye evil because You are good? Do I begrudge Your mercy to others?"*

   • **Action:** Listen for Him to speak to the envy and judgment in your heart and fill it with His divine love and compassion.

3. "What is that to you? You follow me." (John 21:22) Jesus asked this of Peter, refocusing him from comparing his path to another's and back to his own unique assignment. In this chapter, you've witnessed a call to prevail against the gates of hell in a very personal way. You may not be called to Sheol, but you have a divine assignment.

• **Ask Him:** *"Jesus, what is my unique assignment in prevailing against the gates of hell? What is that to me? I will follow You."*

• **Action:** Listen for His guidance to the path He has uniquely designed for you.

Reflect and Respond

Take a moment to record what you received in this time of conversation with Jesus. What did you hear? What did you feel? Let this be a record of your direct experience of His living presence.

____

____

____

____

Next Step

Over the next few days, carry the question that resonated with you the most. As you go about your day, practice listening for Jesus' voice and responding to His truth. Let your newfound spiritual ears guide your every step.

Prayer and Contemplation

Father, thank you for the truth that is Jesus. Thank you for the way you speak to me personally, in ways that I can understand and experience. I choose to lay down my rights and judgment and embrace Your love and Your way. In Jesus' name, Amen.

PLAY SHEET | RULER

Ruler Edition
Redemptive Gifts Summary

THIS CHAPTER IS A HEAVYWEIGHT PLAY, shifting the stadium lights from the stagnant "shallows" of religious trauma to the high-velocity restoration of the heart. It is a call for you to stop holding onto your "right to be angry" and to embrace the Resurrection Life that has the power to solder your family story back together.

THE DNA WRISTBAND AUDIBLE: CHAPTER PLAY-CALL

1. **The Green Dot Helmet** (Individual Redemptive Gift): **Ruler** The frequency for this play is set to the Ruler. This is your gift of the "Architect of Authority" and the "Steward of Legitimate Rights." You are hardwired to recognize when a "Gate of Hell"—like bitterness or a generational grudge—is hindering the flow of your family's legacy. The Ruler in you is being called to stop managing the "Quarry of Anger" and to start using your Sonship Authority to forbid the isolation that bitterness creates. You have the inherent capacity to realize that the "Power of Death" cannot overpower the legislative assembly of your heart when you are One with the King.

2. The Coaches' Booth (*Legacy Anchor*): *More Than a Carpenter* by Josh McDowell In the "Booths" of your spiritual legacy, *More Than a Carpenter* (Ruler/Architecture) represents the investigation into the solid, undeniable reality of Christ's victory. You apply this by moving beyond "marbles in the mouth" sentiment and into a "Structural" confidence that death has been defeated. This anchor reminds you that the "Gates of Hell" are not a final boundary for your loved ones, but a location subject to the King's administration. It proves that the "Story" isn't over just because a life was cut short; the architecture of the Cross is designed for a total rescue.

3. The Play-Call from God

"Child, tune into the headset—I am speaking over the '45 vinyl record' of your bitterness. I see the 'rights' you are clamping tight in your fists, sitting in the dusty quarry of your own 'Hell,' wondering if life will ever be fair.

I am calling an audible: Resurrection life triumphs over every definition of death! I didn't give you the keys to the Kingdom so you could snoop through transgressions; I gave them to you to prevail against the gates of isolation.

I watched My Son, Jesus, descend into the lower parts of the earth to fill all things, and I have given you that same Sonship Authority. That is the C♡♡Lness of our Oneness. When

you feel the 'craggy and hard' edges of an old resentment, I want you to remember that My Love is a vibration that resets the jukebox of your soul.

Stop believing the lie that your anger is an inalienable right. Your DNA is hardwired to be a 'Living Gateway' of honor and restoration. Be Spiritually BRAVE enough to lay your hand on the shoulder of the 'rebellious' parts of your history and speak My Good News. I am so good that I use your 'yes' to solder the broken links of your mother-daughter, father-son, family story. You aren't meant to be a prisoner of trauma; you are meant to be a King's Champion who leads captives away. Run the play, Child. The stairs are open, and I am beaming with joy."

4. The Audible (The Timeline of Now) The enemy wants you to remain "neutral" or "neutralized" by the weight of your unforgiveness.

The Audible is this: The "Pickle" is out of the barrel! Right now, on the timeline of today, I am removing the "limitations of your belief" from your mind. I am releasing the power to climb back to the upper air of My presence. The gates are prevailing *for* you, not against you. How Good is God!

REFORMATION DATA: THE ARCHITECTURE OF YOUR PREVAILING

To understand the "field" you are playing on, consider how to apply these "Ruler" principles to your own "Quarry":

• **The Legislative Assembly:** Jesus called the church His "Ekklesia"—a governing body. You apply this by realizing that you have the Keys of Heaven to forbid on earth that which is forbidden in heaven. Bitterness is forbidden in Heaven; therefore, you have the legal right to forbid it from ruling your family's "Sheol" or your own heart.

• **The "B-17" Reset:** In the story, the "bitterness record" was broken by a single mention of a loved one's name. *Apply this:* by realizing that Love is a Vibration. When you speak the truth of "How Good God Is" into a dark situation, you are literally resetting the frequency of the environment. Memory and umbilical connections are eternal sparks that ignite under the touch of Mercy.

- **Retracing the Steps:** Virgil said the "rub" is the task of climbing back to the upper air. You apply the Higher Law by realizing that Jesus has already done the "rub" for you. By yielding to His "firm embrace," you aren't fighting to climb out of your anger; you are being "drawn up" by the Savior-God who claims the entire world—and your entire heart—as His own.

Sideline Note: Virgil (Publius Vergilius Maro) refers to the ancient Roman poet (70–19 BC) most famous for the epic poem, the Aeneid. Specifically, the "rub" refers to a famous passage in Book VI of the Aeneid regarding the descent into the underworld: "Facilis descensus Averno... sed revocare gradum superasque evadere ad auras, hoc opus, hic labor est."
Translation:
"The descent into Hell is easy... but to retrace one's steps and escape to the upper air, this is the task, this is the toil [the rub]."

HOW GOOD IS GOD!

THE SPACIOUS PLACE

"He brought me out into a spacious place; He rescued me because He delighted in me." — Psalm 18:19 (NIV)

The past can feel like a small room. The binds of history are tight, defining where you stop and where the impossible begins.

But the Father does not build ceilings. He builds horizons. You are not held by what was. You are held by Who is.

Breathe here. The boundaries have fallen. There is room for you to believe.

Chapter 7

So Sad U See: Unraveling the Ancestral Bind

The scroll was signed in dust, long, long ago,
By hands we know not, spirits whispering low.
What if their vow—a sacred, solemn bind—
Still chains the wings of your awakening mind?
A ghost of doctrine, woven in your breath,
Guards freedom's gate, a lock passed down through death.
Break the old seal, where ancient fears convene,
And meet the God your soul has always seen.

"Yeshuat Hashem k'heref ayin."
The salvation of God is like the blink of an eye.
— Pesikta Zutreta

COACH'S CLIPBOARD: THE DEFINITION
Pesikta Zutreta:A collection of Jewish religious commentary (Midrash) on the Torah and the Five Megillot (scrolls). Compiled in the 11th century CE by the Bulgarian scholar and Talmudist, Rabbi Toviyah ben Eliezer.

My Hebraic roots were discovered by that same "blink of an eye" faith found in the *Gates of Time* chapter. The framework of this book is not linear; it is built around a fixed set of Thematic Doorways. All wisdom gained and every experience encountered during the season is filtered and woven through the authority of those singular thresholds.

Salvation of God: In the Jewish mindset, individuals are born pure and face a moral choice between good and evil inclinations. Sin is a conscious decision, and repentance can achieve full atonement. Conversely, the traditional Christian view holds that all humanity is born tainted by Original Sin (inherited from Adam), resulting in an inescapable moral incapacity. Consequently, salvation and justification are achieved solely through faith in Jesus Christ, whose death provides the necessary remedy for this inherited guilt.

I find it impossible to read a Scripture text without curiosity knocking on the door of life. I want to know the people, the disciples, and the Jesus who actually lived it and humbly wrote it down for us to learn how to encounter the threshold of Him.

Time, the Cloud of Witnesses, and Scripture are all accessed through Him—the Door.

"Then Simon Peter also arrived and went straight into the tomb and took a long look at the grave clothes lying there. He also noticed that the cloth that was wrapped around the head of Jesus was not lying with the other strips of linen cloth, but neatly rolled up separately."
— (John 20:6-7, Mirror Translation)

Why would Jesus care to fold up His head cloth?

Some believe this is a symbol from the Jewish culture of the day. When a master was finished with his meal, he would throw the cloth aside. But when he wanted to get up from the table and intended to return, he would fold it up neatly to tell the servant not to clean it up yet because *he was coming back.*

What do you think?

The thought process can be overwhelming; our logic frames it within our inexperience of the text. But I asked Jesus: *"What about those three days Your body spent in the tomb?"*

Sometimes in life, you spend more days in the "Tomb of Learning" before you walk out in the "Day of Resurrection." What if the blood and beliefs of your ancestors act as an accusation the enemy won't let go of?

This is one of those "Tomb Days."

THE BLANKET & THE CAROUSEL

God set a date for this chapter. I received a prophetic word in the midst of "tuning my personal piano" with curiosity:

"Tell her I love her and I have not forgotten her."

Why? And what is the root? It's a question of Time, and Time is the essence.

"A new perspective is always good but you also have to be honest with yourself. It's not all about oneself, but how we fit in a whole... It is always good in this case to go back to the root, to the beginning, to the ancient path... I have the feeling this is not about you but about your family line. The root is not in your life but many generations ago."
— Prophetic Journal Entry

We were like seeds planted together in the same soil, to be co-quickened to life. If we were included in His death, we are equally included in His resurrection.

"The love of Christ constrains us and resonates within us; leaving us with only one conclusion: when Jesus died, every individual simultaneously died. In God's logic, one has died for all, thus all have died. Now if all were included in his

death they were equally included in his resurrection. This unveiling of his love redefines human life. Whatever reference we could have of ourselves outside of our association with Christ is no longer relevant."
— 2 Corinthians 5:14-15 (Mirror Bible)

Whatever reference we could have of ourselves... Hmm?

This chapter is a struggle to articulate the root systems experienced in the story to paper, versus sitting down with you and watching a movie unfold. It is the "whatever reference" that has continually been at the forefront of Holy Spirit's quest with me. He is graciously making me aware of a record—a "whatever reference" of understood logic—and the ever-altering Rhema Mind that changes that "record" as to what is no longer relevant.

If a Higher Law (The Law of the Spirit of Life) repeals a Lesser Law (Sin and Death):

It is similar to receiving a restraining order from the Lesser Law. A restraining order is a civil court order that legally requires one person (the restrained party) to stop harming or harassing another. The primary purpose is to provide a legal layer of safety.

If we walked out of the courtroom with this Higher Law in our hand, waved it at the wind, and did a war dance around it on the lawns of justice, how would the law be employed?

Hypothetically, our DNA, thinking, and actions are a historical white horse on a carousel. It is beautiful, hand-painted with a royal crown, ribbons of valor braided into a windswept mane, galloping up and down—always moving forward, but only in circles.

The Higher Law gives the royal horse the freedom to **eject** from the foundation and monotonous movement of the carousel to canter freely into the picture and liberty of life. (Ha, ha, I just described a scene from the original *Mary Poppins* movie).

But how would the law be upheld? There are parties and parchments involved.
- The Carousel Operator lassoes the horse: *"Where are you going?"*
- The Ticket Taker claims: "I have already sold tickets for rides on this horse."
- A five-year-old boy, sticky with candy, stomps his feet: *"I want to ride the horse with the crown!"*

Who can defy the cycle of the merry-go-round? What happens if the "merry-go-round" denies the upgraded law and the Divine Sponsor?

THE SADDUCEE BIND

I woke up in the morning and sensed I was covered by a blanket. Sensed, not seen. In my morning prayer time, a blanket was continuously perceived. I couldn't shake the thought.

Later that morning, I received the prophetic word about the "Root," which only fueled the flame of getting to the bottom of it. I was elbow-deep in my encountering "Tomb Days." Don't get me wrong, the feeling was not depressing; there was a weightiness of presence.

Blanket... Blanket? Covers me and is unseen? Jewish roots and traditions?

My banner and cornerstone scripture for the "Tomb Days" season became John 6:36:

"But even though you have seen me, you are not persuaded. (You might be happy with the healings and be entertained by the signs, but still you fail to understand who I am! I'm not

here to impress you with me! I'm here to persuade you about you! Your sonship is what I am all about! And the only way that I can persuade you about you is to take you with me into your death and darkness and overcome your fear and hell and birth you again into newness of life in my resurrection!)"

Then Lord, I give You permission to persuade me.

So, I took this "unseen" blanket—the messy, unfolded linens, what covered the "Body portion of Christ"—to the Courts of Heaven. I needed their story! And it's a Jewish thing. Translation in Hebrew, please!

I laid the elements on the bench of His Honor, and the story shook loose.

2 Corinthians 3:14-16: This passage speaks of a "veil" that covers the hearts of people when the Old Covenant is read, preventing them from understanding its true meaning. The scripture states that when one turns to the Lord, the veil is lifted.

My spirit relayed to my understanding that my Jewish maternal line was linked with the sect of the Sadducees.

The New Testament Takeaway:

(Matthew 22:23, Mark 12:18, Luke 20:27, Acts 23:8)

The Sadducees do not believe in the resurrection.

How does a declaration of limited belief impact your spiritual epigenetic line? It binds your freedom.

The Sadducees say that souls die with the bodies. Because they did not believe in the Resurrection, they were... **"So Sad, You See."**

And there I have my Play Call in the huddle of humanity into the lower realms of the earth. Old belief systems, hello Father Abraham. The Jesus in me is coming to do more than offer a finger dip of water.

Courts of Heaven Assignment: Go preach the Gospel of Good News to my Jewish ancestors in Sheol—that Jesus was raised from the dead, my IAMness is raised from the dead— and return back to this courtroom.

Our Super Bowl reset-power quote is always: *Go ask Jesus!* And our question of the hour: *How Good is God?*

We are about to See!

THE BLUE THREAD

I step before Sheol's entrance, turn left, wash my hands in a small marble basin, and tidy my robe. Lifting my voice, I declare:

"Jesus Christ is risen from the dead! I am raised from the dead in and through Him. I have permission to declare Him here to you today! Selah..."

I didn't see anyone around. *Hmm? Waiting?*

So I sang at the top of my lungs: *"Glory to God in the highest, Peace to all men in Him, He is the Lord who decrees our lordship and honors our stand in Him!"*
Still... no one.
Remaining in Sheol, I peeked with my spirit back into the Heavenly Court briefly. I addressed the court and said to the Lord, *"No one is there?"*
Then, as in a mist, I saw the movement of thousands of individuals with prayer shawls around their shoulders, walking from within the cover of the mist. The misty veil looked similar to bird netting you use to protect the fruit of your blueberry bushes in the garden.
I lift the 'veil' of Moses and walk underneath it.

I step to the man closest to me, offer him a wooden cup of water. He drinks. I shake his hand.

The same man passes the wooden cup of water to the next standing in the massive queue. I also shake his hand. The scene and protocol repeat itself again and again. The wooden cup of water provides a drink and is passed to the next. I always shake each individual's hand in the passing.

My vision expands and I perceive four angels lay hold of the corners of Moses' veil, lifting it off every individual who has drunk of this cup and shaken my hand.

Laughter erupts! Joy falls like rain and they begin to remove their sacred clothing. Off with their hats, shoes, pants, shirts, until they were unclothed down to the *ephod and undergarment.* A curious sight, all of them presented in ephod and *tallit* (prayer shawl).

The first man (Patriarch) I interacted with remained in the forefront of this auspicious moment. With joy on our lips and family in our blood, intuitively reaching toward him, *I pulled a single blue thread from his tallit.*

In the "pulling," hanging onto the thread, my steps moved backward. I continued pulling the blue thread as I walked around the company of people—it could be thousands— wrapping or spooling the mass of people in the blue thread from the prayer shawl of that same first individual.

The blue thread responded as a single string plucked on a musical instrument. Strong as silk, translucent, reflecting gold light. Sound, vibration, and light dancing as I continued to walk around and entangle them in a cord of light.

The single thread was pulled from Jacob's tallit.

The first man, a rabbi—*Jacob,* in my family line.

He falls to his knees and begins to weep with thanksgiving. The spool of a single blue thread begins to sing; bliss is vibrated around the mass of men—a remembrance, the Living Torah.

Then I see women and children begin to enter the assembly place in Sheol. One by one, the women and children walk through the tabernacle not made with human hands.

> *"Now we know that if the earthly tent we live in is dismantled, we have a building from God, an eternal house in Heaven, not built by human hands."*
> *— 2 Corinthians 5:1*

Each member of this massive family walked through the tabernacle, divinely spooled around a family provision: a single blue thread of one man's tallit. Jacob was still on his knees.

They walked through the Way.

They walked through the Truth.

They walked through the Life.

Because I was in the front of the queue, I didn't notice Jesus shaking each family member's hand as they were withdrawn and deposited in Heaven.

The paradigm continued until the women and children had all walked through. Slowly, the threaded circle pattern invited every man spooled in blue thread to walk into and through the tabernacle of light. Until only one remained: Jacob, still on his knees, and me.

The thread supernaturally remained suspended in position even though no individual was there to shore it up. It waited. The thread waited for Jacob.

Jacob gazed at the wooden cup in his hands, before giving it back to me, and gave me a bear hug—the kind that lasts until we meet again. While looking into his eyes, he pulled a small boutonniere-size cutting of the tip of an olive branch—from where, I do not know—and pinned it to my lapel with a tiny gold dove.

We embraced one more time as the rain of joy, which continually misted over us, began to recede from the surface of the ground we stood on in Sheol. Jacob smiled at me as he proceeded to walk the path.

I noticed when he stepped, the ground was flooded by the weight of his foot; water squished up from the surface. But when his foot lifted to take the next step forward, the ground was dry. Each step evaporated the moisture from the soil until he was through the path.

Jesus, with tears of joy and His hand stretched out to Jacob... they both turned their gaze simultaneously to see the remains behind.

The soil was dry. The blue thread, commanded to disembark from its pattern, flew as threads of light to the hem of Jesus' garment. Heaven's door closed behind.

My spirit stood in an empty place.

My spirit filled with the love of God.

I unpinned Jacob's gift—the small clipping of olive branch and dove—from my shoulder, and laid them in the center of this empty place. *Selah...*

THE PRIEST'S GARMENT

I step back into the courtroom. The room is filled with huge white pillars, and many men are now standing present.

"Father," I say.

I hand Him the assignment, completed, and ask for it to be recorded. Very interesting: as I wait...

Weary from the emotions that transpire in the work of repentance, I notice the earlier perceived, invisible blanket is gone.

My grave clothes—the "linens"—are still resting on the bench top. Father God reaches over and picks them up, stretches them, and then proceeds to put the soiled cloth on Himself.

Can I say magically?

They become the High Priest's dressings.

And God sits back down, smiling.

My emotions spent, I step out of the courtroom back into the prayer closet of my living room. Four hours have passed.

COACH'S CLIPBOARD

"If you don't change with the times, the times are going to change you."— Marv Levy, Legendary Hall of Fame Coach

The Ancestral bind, a doctrine cold and thin,
Woven across the years to hold the lineage in.
A faith that feared the angel, spirit, and the rise,
The limiting lament seen through ancestral eyes.
We heard the whisper from the lie that held the key:
"The spirit is extinct, the promise lost, So Sad U See."
But the Great Persuasion breaks the grip of fear,
The Higher Law of Life declares the lineage clear.
With Blue Thread spun from Jacob's ancient shawl,
The accusation falls away from one and all.
The empty cup of silver holds no greater grace,
Than simple wood that sanctifies this place.
We raise the plain wooden cup—a truth of humble worth,
That celebrates the New Birth and Heaven's open earth.

ACTIVATION

So Sad U See: Unraveling the Ancestral Bind

This chapter offers a powerful framework for addressing any ancestral bind or inherited limitation in your life. Kristen's experience teaches that God's authority is absolute (Higher Law), His provision is simple (Wooden Cup), and His redemption is expansive (Blue Thread).

Now, let's step into this revelation and allow the questions of Jesus to open a personal conversation with Him, inviting you to search out any generational limitation for the complete liberty of your Co-Resurrection.

A Direct Conversation with Jesus

1. **"What do you want me to do for you?" (Mark 10:51)**

Kristen's assignment began with a vague sense (the invisible blanket, "Tell her I love her") but escalated into a powerful, specific mandate. You must move from vague desire to specific demand when confronting generational issues. Bring the specific area of limitation in your life (sickness, mindset, fear) to Jesus.

   • **Ask Him:** "Jesus, what is the specific, tangible thing You want to achieve through this situation? Give me the language and mandate I need to declare the Higher Law over this limit today."
   • **Action:** Be clear and listen for His direction.

2. **"If I have told you earthly things and you do not believe, how will you believe if I tell you heavenly things?" (John 3:12)**

This question challenges the "So Sad U See" limitation in every form—the mind that cannot believe what it cannot see. Kristen's journey involved perceiving the language of the spirit: the Blue Thread and the Wooden Cup—spiritual reality made tangible.

- **Ask Him:**"Lord, where is my earthly logic limiting my growth in heavenly perspectives? Show me the simple, tangible tool (a word, a gesture, a memory) You want me to use to enact the Higher Law in my life, knowing that Yeshuat Hashem k'heref ayin (the salvation of God is like the blink of an eye)?"

3. **"Do you not know that you are God's temple and that God's Spirit dwells in you?" (1 Corinthians 3:16)**

The Ancestral Bind is simply an attack on your inherent identity and the sovereignty of the Spirit who dwells in you. Jacob's family was bound by doctrine, but Kristen's Co-Inclusion in Christ set them free.

- **Ask Him:**"How does the knowledge that Your Spirit dwells in me give me a 'Restraining Order' against specific generational patterns? Show me what I must forbid on earth that is already forbidden in Heaven because of my Oneness with You."

Reflect and Respond

Take a moment to record what you experienced through this encounter and in this time of conversation with Jesus. What was the feeling of the Higher Law overriding the blockages in life? How did the simple truth of a heavenly communion (*Wooden Cup: Kiddush cup, a ceremonial goblet for sanctifying the Sabbath*) sanctify this moment for you?

Let this be a record of your direct experience of ejecting from the carousel and employing the liberty of the Higher Law.

Next Step

Carry the question that challenged your limitation the most. Practice seeing your life through the lens of *How Good God Is!* Declare that you are no longer operating on the slow cycle of the carousel but on the instantaneous, Higher Law of the Spirit of Life.

Prayer and Contemplation

Father, thank You for the truth that spans across time and place. I choose the Higher Law over every ancestral bind. I believe You have cleared my lineage with Christ's righteousness. I am ready to see the invisible and trust that the Spirit who dwells in me has given me authority. In Jesus' name, Amen

---

PLAY SHEET | TEACHER

Teacher Edition
Redemptive Gifts Summary
THIS CHAPTER IS A HIGH-STAKES LEGISLATIVE SESSION in the Courts of Heaven, targeting the "Ancestral Bind"—those invisible defensive schemes passed down through your spiritual DNA.

It is a call for you to recognize that the "vows of the fathers" are not a permanent lock when you serve the Higher Law of the Spirit of Life as a Restraining Order over your lineage.

The DNA Wristband Audible: Chapter Play-Call

1. **The Green Dot Helmet** (Individual Redemptive Gift): **Teacher** The frequency for this play is set to the Teacher. This is your gift of the "Architect" and the "Reformer."

You are hardwired to search out the "roots" and the "ancient paths" of your life. You have an internal drive to understand why things aren't "adding up"—why ABC does not equal 123 in your breakthrough.

The Teacher in you is being activated to dismantle the "So Sad U See" (Sadducean) mindset—the voice in your blood that says the supernatural is extinct or that the resurrection doesn't apply to your situation. You are being called to stop circling on the "carousel" of inherited logic and to employ the Higher Law that clears your entire lineage.

2. **The Coaches' Booth** *Legacy Anchor: The Prayer of Jabez* by Bruce Wilkinson In the "Booths" of your spiritual legacy, The Prayer of Jabez (Teacher/Structure) represents your breakout play: "Enlarge my territory and keep me from evil." *Apply This:* Realize that you are not a victim of the "pain" or the structural limitations your ancestors signed in the dust. This anchor reminds you that the Divine Sponsor is ready to upgrade your law. Just as Jabez broke out of a legacy of sorrow, you are applying this truth to break out of the "Ancestral Bind." It proves that God is more concerned with your "New Birth" and your "Expanded Territory" than He is with the "Grave Clothes" of your past.

3. **The Play-Call from God**

"Child, check your helmet—I am speaking a 'Blink of the Eye' change into your situation. I see you feeling 'hope-exhausted,' ticking the boxes of inner healing while still sensing an 'invisible blanket' of limitation over your heart.

I am calling an audible: Yeshuat Hashem k'heref ayin
—My salvation is as fast as the blink of an eye!
I watched My Son, Jesus, neatly fold His head cloth in the tomb as a signal to you that the 'tomb days' of your learning are over. That is the C♡♡Lness of our Oneness.

When you feel the weight of an old family vow or a doctrine that denies My power, I want you to reach for the Blue Thread. I have already spooled your entire family in the 'Chord of Light' from the Master's tallit.
Stop believing the lie that the 'Spirit is extinct' in your family tree.
Your DNA is hardwired for the Higher Law of Life. Be Spiritually BRAVE enough to wash your hands of the old protocol and step under the 'veil' of My presence. I am so good that I pick up your 'soiled linens' and wear them as My own High Priest dressings just to show you how clean you are.
You are the one I have authorized to unpin the 'olive branch' of peace and lay it in the empty places of your history. Run the play, Child.
The carousel has stopped and the gate is open."

4. The Audible *The Timeline of Now*

The enemy wants you to remain "bound" by the scrolls and the spirits of the past.

The Audible is this: The Restraining Order is served! Right now, on the timeline of today, I am removing the "Ancestral Bind" from your mind. I am releasing the power of the Wooden Cup—the humble, simple authority of My finished work. The veil is lifted. The lineage is clear. You are free to canter into the liberty of life. How Good is God!

REFORMATION DATA: THE ARCHITECTURE OF YOUR UNRAVELING

To understand the "field" you are playing on, consider how to apply these "Teacher" principles to your own "Lineage":

• **The Restraining Order:** In the spirit, a "Restraining Order" legally requires the "Lesser Law" (Sin and Death) to stop harassing you. *Apply This:* Take the Higher Law (The Spirit of Life) and "wave it at the wind." When you declare that you are "In Christ," you are legally ejecting from the monotonous movement of your generational carousel.

• **The Blue Thread** (Techelet)**:** The *Techelet* was a reminder of heavenly identity. *Apply This:* "Pull the thread" of Co-Inclusion. Just as the single thread spooled thousands in the story, your one "yes" to the Truth of the Resurrection can entangle your entire family in a chord of light. One has died for all; therefore, all have died to the old bind.

• **The Wooden Cup** (Humble Authority)**:** *Apply This:* Trade "popular opinion" for the "Wooden Cup" of simple communion. You don't need a silver chalice or massive amounts of "inner healing" to be rescued; you need a face-to-face encounter with the Living Torah. When you "drink" from the truth of His goodness, the angels are authorized to lift the veil off your heart.

HOW GOOD IS GOD!

THE SACRED SEAT

"He prepares a table before me in the presence of my enemies; He anoints my head with oil; my cup runs over." — *Psalm 23:5 (NKJV)*

The pew is not a parking spot. It is a place of communion.

Here, in the quiet row, the Bread is broken, and the Cup is poured. Here, we do not watch a performance. We taste a Person.

Do not rush past this seat. It is where the King serves you. Sit down. Eat. Remember Him.

Section II

Gates of Pew

How Good is God!

ALIVE IN THE HOUSE

"But I am like a green olive tree in the house of God; I trust in the mercy of God forever and ever." — Psalm 52:8 (NKJV)

Growth is not a deadline. It is a daily drink.

In a world that demands finished products, God delights in the unfolding leaf.

To be green is to remain soft, open, and alive to His voice. Do not rush the fruit. Trust the root.

Stay open. Let Him hold the pen.

Chapter 8

The Ready Scribe: Green and Growing

Not Ripe and Rotting

"You're either green and growing or ripe and rotting. Get a moving target. You have to be in motion. The moment you think you've figured it out, you've stopped growing."

— **Lou Holtz,** Former NCAA and NFL Head Football Coach

Psalm 45:1 (Author Inspired) *My heart is not merely composing a good song; it is bursting with the finished matter of our King! I speak of nothing but the design of our co-union—the mutual indwelling realized in Him. My tongue is now completely yielded, a skilled instrument articulating the thoughts of the Spirit; it is the fluent pen of a ready scribe, perfectly mirroring the logos of our identity.*

Two sections that rearrange every particle from the human score: *Pew & Pulpit.* Take your shoes off and walk barefoot in the most luxurious green grass you can imagine. It is cultivated and groomed with no surprises—no pebbles for concern. It is easy to walk with your eyes closed and senses fully exhaling.

187

Maybe your bare feet find rest in natural, loose blades of grass that get tangled between your toes in every stride. The grass is cool; you draw from the sun on your face and a gentle warm breeze tickling the hairs on the back of your neck. You are regulated and refreshed.

Reset. Allow breath to come up through your feet, grounding you.

Goûter aux plaisirs de la vie. To taste the pleasures of life. The physical contact with the Earth's surface transfers free electrons into the body. Free? Pause. Question. Electrons which can neutralize "free" radicals and reduce chronic inflammation. Some people call it "Earthing."

I have settled into a deep, contemplative rest—a stillness born from years of seeking, where thought finally solidifies into the tangible. I have placed this book, in its weighty, hardback form—my preference—on my left. The truths within were forged over a lifetime. I can see this *How Good Is God* edition resting there now, the final, definitive view that has irrevocably altered the perspective gathered from every single Pew my history has known.

Pew history? To taste the pleasures of life. Free? Pause. Honored. Grateful. Community. In love.

Our verse... ready?

SPITTING DISTANCE

It was spitting distance, upwind and across the street from "Norm's."

Ready or not, this verse attached itself to me inside this place: a house that needed a paint job, faded dark, Ranch style, built on a lower berm off street level on Highway 99E, Aurora, Oregon.

The first thing—or the only thing—you may see while driving by without real intent is the roof. "Norm's" was a Mom and Pop local market icon. Push the door open—*clank* of the tin bell on the glass to announce "you're here"—and hit a wall of cigarette smoke blended with the residue of fast-food fryer oil.

If you were a local, you were on a first-name basis with Norm and Ethel. Nothing sets memory better than the burnt coffee you continued to buy because everybody loved "Norm's." I cherish my quilt table runner—mixed browns and whites in a Longhouse pattern—that Ethel made for me.

Norm's is the pin-marker for the house that I was invited to but once. I have no recollection of the *why* or *who* of the people who gathered there. But that day, a dark-haired, European-looking man—about the same "30-ish" age as myself—came up to me in the kitchen.

Without fanfare or explanation (because I didn't have a clue), he gave me a *"Word from the Lord."*

My very first word from the Lord. Just as "Norm's" is pin-marked, so was this first scripture declaration of my Divine Attributes.

THE AUDIT

How Good is God... in my attempts to create thinking, reflection, and press the corporate bandwidth of His inerrant goodness? I am asking you to travel from your first prophetic word to today.

Identify the areas where your readiness was *Green and Growing* like our header quote, or stuck at *Ripe and Rotting*.

Sounds harsh, the "rotting" part, doesn't it? But let's remind ourselves: what do the traditions of men do to the Word?

COACH'S CLIPBOARD: THE NULLIFICATION
"The traditions of men make the Word of God of no effect."(Mark 7:13, Matthew 15:6)

This highlights a conflict where human-made rules and customs are elevated above God's actual commandments. It means that elaborate traditions (like ritual handwashing or religious hierarchy) are often prioritized over core principles (like honoring parents or the movement of the Spirit). If our traditions are not aligned with the Living Message, they become a barrier to true faith.

The history of the Church Pew is a quiet, profound story of settled purpose and surprising complication.

For centuries, believers stood or knelt, free to move and flow during worship. As the need for order grew—particularly after the Reformation—the simple bench evolved into the fixed wooden pew. What began as structure soon bore an earthly cost: many pews were "rented" or privately owned by wealthy families, creating divisions where status dictated seating.

This contrast is striking when we consider the original design of worship: of all the sacred furniture in God's house, *the Tabernacle contained no chairs.*

The sacred furniture of the Tabernacle was designed for *active participation:*

- The **Altars** for offering.
- The **Table** for communion.
- The **Basin** for cleansing.
- The **Ark** for covenant presence.

There was no passive seating. The focus was on continuous worship, prostration, reflection, transformation, and the ultimate removal of that which is out of tune with our original design.

Yet, even with the Pew's history of earthly pricing, it remains an anchor—a stable Gate for the heart to receive the weighty, enduring truth of the Gospel across generations, reminding us that even in our seated rest, the work of the Spirit is always in motion.

My point is this: The same Author writing this book is the same "prophetic-word-infant"—literally spiritually blind and dyslexic at that time—who received a word that she would be writing for Him.

Green and Growing, or Ripe and Rotting. That is my takeaway of the Pew.

If the Lord laid a hardback book that contained the finished work of His faith in you, does that book—laid next to you on any historic pew, chair, or furniture piece you may have had the privilege to sit in—give voice? Does it make itself ready to who you are today?

How Good is God in your book?

THE PROPHETIC MANDATE OF THE READY SCRIBE
My friends, the spirit of that verse—the profound, urgent necessity of the declared word—does not simply live in a book; it lives within the yearning soul of the Redemptive Gift Prophet!

The verse you seek, this declaration of divine readiness, comes to us from the royal treasury of the Scriptures, from Psalm 45, the very first verse:

"My heart is inditing a good matter: I speak of the things which I have made touching the king: my tongue is the pen of a ready writer."
— Psalm 45:1 (KJV)

The Meaning: Urgency and Divine Service
You see, this is not merely an ancient lyric about a king's celebration. Oh, no. It is a powerful mandate for every soul called to truth!

- **The Inditing Heart:** It begins not with the hand, but with the heart—a heart set on fire, ready to conceive a good matter. Before the voice can sound the clarion call for justice and love, the inner man must be ready, must be prepared to receive the divine instruction.
- **Speaking of the King:** The tongue, the voice, is not to be wasted on frivolous pursuit or cheap distraction. It is reserved for the most urgent business of the cosmos: speaking of the King! It is the testimony that transcends the moment and points toward the eternal power seated on the throne of grace.
- **The Pen of a Ready Writer:** And here is the urgency! The writer is *ready*, prepared, equipped. This metaphor does not speak of sluggishness or hesitation. It speaks of a swiftness of spirit and an eloquence of purpose.

When the truth wells up from the heart, the tongue must deliver it with the precision and the force of a perfectly wrought instrument.

The question for us today is not whether the pen is ready—but whether **we** are ready to let our lives be the pen that writes the final chapter of freedom, justice, and beloved community upon the face of this earth!

The message is urgent, and the hour demands our declaration.

ACTIVATION

The Ready Scribe

This chapter calls you to audit your spiritual life, challenging you to move beyond the limitations of "Pew history" and passive observance into the active motion of a Ready Scribe.

You are invited to embrace the discipline of perpetual growth, knowing that your heart is bursting with the finished matter of our King.

The Audit

Look at the "Pew" you are currently sitting in—is it a place of true, restorative rest, or is it a place of stagnation? Identify where you have become "Ripe and Rotting" by relying on yesterday's revelation. To be "Green and Growing" is to pursue a moving target; it is to stay in the perpetual flow of the Spirit's current instruction.

(*The Author did juggle that there may not be a "pew" present! Does that change the audit?* No. The Pew is a mindset.)

A Direct Conversation with Jesus

1. **The Temple in Motion "Do you not know that you are God's temple and that God's Spirit dwells in you?" (1 Corinthians 3:16)**
The Tabernacle had no fixed seating because the Spirit is always in motion. This reality challenges the belief that you can passively "receive" Truth without actively participating in it.
   - **Ask Him:** "Jesus, where is my spirit sitting in a fixed 'pew' of comfort or tradition? Where have I allowed 'Pew history' to dictate my status in Your house? Show me how to implement the purposes of the 'sacred furniture' and my body for constant worship and transformation."
   - **The Move:** Listen for the instruction to move.
2. **The Moving Target "Why do you stand here idle all day long?"** (Matthew 20:6) Lou Holtz warned that the moment you think you've figured it out, you've stopped growing. Idleness is often not laziness, but a spirit paralyzed by the fear of losing what it has already "ripened."

- **Ask Him:**"Lord, in what area of my life—ministry, health, or relationship—am I stuck in a 'ripe and rotting' cycle? Reveal the 'moving target' that requires me to be green and growing right now, regardless of whether I feel ready."
- **The Move:** Listen for the immediate next step He wants you to take.

3. The Mandate of the Scribe "Who do you say that I am?" (Matthew 16:15)

We all have received words in the kitchens of life that defined our Original Design. Your logos is the finished matter; your tongue/offering or self must be the fluent pen.

- **Ask Him:** "Jesus, what is the 'finished matter' in my heart that is bursting to be written or acted upon? How does Your identity as King compel my tongue to be a 'Ready Scribe' today? What is the urgent declaration I must articulate?"
- **The Move:** Listen for the specific word or truth to declare.

Reflect and Respond

Physically or spiritually, ground yourself in the "free electrons" of His goodness. Take a moment to record what you received in this time of conversation. What was the feeling of the green grass upon your feet? What conviction did the Pew vs. Tabernacle analogy bring to the surface? Let this be a record of your direct shift from stagnation to divine motion.

Next Step

Act on the principle: *"You're either green and growing or ripe and rotting."* Today, choose one step that requires motion —physically, spiritually, or intellectually—that moves you past a point of comfort. Let your heart burst with the finished matter and speak the truth with the fluent pen of a ready scribe.

Prayer and Contemplation

Father, my heart is bursting with the finished matter of our King! I refuse the destiny of being ripe and rotting. I choose to be green and growing and accept the IAMness mandate of the Ready Scribe. I ground myself in Your goodness and yield my tongue as a skilled instrument to articulate the thoughts of the Spirit. My tongue is the pen of a ready writer; I am in motion; I am actively restoring with You, all things. In Jesus' name, Amen.

PLAY SHEET | PROPHET

Prophet Edition
Redemptive Gifts Summary

THIS CHAPTER IS A HIGH -VELOCITY PLAY for your Spiritual Senses, designed to move you from the "Rented Pew" of observation into the active "Pulpit" of your own life. It is a call to stop being "Ripe and Rotting" in old religious traditions and to become a Ready Scribe who is "Green and Growing" in the fresh, daily revelation of the Father.

THE DNA WRISTBAND AUDIBLE: CHAPTER PLAY-CALL

1. The Green Dot Helmet (Individual Redemptive Gift): **Prophet**

The frequency for this play is set to the Prophet. This is your gift of "Design and Perception." You are hardwired to see the "Blueprint" of what God is doing before others do.

When you feel "Ripe and Rotting"—stagnant, bored, or trapped in a religious system that no longer has a pulse—your Prophet gift is signaling you to change the play. You are being called to be *Spiritually BRAVE* enough to trust your "Inward Eyes" and your "Gems of Knowing." You are the one designed to declare that the "Veil is Open," moving your environment from a "museum of the past" into a "garden of the present."

2. The Coaches' Booth (*Legacy Anchor): The Shack* by William Paul Young

In the "Booths" of your spiritual legacy, *The Shack* (Prophet/Design) represents the deep, mystical meeting point where "Conventional Religion" is dismantled by "Living Relationship."

Apply This: **Realize that God is not a "hardback book" sitting on a shelf; He is a Living Person who wants to walk with you through your "Great Sadness" and into your "Great Discovery." This anchor reminds you that your Sonship is a relationship of "Face to Face" intimacy, proving that the "Logos" (Word) is only truly understood when it is experienced as "Rhema" (Breath).**

3. The Play-Call from God

"Child, check your helmet—I am speaking a 'New Beginning' into your ears. I see you sitting in the shadows of the choir loft, feeling like your gifts have been mothballed by the 'Order' of the institutions.

I am calling an audible: You are a Ready Scribe, not a relic! I didn't give you the ability to 'see in the spirit' so you could manage a cemetery; I gave it to you so you could water a garden.

I watched My Son, Jesus, bypass the 'Sanhedrin logic' to speak directly to the hearts of those who were thirsty for Truth. That is the C♡♡Lness of our Oneness. When you feel the 'Green Dot' frequency vibrating in your spirit, don't wait for a committee to vote on your revelation. I want you to pick up your 'Scribe's Pen' and begin to write the story of How Good I Am in your own life.

Stop believing the lie that you have to be 'polished' to be used. Your DNA is hardwired for Constant Growth. Be Spiritually BRAVE enough to kick off the 'Saddle Shoes' of your past and walk into the 'Thick Atmosphere' of My Presence. I am so good that I have removed the 'Door' of the temple so that you and I can be inseparable. Run the play, Child. The ink is fresh and the page is turning."

4. The Audible *The Timeline of Now*

The enemy wants you to remain "blasé" and "ripe," waiting for a future Heaven while missing the present Kingdom.

The Audible is this: *The "Windows to the Supernatural" are wide open!* Right now, on the timeline of today, I am removing the "Religious Shroud" from your mind. I am releasing the power to move in the "Liquid Glory" of My Spirit. You are not a corpse in a pew; you are a King's Champion in the field. How Good is God!

REFORMATION DATA: THE ARCHITECTURE OF YOUR GROWTH

To understand the "field" you are playing on, consider how to apply these "Ready Scribe" principles to your own "Pulpit":

• **Green and Growing:** In biology, anything that stops growing begins to die. *Apply This:* Choose a "1% Change" every day. Whether it's a new way of praying or a fresh perspective on a "Line Strategy" of your past, your growth is found in your willingness to be a "Student of the Spirit" rather than a "Master of the Tradition."

• **The Scribe's Pen:** Psalm 45:1 says, "My tongue is the pen of a ready scribe." *Apply This:* Speak what you See. When you receive a "Gem of Knowing" or a "Prophetic Screen" drop over your eyes, use your words to "etch" that reality into the earth. Your authority is found in your authentic expression of the Father's heart.

• **The "Veil" Removal:** You apply the Higher Law by realizing that the "veil" was torn from top to bottom. This means you no longer need an "intermediary" or a "Sadducee" to interpret God for you. *Apply This:* Take "Communion" (Common-Union) as a daily lifestyle of Relational Discernment, trusting that you are fully authorized to hear and see for yourself.

Section III

Gates of Pulpit

HOW GOOD IS GOD!

THE UNBOUND LIFE

"And he who had died came out bound hand and foot with grave-clothes... Jesus said to them, 'Loose him, and let him go.'" — John 11:44 (NKJV)

The shroud has served its purpose. It held you in the quiet of the tomb, but it cannot hold the breath of the living.

You do not have to fight the linens. You simply have to outgrow them.

The Altar is not a place to die again. It is the place where the wrappings fall, and the son stands free.

Step out of the gray. The Air is waiting.

Chapter 9

The Shroud and the Altar:

Unwrapping the Live Body

"A revival is nothing else than a
new beginning of obedience to God."
— **Charles Finney**, Father of Modern Revivalism

Many of us have had an opportunity to touch Revival in our lifetime; few have encountered a Reformation.

The UnFinished Book, in its earliest stage, crossed my path a little over ten years ago. Kristen wrote me a letter asking if I would read and consider endorsing her first book. I responded with a massive yes. Many intervening years passed, but she hung onto that letter of hope. That same request, copied and mailed to me, resurfaced as she crossed the finish line, removing the "Un" to her Finished work.

I'm inspired by her journey, as if she had met Martin Luther himself somewhere in the pages penned. She has wrestled and nailed many theses upon the door of what we call "church." Her text will challenge the "established boundary line of eternity" with experiences that could only be authored by the Master. The race she has run is one that I am honored to be part of.

*— **Pastor Tommy Barnett***
(Author, Co-Pastor Dream City Church Phoenix, Founder of the Los Angeles Dream Center)

Legacy Note: At the age of 60, Pastor Barnett ran across the Mojave Desert to raise the funds needed to open the Dream Center. It took him 19 days—the equivalent of running a marathon per day.

REVIVAL VS. REFORMATION

Let me ask you a couple of questions: *What is the difference between Revival and Reformation?*

Revival: The act of reviving, or the state of being revived.

Revival is akin to the breath of God—an inner awakening, a divine wind that sweeps through the hearts of individuals. It awakens the spirit, rekindling a fervent love for the Almighty. It is personal, intimate, like the flicker of a candle in the darkness that spreads its light, igniting passion and repentance within the soul.

Reformation: An improvement in the existing form or condition of institutions or practices.

Reformation is the hammer that strikes the nail of change into the very fabric of our institutions and doctrines. It is systemic, communal, like the grand architecture of a cathedral being reshaped from its very foundations. It demands courage, action, and a steadfast heart to challenge the status quo.

Honestly, between the two, which one does the church need? Which one do you hunger for?

(Sorry, I did not offer "Both" or "All of the Above" as an option.)

Are we not individually responsible to sit down at the table of communion?

"Do this in remembrance of me." (Luke 22:19).

If communion revives the soul, then my conclusion suggests that *Revival is as close as your next "meal" with the Lord.*

"Anyone who partakes of this meal in an indifferent manner... eats and drinks judgment upon themselves... The human body of Jesus represents the judgment of every single human life... This is the reason why many of you are suffering unnecessarily with weaknesses and illnesses, and many have already died."
— 1 Corinthians 11:29-30 (Mirror Bible)

**Does the church require improvement on the existing form, condition of its institutions and doctrine?*

(Church: His own Living Body—the visible, physical extension of His life on earth.)

In the history of our faith, there have always been those courageous enough to stand up and say, *"The view from this seat must change."* They were the architects of Reformation, the ones who looked at the rigid structures of their day and demanded they be realigned with the Truth.

THE ARCHITECTS OF THE SHIFT

- **Martin Luther (1483–1546).** He was the **Hammer**. He looked at a system built on religious merit—a "pay-to-sit" salvation—and tore down the veil. By putting the Word into the hands of the common man, he moved the Logos out of the shadows and into the light.
- **John Calvin (1509–1564).** He provided the **Structure**. He wasn't interested in a fleeting moment; he wanted a settled foundation. He sought to build a life where the sovereignty of God wasn't just a theory, but a physical reality that governed every aspect of our existence.
- **Huldrych Zwingli (1484–1531).** He was the **Simplifier**. A leader of the Reformation in Switzerland, he believed that if a practice wasn't explicitly found in the Bible, it had no place in the house of God. He literally stripped the "active" participation (statues, music, elaborate altars) out of the buildings, leaving only the stark, grounded weight of the Word.

• **Catherine of Siena (1347–1380).** She proved that reformation often begins in the *Secret Place.* She was a mystic who used her voice to call the highest authorities back to spiritual integrity. She understood that before you can reform a building, you must reform the heart.

THE WEIGHT OF THE HIGHER LAW

When we weigh these reformers against the *Law of the Spirit of Life,* we see the true nature of their work. Reformation, on its own, is a necessary realignment of the *Logos mind*—it fixes the legal framework and settles the doctrine. It moves us from a chaotic, lawless state into a disciplined, structural one.

But we must settle this in our spirits: The Bible is not the Boss. The "Word of God" is not ink on a page; the Word of God is a Person.

The Book itself cannot love, save, or breathe life into you. It isn't kind, and it isn't generous—those are the empowerments of a Living Being. By the Rhema Mind, we recognize that while the letter kills, the Spirit gives life!

THE HEAVY ANCHOR OF THE REFORMATION

We have to look at the shadow side of the Reformation's "grounded" nature. While John Calvin built a structure that was undeniably weighty, he also hammered down the floorboards so tightly that he inadvertently boarded up the windows to the supernatural. In his quest for a settled, sovereign Logos, he authored a "cessationist" view—effectively declaring that the gifts of the Spirit and the miraculous moves of God had served their purpose and retired from the field.

He gave us a magnificent, solid Pew, but then he told us that the Active Participation—the dancing, the healing, the Rhema-fire—was a closed chapter of history.

THE DANGER OF REFORMATION WITHOUT REVIVAL

The danger is exactly this: you end up with a beautiful, expensive hardback book that you aren't allowed to open.

You end up with a Pew View that sees the throne but isn't allowed to feel the electricity of the One sitting on it.

We don't just want a God who *was* good; we are here for the **How Good IS God**—the present, vibrating, gift-giving reality of a Father who never stopped moving.

THE WITTENBERG VISION

The writer of the endorsement (Pastor Barnett) said: "I'm inspired by her journey as if she had met Martin Luther himself..."

You do know where this is going?

Only a reformation of thought and experience could declare such an account.

Two things I learned by meeting Martin Luther:
1. The writer has stood in his pulpit.
2. I saw the Shroud of DEATH.

God obliged my request to meet Martin Luther. "Hopefully," I thought, "the conversation could shed light on the sticky-note dilemma." A couple of weeks later, He sent His Son to do the introductions.

My "tour guide," Jesus, grabbed the iron handle, opened the door, and we stepped into *All Saints' Church* in Wittenberg, Saxony-Anhalt, Germany. Somewhere on the timeline of the 1500s (give or take).

I was shown to the front pew. Nothing was said about waiting, so I sat down, rested, and let the spirit of my imagination hone in on my surroundings. Light and Spirit were moving in the heart of understanding. Time on bended knee is precious "waiting" which removes the barriers that diffract the view.

And there he was.

A well-fed, mid-height man in typical period rector's clothes. Jesus grinned, always delighted with Himself in the watching. Martin Luther was warm, intelligent, and gracious. He motioned for me to ascend his pulpit.

Pulpit indeed. Ornate and raised to the clouds in my opinion. Martin Luther made a disagreeable *hmm* in our conversation. "And my tomb and gravestone on the floor right underneath. Hmm?"

I kicked my shoes off and began my humble ascent. Jesus and Martin Luther waited at the bottom, watching me. The stairs appeared pillowy to my senses. My hand reached to hold the solid rail to assist me step by step as my climb curved upward.

Ascending the platform, it became a window, for which I was part of the glass. I saw myself looking out at the town of Wittenberg. A light being guided my view, as a broad telescope points the gaze.

THE VISION OF THE CAPE

The people walking on the sidewalks were covered in a black cape and hood, walking bent over. The fabric on the inside of the capes was a beautiful red satin lining, but the outside was a dull matte black.

Entering back to the pulpit, Jesus' thoughts were saying:

"The body of Christ wears the Gospel as a shroud which has been darkened. My blood is only on the inside next to the skin, not worn or appropriated to the earth."

Shroud: A length of cloth or an enveloping garment in which a dead person is wrapped for burial.

I descended the grand steps, a bit baffled. The Lord asked me what I saw. I responded: *"I noticed the people of the town were walking around with black fabric with eye cutouts over their heads."*

Without a facial flinch, Jesus asked me to ascend into Martin Luther's pulpit once more, and made an interesting request:

"When you look, look into TODAY. Today's timeline."

How does all this mystical woo-woo happen? The closest clue I can offer is similar to the movie *Tomorrowland* (2015). When Casey, the vibrant heroine, is allowed to steer the "earth wheel" changing timelines to see into a moment. Grace, my dear friend, grace for the gifts He bestows.

Back up the honorable staircase I went. The platform, again, became a window, and I looked.

The townspeople were of "modern" age—100% denim everywhere, t-shirts, baseball hats, yoga pants. Yet, they too were walking around the village *still with their heads cloaked in the black sack.*

It doesn't take a rocket scientist to gather the interpretation. The church—which includes me—is still walking around in her grave clothes.

"And the dead man appeared with his hands and feet swathed in linen cloths also his face was covered in a cloth. Jesus said to them, 'Unwrap him so that he can move around freely.'"
— John 11:44 (Mirror Bible)

Is the Body still walking around with their grave clothes on?

"This will happen in an instant, in a blink of the eye: the final trumpet will sound, then the dead shall be awoken out of their sleep and we, who are still alive, shall be instantly changed into a different kind of body. For this corruptible must be clothed with incorruption and this mortal must be clothed with immortality."— 1 Corinthians 15:52-53 (Mirror Bible)

The pulpit view, no matter the timeline, is still a people wrapped in grave clothes. How does that make you feel?

Selah... The pew and pulpit covered in a language of death.

THE ALTAR GEOMETRY

Thoughts were racing around my mind as I stepped back into the spirit to finish what the Father had granted. Jesus and Martin Luther just looked at me. Then Jesus grabbed my hand and simultaneously motioned to Martin Luther, *"Over here."*

We walked to the glamorous altar that was shadowed by the pulpit.

Jesus motioned us: *"Kristen, you lay down here, center. Martin Luther, you lay situated here, on the right."*

And He rested Himself, left-side and lower than either of our heads.

At His direction, I was laid into the altar of Him!

Our "Grace-man" Martin Luther as the scapegoat, freed, presented before the Lord alive.

COACH'S CLIPBOARD: THE THIEVES & THE GOATS

"I promise you—this very day you will enter paradise with me." (Luke 23:43)

In the profound geometry of the Cross, we find a living portrait of Leviticus 16 reaching its cosmic conclusion. Suspended between Heaven and earth, Jesus stands as the High Priest, flanked by two robbers who represent the dual nature of the human journey.

- **The First Thief:** Mirrors the *Lord's Goat* (Yom Kippur). His heart yields to the proximity of Grace. He recognizes his own "DNA" is being reclaimed in the shadow of the Innocent One.
- **The Second Thief:** Mirrors the *Azazel (Scapegoat)*. Tethered to the "Logos mind" of accusation and earthly demand.

As Jesus breathes His final "Rhema" of forgiveness, He occupies the space where our guilt is separated from our identity. He becomes the ultimate Scapegoat, carrying the collective weight of our "missing the mark" into the wilderness of forgetfulness.

Grace Lessons:
1. **It's never too late:** Invitations are eternal.
2. **We all have fallen short:** All people are saved by grace.
3. **Faith is important:** One thief was saved by faith; the other condemned by unbelief.
4. **We can be with Jesus NOW:** We are with Him in His death and His resurrection.

ACTIVATION

This chapter invites you to move past the "rented seat" of religious tradition and step into the active participation of the Tabernacle. It is a call to recognize where you have worn the Gospel as a shroud rather than a garment of life. You are not meant to merely observe the Reformation; you are called to be the carpenter who nails the thesis of Resurrection onto the doors of your own world.

A Direct Conversation with Jesus
1. **"Unwrap him and let him go."** (John 11:44)
Jesus spoke this to the bystanders, not to Lazarus. It was a communal command to remove the evidence of death.
*   **Ask Him:** *"Jesus, who have You placed in my life that I am called to help 'unwrap'? And where am I still waiting for You to do what You have already commanded me to do —to step out of my own shroud and move freely?"*
*   **Action:** Listen for the specific "grave cloth" (shame or religious rule) He is pointing to.

2. **"I promise you—this very day you will enter paradise with me."** (Luke 23:43) The thief on the cross didn't have time to "clean up" his life; he simply recognized the Person next to him. This question challenges your "religious merit" mindset.

- **Ask Him:** *"Lord, in what area of my life am I still 'paying-to-sit'—trying to earn my salvation through works? How can I shift today into the thief of Grace who simply asks to be remembered?"*
- **Action:** Listen for His immediate invitation into "Paradise" (Oneness) right now.

   3. "Who do you say that I am?" (Matthew 16:15) Martin Luther tore down the veil so the common man could hold the Word. But the Word is a Person, not a book.
- **Ask Him:** *"Master, how have I made the Bible my 'Boss' while ignoring You as my 'Friend'? Teach me the language of the Spirit that can be felt, tasted, and smelled, moving me beyond the paper and into Your Presence."*
- **Action:** Listen for the "vibration" of His life within you.

Reflect and Respond

- **The View from the Pulpit:** Consider the "black cape" imagery. Where in your spiritual walk are you wearing the Blood of Jesus on the inside (private safety) but presenting a "shroud of death" (religious dullness or gloom) to the world?
- **The Weight of the Pew:** You've sat in many pews. Reflect on the difference between "renting a seat" in a system and "occupying a space" in the Body. Does your current "seating" allow for the electricity of the Spirit?
- **The Altar Geometry:** Imagine yourself laying in that altar at Wittenberg. On one side is the Hammer of Reformation; on the other is the Person of Christ. Feel the weight of the "Great Exchange."

The Next Step

Identify one "Grave Cloth" (a thought of shame, a religious rule, or a "Logos" limitation) that has been binding your hands or feet. Consciously "unwrap" it this week by declaring: *"This no longer fits the living. I am clothed in His immortality now."*

Prayer and Contemplation

Jesus, I thank You that You are not a dead word on a page, but a Living Person who calls me Friend. Thank You for the Reformers who fixed the view, but thank You more for the Spirit who invites me to stand up. I choose today to move past the shroud. I choose to be clothed in Your immortality now, not just in a distant 'blink of an eye' future. Let my life be the 'active participation' of Your goodness. Amen.

PLAY SHEET | EXHORTER

Exhorter Edition
Redemptive Gifts Summary

THIS CHAPTER IS A HEAVYWEIGHT PLAY, shifting the stadium lights from the "Order" of the institutions to the "Electricity" of the Living Body. It is a call for you to stop being a corpse wrapped in a religious shroud and to start being a Son activated by the Spirit.

THE DNA WRISTBAND AUDIBLE: CHAPTER PLAY-CALL

1. The Green Dot Helmet (*Individual Redemptive Gift*): **Exhorter** The frequency for this play is set to the Exhorter. This is your gift of "Reality" and "Relationship." While the Reformers built the structure (Teacher), the Exhorter brings the life.

You are hardwired to dismantle the "pay-to-sit" spectator mentality by demanding active participation.

The Exhorter in you is being called to hammer the thesis of Grace onto the doors of your own heart. You are designed to move the Logos (the written word) out of the shadows and into the light of your daily experience, refusing to settle for "shrouded" information and demanding the "Electricity" of a face-to-face friendship.

2. The Coaches' Booth (*Legacy Anchor*): *Jesus Calling* by Sarah Young In the "Booths" of your spiritual legacy, Jesus Calling (Exhorter/Intimacy) stands as the beacon for this frequency. Sarah Young removed the "shroud" of distance by penning words as if Jesus were speaking directly to the reader. *Apply This:* Realize that the Altar in this chapter is your invitation to do the same. This Light on the timeline proves that the Reformation isn't just about correct doctrine; it is about "Hearing God's Voice" for yourself. The shroud falls off when you realize the King is speaking directly to you.

3. The Play-Call from God

"Child, check your helmet—I am speaking a new beginning of obedience into your ears. I see you hesitating at the Altar of tradition, feeling the weight of the burial clothes that religious expectation has wrapped around your potential. I am calling an audible: Unwrap the Body! I watched My Son, Jesus, neatly roll up His head cloth in the tomb to tell the world He was finished with His mission, but He is not finished with the mission of you, His Body. I didn't save you so you could sit in a 'rented pew' wearing the Gospel like a black burial shroud. I am not a dead word on a page or a 'hardback book' you aren't allowed to open. I am a Living Person who calls you Friend. That is the C♡♡Lness of our Oneness.

When you feel the pull of 'Logos guilt,' I want you to remember the Great Exchange on the Altar. You aren't meant to carry the weight of the rules; you are meant to carry the Rhema fire of My Resurrection. Be Spiritually BRAVE enough to kick off the shoes of your 'pew history' and walk in the immortality I've already clothed you in. Your DNA is hardwired for this Reformation. I am so good that I have moved the river of My Spirit to water your entire field. Rise from the Altar, Child—the game has moved into a new dimension."

4. **The Audible** (The Timeline of Now) The enemy wants you to remain "blasé" about your identity, stuck in a view where the gifts of the Spirit are retired. The Audible is this: The Windows to the Supernatural are wide open! Right now, on the timeline of today, I am calling for a "Blink of the Eye" change. Unwrap the shame, unwrap the rules, and step out of the shroud. You are not a corpse; you are a King's Champion. How Good is God!

REFORMATION DATA: THE ARCHITECTURE OF YOUR MOVEMENT

To understand the "field" you are playing on, consider how to apply these "Exhorter" principles to your own "Pulpit":

• **The Literacy Surge:** Just as the Bible moved from Latin to the common tongue, your faith must move from "Religious Jargon" to your own "Heart Language." *Apply This:* Read the Word for yourself. Trust that the Exhorter gift in you allows you to see the Person behind the text without an intermediary.

• **The Living Body**: Over 2 billion people partake in communion, yet many do so under the "shroud" of ritual. *Apply This:* Move from being a "Christian in name" to a "Living Body in function." Treat the "Meal" not as a routine, but as a real-time infusion of Jesus' humanity and your own Sonship.

• **Unwrapping the Shroud:** Historically, "Revivals" happen when the "shrouds" of tradition fall away. *Apply This:* Identify one "religious rule" that makes you feel dead or limited, and trade it for a Spiritually BRAVE action of life.

215

Section IV

Gates of Heaven

.HOW GOOD IS GOD!

THE OPEN SKY

"Assuredly, I say to you, unless you are converted and become as little children, you will by no means enter the kingdom of Heaven." — Matthew 18:3 (NKJV)

The windows of Heaven are not locked. We often stand outside, analyzing the glass, waiting for permission to peek in.

But the Father has thrown the sash wide. He is not hiding the view. He is inviting the **Wonder**.

To the child, the kingdom is not a theology to study. It is a playground to experience.

Do not analyze the wind. Feel it. The geography is simple: It is Open.

Chapter 10:

The Gates of Heaven:

The Geography of Simple

"If you can't explain it simply, you don't understand it well enough."
— **Vince Lombardi**

"If you can't explain it to a six-year-old, you don't understand it yourself."
— **Albert Einstein**

Learning about Heaven is like learning to ride a bike. At first, you just look at the bike and hear people talk about it—that's like reading a book. Remember, you learned to read, and every day you learn the meaning of different words. But Heaven isn't only a living story made by God; it's a ride that takes you through the video games of life.

When you get on, you realize you aren't doing it alone. It's like having your Father's hand on the back of the seat, running right beside you. You stop worrying about the "how" and start feeling the wind on your face. Suddenly, you aren't just on the bike; you and the bike are moving together as one.

That "In-With-in" feeling, where you feel safe, fast, and fully alive because your Father is right there with His hand on the seat—that is what Heaven feels like every day.

And the cool thing is... once you have experienced "riding a bike," nobody ever forgets. Your heart just knows. You and the bicycle ride together, and your Father's hand is always "magically" there to assist you on the path you choose to take.

To go back to the very beginning is to find the Word already present there, face to face with God. The one mirrors the other. The Word is I AM; God's eloquence echoes and concludes in Him. The Word equals God.

As an avid note-taker and writer, the first mark I place on the blank note page is a divider line. This separates the "actual text" from the "thinking or research text."

Creatively penned, I'll write the John 1:1 verse again... *"In the Beginning was"... we will thread the commentary with personal inspiration of the individual words underlined.*

In the beginning—the first in order, time, place, or rank | is to find the Word—Living word with a name, filled in intelligence, interconnected network of things known; the sum total of logic | already present there with God, face to face, mirror, no beginning no end. The Word is (His name) IAM—present-there, no beginning, no end. Echoes and concludes in Him. "The light/sound/knowing bounces back and forth." Mirror.
"If you have seen Me, you have seen the Father..."

The divider line isn't present on the page within the LOVE of God.

THE GEOGRAPHY OF GRACE

My last physical chapter to write was The Geography of Grace. It was a push-pull, a "put off," simply because of the vast sum of things to cover. Which equals: Grace is exhaustive.

This past week, Don and I were invited to a gathering of family and friends. One of the family guests had recently lost a parent. Very recent. To our surprise and compassion, this very conservative guest felt comfortable enough to unpack and share her thinking-out-loud grief with us. Throughout their visit, with grief sitting on her shirt sleeve, it was easy to overhear a particular problem. Her family's lack of clarity over heavy and hurting processing conversation via phone calls, texts, and the like. Their grieving concern was: how do we communicate and comfort a five-year-old member of the family?

How do you explain the end of life, separate from the language of Christ?

The divider line once again appears on the page of humanity...

Actual TRUTH "text" above versus thinking or research text below.

You can feel the weight, emptiness, and confusion when faith and hope are missing ink in the conversation. Many readers would ask, Kristen, why didn't you tell them?

Grief always tenderizes the heart; experience has taught me to wait and allow the soul to pour out the tangible burden. Comfort is in the listening. Answers before questions open the door before they consider the window. Holy Spirit is a faithful guarantor, and five-year-olds still hear and discern truth from the unseen. We never forget how to "ride a bike." God is really that good!

Santa Claus, the Easter Bunny, and the Tooth Fairy are spoken from the same parenting mouth. Yet we all know the difference between TRUTH and make-believe. Nothing can separate us from the LOVE of God.

THE TOPOGRAPHY OF HEAVEN
So, what is the geography we are invited into?

The kingdom of Heaven is stepping through the veil of His flesh. When you enter, you encounter types and shadows of the Tabernacle, but you also walk a river, cross the bridge, and go upstream to His mountain.

Heaven is full of intimacy, gardens, and sanctuaries. It is full of courts, governance, and rule—the good kind of rule where righteousness prevails, not separation. The kingdom of Heaven is like family, church, and picnics; it is filled with people from all walks and all time zones.

The kingdom of Heaven is like quiet prayer, loud joy, and sitting with Jesus on the bench next to the waterfall of His headwaters. There are thrones, and mountains, and rivers. There are benches, balconies, and witnesses.

It is vast, overwhelming at times, but it is not confusing. However, to help us navigate this infinite geography here on earth, it is easier to explain within a story and map out on a 100-yard field.

THE 100-YARD MAP OF ONENESS
0–20 YARD LINE: THE DEFENSIVE STANCE
(The Shadow of the Goalposts)
"10 Yard Line" – The Window (Vision & Invitation):
• **The Parable:** The kingdom of Heaven is like a Mustard Seed.
• **The Goodness:** You start small. You may feel insignificant on the field, a tiny speck against a giant defense. But the goodness is in the DNA. You don't have to be big to be potent.
• **The Outcome:** The smallest faith inevitably grows into the largest shelter. It becomes a tree where the birds of the air (thoughts of peace and rest) come to nest in your branches.
• "20 Yard Line" – The Door (Intimacy & Passage):
• **The Parable:** The kingdom of Heaven is like Leaven (Yeast) hidden in the meal.
• **The Goodness:** This is the quiet work. You shut the door, and the influence spreads. It isn't loud; it is pervasive.

- **The Outcome:** The whole loaf gets raised. Your private intimacy with the Father "infects" every other area of your life until the heavy atmosphere becomes light and airy.

30–40 YARD LINE: THE TRANSITION (Gaining Momentum)

"30 Yard Line "– The Go-Zone Door (Learning the Language):

- **The Parable:** The Kingdom of Heaven is like Treasure hidden in a field.
- **The Goodness:** You stumble upon something so valuable at the 30-yard line that the defensive struggle suddenly loses its appeal. The joy of the discovery hits you.
- **The Outcome:** You joyfully sell all that you have—you trade your worry, your "rights," and your old playbook—just to buy that field. It's not a sacrifice; it's the smartest trade of your life.

"40 Yard Line"– The Frontier Gates (Following His Authority):

- **The Parable:** The Kingdom of Heaven is like a Merchant seeking beautiful Pearls.
- **The Goodness:** You are no longer satisfied with synthetic imitations. You have seen the Pearl of Great Price (Christ in You).
- **The Outcome:** You stop bargaining. You realize that one true thing is worth more than a million "good" things. You focus. The clutter drops away.
- 50 YARD LINE: THE CORE
- (Identity & Alignment)

"50 Yard Line" – Doors to Rooms (Dying Once and For All):

- **The Parable:** The Kingdom of Heaven is like a Dragnet cast into the sea.
- **The Goodness:** The net gathers everything—your past, your mess, your victories. But when it hits the shore (the Cross), the Father sits down to sort it.

• **The Outcome:** He keeps the Good (your true identity in Him) and throws away the Bad (the shame, the false self, the 'I-am-not'-tree). You don't have to sort yourself; He does it. You are left only with what is edible and alive.

60–80 YARD LINE: THE OFFENSIVE STRIKE
(Occupying Domain)

"60 Yard Line "– The Gate (Authority & Domain):

• **The Parable:** The Kingdom of Heaven is like a King who prepared a Wedding Feast.

• **The Goodness:** The invitation is sent. The oxen are killed; the dinner is ready. The King says, "Come."

• **The Outcome:** The highways and hedges are emptied. You realize you aren't just a player on the field; you are a Guest at the Head Table. The only requirement is the Wedding Garment—the righteousness of Christ that fits you perfectly.

"80 Yard Line" – The Red Zone (Oneness in Motion):

• **The Parable:** The Kingdom of Heaven is like a Householder bringing out treasures New and Old.

• **The Goodness:** You have mastery now. You can reach back into the "Old" (the Law, the history, the lessons) and the "New" (Grace, Spirit, Freedom) and blend them into a winning drive.

• **The Outcome:** You become a scribe of the Kingdom. You have the resourcefulness to handle any defense because your playbook is infinite.

"90 YARD LINE" TO THE END ZONE: THE SCORING REALITY

(Rest & Union)

The End Zone – The Sabbath Open Door (The Eternal Now Rest):

• **The Parable:** The Kingdom of Heaven is like a Sower.

• **The Goodness:** The Seed (The Living Word) found the Good Ground (Your Heart). It wasn't about the rocks or the thorns; it was about the harvest.

• **The Outcome:** Thirty, sixty, a hundredfold. You crossed the line. You didn't just survive the game; you multiplied the Life. You are dwelling in the absolute rest of the Father's face, producing fruit simply by being planted in Him.

THE SNAP: LIVING IN THE MULTI-DIMENSIONAL

"Relocating your heart means realizing you are never standing in just one dimension. Experiencing the Kingdom is knowing that the Windows are always open for vision, the Door is always yours to shut for privacy or open for restoration, and the Gate is simply the place where you decide to stand in your authority. You are the portal where the Coach's voice becomes the play on the field."

ACTIVATION

THE GATES OF HEAVEN: THE GEOGRAPHY OF SIMPLE

A Dircct Conversation with Jesus

1. The Window (10-Yard Line: The Mustard Seed)

"Jesus, I sometimes feel small and insignificant against this giant defense. Remind me that the Kingdom in me is like a Mustard Seed—tiny but explosive with life. Show me the forest of peace and rest that is sleeping inside this single seed of faith today."

2. The Frontier Gates (40-Yard Line: The Pearl of Great Price)

"Lord, I am tired of collecting cheap imitations and settling for less than Your best. I trade my anxiety and my need to be 'right' for the Field where You are hidden. I joyfully sell out my old playbook to possess the true Pearl of Your presence."

3. The Core (50-Yard Line: The Dragnet)

"Jesus, my life feels like a net that has gathered everything —the good, the bad, the victories, and the shame.

I surrender the net to You. Let me rest at the Cross, knowing that You are the One who sorts it out. Help me to keep only my true identity in You and throw away the 'I-am-not'-tree logic once and for all."

4. The End Zone (The Sabbath Rest: The Sower)

"Father, bring out of me treasures new and old. Let me rest in the End Zone, knowing that I am the Good Ground. Teach me that I don't have to force the seed to grow; I just need to rest in Your face and allow Your Living Word to produce the thirty, sixty, and a hundredfold harvest."

Reflect and Respond

- Which "Parable of the Field" resonates with your current season? Are you in the "Hidden Treasure" phase (learning to joyfully trade your worries for His presence) or the "Wedding Feast" phase (learning to wear your identity as a guest of honor)?
- How does knowing that the "Dragnet" of God throws away your shame (the bad fish) change the way you view your past mistakes?

____

____

____

____

Next Step

Identify one "divider line" in your life—a place where you have separated your "sacred" spiritual life from your "secular" daily grind. Smudge that line today. Choose one task (like driving, answering emails, or cooking) and consciously practice the "In-With-in" movement, knowing the Father's hand is on the bicycle seat, assisting you on the path you choose to take.

Prayer and Contemplation

Father, I thank You that the bike ride has begun. I lift up my head as a living gateway and welcome the King of Glory into every yard of my day. I refuse to live in the "thinking text" of doubt; I choose to live in the "Truth text" of Your Love. Thank You for the 50-yard line reality—that the net has been sorted, and I am kept safe in the basket of Your love. I am safe, I am fast, and I am fully alive in the Geography of Your Grace. Amen.

PLAY SHEET | GIVER

Giver Edition Redemptive Gifts Summary

THIS CHAPTER IS THE "TRUST FUND" REVELATION. It takes the infinite "Geography" of Heaven and stewards it down into a simple, rideable map. It calls you to stop hoarding complex theological theories and to start stewarding the simple, present-tense reality of the Parables of the Kingdom.

THE DNA WRISTBAND AUDIBLE: CHAPTER PLAY-CALL

1. **The Green Dot Helmet** (Individual Redemptive Gift): **Giver**

The frequency for this play is set to the Giver. This is your gift of "Stewardship" and "Supply." You are hardwired to govern the resources of Heaven and manage them with practical wisdom. The Giver in you hates the "waste" of over-complication. You are being activated to take the vastness of the Kingdom and simplify it into a "Mustard Seed" birthright that even a child can inherit. You are called to prove that God is good not by arguing theology, but by "riding the bike" of His provision.

2. The Coaches' Booth (*Legacy Anchor*): *Heaven is for Real* by Todd Burpo

In the "Booths" of your spiritual legacy, *Heaven is for Real* (Giver/Generational) stands as the beacon for this frequency. Just as Todd Burpo had to listen to the simple, un-shrouded testimony of his four-year-old son Colton to understand Heaven, this anchor reminds you that the Kingdom belongs to the childlike. *Apply This:* The Giver gift flourishes in the safety of family and generational blessing. You don't need a doctorate to explain Heaven; you just need the honest, simple trust of a son or daughter.

3. The Play-Call from God

"Child, check your helmet—I am entrusting you with the 'Keys to the Parables.' I see you standing at the 10-yard line, looking at your Mustard Seed, wondering if you have enough 'spiritual currency' to buy a ticket to the game. But I am calling an audible: The Ride is Free! I didn't give you the 'Geography of Grace' to confuse you; I gave it to you to sustain you. I am the Father running beside your bike, and My hand on the seat is your unlimited supply of safety. Stop trying to 'earn' the wind in your face. The Giver in you knows that true wealth isn't in what you know, but in Who you are with. Don't let the enemy clutter your mind with

'Thinking Text' debt. Cash in on the 'Truth Text' of the Pearl of Great Price. Be Spiritually BRAVE enough to play the 'video game' of life knowing you have infinite life and infinite help. Run the play, Child. The supply is already on the field."

4. The Audible (The Timeline of Now)

The enemy wants you to believe that Heaven is a "Future Reward" you have to wait for. The Audible is this: The Kingdom is Here! Right now, on the timeline of today, I am releasing the "In-With-in" reality. You don't have to wait to die to go to Heaven; you can ride the bike of Heaven right through your Monday morning. How Good is God!

REFORMATION DATA: THE 100-YARD MAP OF YOUR STEWARDSHIP

To understand the "field" you are playing on, consider how to apply these "Giver" coordinates to your own life:

• **The 10-Yard Line (The Mustard Seed):** The Giver operates from small beginnings. *Apply This:* When you feel insignificant, look at the seed. The "forest" of provision is not a promise for someday; it is already coded into your current DNA. Steward the small vision He gives you, and it will grow into a shelter for many.

• **The 50-Yard Line (The Dragnet):** Stewardship of Identity. *Apply This:* The greatest resource you have is your Sonship. Stop "wasting" energy trying to sort out your own flaws. Let the Father sit on the shore and sort the net. Steward the Good Fish (who He says you are) and leave the Bad Fish (your past shame) on the beach.

• **The End Zone (The Sower):** The Giver knows that Rest produces the harvest. *Apply This:* You cannot force the seed to grow; you can only provide the Good Ground. You cannot give what you do not have. Occupy the End Zone of Rest so you can be a generous, thirty-to-a-hundredfold conduit of life to others. The bike ride isn't a race; it's a relationship.

HOW GOOD IS GOD!

THE SAFE PLACE

"Trust in Him at all times, you people; Pour out your heart before Him; God is a refuge for us." — Psalm 62:8 (NKJV)

Secrets grow heavy in the silence. We hide the "Scared" and the "Mad" because we fear they are too much for the room.

But the Father is not intimidated by your chaos. He is not fragile. He does not need you to tidy up your history before you sit at His feet.

Bring the anger. Bring the secret. Bring the song you threw away.

There is no judgment here. There is only a Refuge.

Chapter 11

"Hello" Scared, Mad, Angry, Done:

YOU ARE BRAVER THAN THE SUM OF YOUR SECRETS

"Everyone has that moment I think, the moment when something so momentous happens that it rips your very being into small pieces. And then you have to stop. For a long time, you gather your pieces. And it takes such a very long time, not to fit them back together, but to assemble them in a new way, not necessarily a better way. More, a way you can live with until you know for certain that this piece should go there, and that one there."

— **Kathleen Glasgow**, Girl in Pieces

JOHN 3:16 RESURRECTED

Heaven was a distant land of confusion and comfort. It was spoken of in the church as a promised, unseen location to those who "believe," or a tearful and sometimes tragic celebration at funerals.

And if you don't fall into those categories, what's next? We circle back around to hell as the heavy push-stone to coerce the belief system. It was an institution this Baptist farm girl didn't question until the pieces of her life were unrecognizable.

Where did we leave ourselves on the timeline of life?

I'll start from the aftermath. I returned home to Oregon with arms and responsibilities a little fuller than when I left just five years before. Married for the second time, a second son on the way, a stay-at-home Mom; all time and resources were focused on raising our little family. Those fractured puzzle pieces, which were a part of me, had been swept under the carpet of time. Time now existed for changing diapers, paying the bills, and the upkeep of a young family infrastructure.

Holy Spirit was drawing me to Himself. The unknown is uncomfortable, but life's noise acted similarly to the floating "snow" debris inside a snow globe. My life was a snow globe: disrupted from any shaking, with a slow gravitational settle until the next jostle. It was hard to hear, and even harder to believe, that God had a plan for me. But John 3:16 was about to be resurrected, as the Guarantor Himself held my hand and walked me through it.

"Now it is God who establishes both us and you in Christ. He anointed us, placed His seal on us, and put His Spirit in our hearts as a guaranteeing pledge of what is to come." (2 Corinthians 1:21-22)

He put His Spirit in our hearts. How many times are we, in theory, going to say it isn't there? Nothing can separate us from the Love of God!

THIS IS THE STORY OF MY CHOICES

"May your choices reflect your hopes, not your fears."
– Nelson Mandela

He was charismatic, talented, with dark eyes and brows like Magnum P.I.—a hometown boy who paid me the attention that touched my heart. Those characteristics I loved about him, and his love's intent, never changed throughout our short marriage.

They weren't enough, however, to cover the pain that he suffered as a boy. Abuse's hand polluted God-given gifts into manipulation and deceit. At twenty-one years of age, my own immaturity and ignorance about the assaults of life pushed him, shoved me, and pushed any relationship I had with God away.

Tom and I were in the thick of deceptions and broken promises. I had never experienced being at risk in any relationship. "Get out" was the only mechanism I was functioning on.

It was my twenty-third birthday. Tom, in a last-ditch effort to make amends, convinced me to take a day trip to the coast. The only remaining part of my memory around that day is that the same charismatic, convincing nature also persuaded me to have sex with him. The last time was a blindsided last time. I got pregnant.

Scared, mad, angry, done.

Scared, Mad, Angry, Done.

I wanted no part of him and didn't give him any part of what happened. "Scared, mad, angry, done" had already made her bed. Heaven, or the threat of hell, couldn't dislodge "scared, mad, angry, done." I felt cheated, lied to, misrepresented, entitled to the Cinderella dreams carried in my heart. How did hate get such a hold?

My decision was made. Abortion was the only way I could rid myself of the Fearsome Foursome: Scared, Mad, Angry, Done. Time has put an eraser over many of the details of that horrific season. I don't remember the road to the appointment in Portland or even how it was paid for, but the institution's name runs contrary to its text: The Lovejoy Center.

The next intrusive horror—why I did this I couldn't say, except I have always been level-headed in emergency situations—I asked to see the fetus remains that were suctioned out of me.

One powerful testament I am privileged to honor is my Mom. Here, her only girl was walking numb, breaking every evangelical rule known to her that existed behind the doors of denominations, and she chose to be there. She drove me to my abortion appointment, sat in the waiting room praying for me, drove me home, and cared for me. That care never found an excuse, never came up in blame, and never quivered over a lifetime.

You could say that a part of me was buried alive!

Later—much later—my murky "snow globe" was frequently shaken in the trials of parenting. An emptiness appeared. An invisible umbilical cord was blocked, soul nourishment depleted.

Loving our boys was easy; I could relate to how they discovered life. Simple applications. Tonka Trucks moved dirt; anything motorized made it go faster, even if it was just the "vroom" coming from their lips. Sticks, rocks, fists—things the imagination supplies—never without a weapon, wonders that could take out imagined or real enemies. If you can take it apart, you can put it back together better. Each one of our boys has their own unique kinetic flare and wonder.

Blinded by "busy," God's restorative love was right in front of my nose.

The "snow globe" suffered a hairline fracture during a miscarriage. The glycerol liquid, which quietly cradled the snow-shame of yesterday's debris until they floated and rested on the bottom, was gone. "Siri," volume 9, my unrecognizable remains tossed audibly in the clothes dryer. The noisy cadence flipped around and around. You try to deal with it: open the door to search for the tiny perpetrator, remove the chip hiding in the dryer drum air holes, slam the door shut, and walk away. If only the broken and anorexic soul could stop throwing up rock chips into your shoe, sock, and the cuff of your jeans.

THEN HOLY SPIRIT...

There is an unspoken cry born in each of us. A wail entwined in the remembrance of our Oneness. I finally remembered. Holy Spirit faithfully reminded me until I listened.

How do you "become" who you really are?

Born anew, born from above, born again. I became the Jesus Freak of my own generation. An immature Jesus Freak, but a revolution was occurring nonetheless. The walls of church that brought me generational comfort were now floating walls—moveable, questionable. Not acceptable. But the pain of man's approval or the brick-and-mortar systems that governed were no match for the ignited flame of Holy Spirit.

Pain that produces growth gives faith stature.

Nothing can separate us from the LOVE of God.

This book is a personal letter. As shared prior, *how-I-arrived-here (my memoir journey)* is written in *The UnFinished Book*.

- A memoir shares how you journeyed to seeing in the Spirit.
- A letter writes what you have learned from seeing.

Love reveals the unseen. "Unseen" should not suggest it is in darkness or without light. Fear is attached like a light switch on the wall; trauma cut the hole, memory laid the light-switch plate, and twisted in the screws. When you walk into a room, what you see depends on what light source you flip on. Shame and guilt constantly reverberated filth, stealing light to make shadows.

Until Love bathed me in a "baptism" in Holy Spirit. He/She/God's Spirit (*Ruach HaKodesh, Jehovah El Shaddai—the Many-Breasted One*) gave me the power to remove the archaic light switch.

This is different from the immersion baptism that washes away our sin and brings us up and out tasting redemption.

I no longer believe that the only evidential sign is speaking in tongues.

Theology is not the rule when the power of life is present.

I know many people who have been "baptized" in Holy Spirit and show living evidence of transformation and power, yet they have struggled with producing an utterance we call "language."

Theology is the privilege to study God.

In Ideas and Opinions, **Albert Einstein** said,

"Pure logical thinking cannot yield us any knowledge of the empirical world; all knowledge of reality starts from experience and ends in it."

He also said, "Information is not knowledge. The only source of knowledge is experience. You need experience to gain wisdom."

Let's draw a simple metaphor: a score of music. Treble clef —Transformation—Bass clef. Ten lines, nine spaces that hold a life-symphony or a simple redemptive song.

We, the Godhead and I, were no longer having a conversation about sin-consciousness. My first note or song to Him was: *I am sorry I ran from You.* Seven profound notes. Together, we dealt with the pain that persuaded wrong choices. He sang over me, bathing me in liquid glory. Not a bath to make you clean from the action, which is the law; He bathed me with grace so I could begin to live and experience the life We had agreed for me.

Consider your life now; there are no outstanding debts; you owe sin nothing. A life bonded to God yields the sacred expression of His character and completes in your experience what life was always meant to be. The reward of the law is death; the gift of grace is life. The bottom line is this: sin employs you like a soldier for its cause and rewards you with death; God gifts you with the highest quality of life all wrapped up in Christ Jesus our Leader. (Romans 6:22, 23 MTB).

HEAVENLY GODIVA KANDY NURSERY

That is just under 2,000 compressed words to encompass ten-plus years. Picture it like this: Papa and I are sitting in the Holy of Holies, Jesus is the Mercy Seat of Himself, and my spirit is being led by Holy Spirit on a journey through the tabernacle. For me, a symphony in only seven notes.

Daily. Seasonally. Within time and outside of time.
- I am no longer in the outer court.
- I am walked through the Brazen Altar; fire is an amazing tool.
- I am escorted around with the mirrors of water in the Laver, to see.
- I am in communion with His Showbread (tasting and seeing).
- I am introduced to the Tree of Life.
- I am a song that He breathes in and exhales over me. (His remembrance over me.)
- IAM in, on, within, beside, here and there, experiencing My Father's yes and amen!

Funny how you remember it clear as a bell. And funny-odd how the spiritual place Holy Spirit took you to resembled the Sunday School nursery room in your "Miss-the-Mark-Church-House-of-Pain"! (See: The UnFinished Book, Chapter 9, Halfway).

Miracles of pain and freedom occurred at the cross of suffering.

As was my routine, I was up early having my devotional time with the Lord. I call it Ascended Prayer. We were always meant to walk with Him in the cool of the day. Our spirits are not bound by time or the body. In my earlier "kindergarten" years of seeing in the Spirit, Jesus was always visually present as a friend and teacher. Whenever I am experiencing a "New" place, I ask for His visual presence to guide me. The first words out of my mouth are, *"Would You show me?"*

Today I was being shown in the Spirit. We walked down a familiar corridor: Sunday School hallway nursery room, Anywhere circa 1960s+ USA.

Jesus and I stepped past the threshold and stood watching the activity inside the nursery room of about fifteen or so active toddlers.

Ages ranging from just walking to about three-ish.

Some sitting, others playing, and others distracted from their next ten-second attention span. I don't remember perceiving "attendants," so to speak, but the room was orderly and felt well cared for. The obvious Church scenario (the parents are in the sanctuary for a well-deserved break): worship, offering, message, etc.

Jesus stood there with a delighted-with-Himself look on His face. Not a word being said, but watching me out of the corner of His eye. In curious compliance and wonder, I began to study a couple of girls playing with each other, recognizably sisters. The elder is standing, the younger sitting on the floor, both playing and exchanging similar toys. Delightfully dressed in soft pink dresses, wavy blonde locks, and fair skin. The older had intense brown eyes, talked with her hands, and commanded the room of children around her. Her little sister was comfortable with big sister's overshadow, bouncing her head like she was singing a song to herself. She never looked up or was distracted from her toy.

My spirit began to overflow a profound feeling of love into my understanding, and tears started to well up. I looked at Jesus, the first tear still building saline in my eye. *"What are the two sisters' names?"*

He answered me: *"Kandy and Briady."*

The floodgates opened. The second name He used, *Briady,* was the name that my husband Don and I had set aside for our girl, four boys ago!

"And Kandy?" I asked in a broken voice.

He said, *"You never named her, so We did!*

And spelled with a *K."*

My composure was gone. At that moment, Kandy and Briady looked up at me as if I had just returned from the sanctuary to collect them. Briady quickly put down her toy and leaned on her hands, bum up, and toddled to me. I grabbed her into my arms and carried her to her sister, who was still orchestrating the room.

Time was irrelevant, distance never happened, the decisions over my body never spoke, a former miscarriage wasn't crying, and GRACE had carried both of my girls into divine care. My choice was nailed to the cross. There was no residue.

THERE WAS NO RESIDUE!

Only LOVE; like we had always existed together. Complete Oneness!

OUR 4 BOYS

"To uncover your true potential you must first find your own limits and then you have to have the courage to blow past them."

— **Picabo Street** (Former American World Cup alpine ski racer and Olympic gold medalist).

Amongst all the noise, Don and I managed to get past diapers—barely. We enjoyed the freedoms of our almost-teenage boys being able to camp, hike, hunt, fish, and sail.

Nobody informs you of the "sports" comma your schedule experiences. Not to mention your pocketbook if you find the sweet spot in your child's talent: Baseball. Somehow you acquire a secret IV solution of energy to schedule, score-keep, traffic grandparents, and wash uniforms. I had some of the best Baseball-Mom-tans sitting in ninety-plus degree temperatures for weekend double-headers. With four boys, we bedraggled through four little league teams, summer and fall ball.

One year the most amazing answer to prayer came when Jace and Jacob, our two middle boys—closest in age—were signed to the same team. The coaches thought they were twins; I knew Heaven had mercy.

Dear reader, if you walked into my office right now, this proud Mama could pull out from underneath her desk a large apothecary jar with every single home-run ball, best outfield-fly caught ball, best games-pitched balls, the baseball bat my Marine made from Afghanistan wood, and (before he signed for the Corps) the baseball he threw first time on the mound, spring training in Arizona.

Nothing is sweeter than a lefty's change-up dropping in the catcher's mitt.

Is that enough proud parent for you?

Now somewhere in there—between football, baseball, girls, academics, girls, cars, fixing cars, girls, kids carrying cell phones, and band practice—shame and guilt decided to invite themselves to batting practice.

Is it a test? Yes! Who sent the test? Yes.

Right in the middle of "Seeing in the Spirit" Jesus-lessons, dismantling false doctrines that had built floating walls, shame-FEAR-guilt hit. Fear… hard stop. *What if my boys found out that I had had an abortion?*

This is the same Mom that boasted her love-trophies in the paragraph before, with a big scary **BUT** that could disqualify me in every area God's passion had called me. Being their Mom is at the top of the list. This was a masked secret. I was called by Heaven to dismantle shame and guilt. His love had introduced me to grace, and she didn't have any dark corners or rules. Righteousness is about Him; there is no measure withholding when one decides to know Him, and then past choices are governed by His love for them. I believe He had a discussion about that.

LABORERS IN THE VINEYARD

"For the kingdom of heaven is like a landowner who went out early in the morning to hire laborers for his vineyard...
And about the eleventh hour he went out and found others standing around... He said to them, 'You go into the vineyard too.'

When evening came... 'Call the laborers and pay them their wages, beginning with the last group to the first.' ...When those hired first came, they thought that they would receive more; but each of them also received a denarius... But he answered and said... 'Is it not lawful for me to do what I wish with what is my own? Or is your eye envious because I am generous?' So the last shall be first, and the first last."
(Matthew 20:1-16 NASB, condensed)

The Kingdom of Heaven is still like this. Righteousness is still generously paid out to the first and the last. We do not begin to look like, and respond like Him, until we know Him.

Choice is once again calling my "IAm" name, and it's a name I didn't answer to many years before. Do I recognize that name today?

My heart shook through a serious season of prayer and inquiring of the Lord His timing. Of course, my husband Don was aware of the different sortings of my past. A few family members could shake the liquid-less snow globe.

   • **Guilt** involves the awareness of having done something wrong; it arises from one's actions.
   • **Shame** is the painful feeling about how one appears to others (and to oneself) at times even if error or action hasn't occurred. That wasn't the case for me.

"If you put shame in a petri dish, it needs three ingredients to grow exponentially: secrecy, silence, and judgement."

— Brené Brown

I knew I carried the key of freedom because women were naturally drawn to me for help and ministry. Now I had to use the same key and walk through my own door again. And yes, I cared very much how I appeared and who I was to our boys. Who do you think did all the "dragging" the family to church?

A SERIOUS NOTE FROM THE AUTHOR, before we adopt any decisions of transparency: Use Wisdom to counsel each of us to have clear peace and direction from the Lord before re-exposing what He has forgiven.

The plan arrived in my heart. Courage must have been rolled up with it.

John 3:16, for God so loved that He gave...

It's time to look in the mirror and see His reflection.

I asked each of our boys individually to take a walk with me. The weather was inviting enough to walk without a coat; we were still newcomers to Corvallis but settling into the community quickly. Sports are a great "how-do-you-do." Shaking in my boots, with the blatant understanding that this was costing me everything. I mean everything I held dear.

Easiest to go from the eldest to youngest. I asked Joseph to go for that first walk. My oldest is so much like me: inquisitive, brave, bull-headed at times, loves to dig up truth.

A flashback: How does this mother of four strapping young men, who held each one of them to her breast, have anything in common with the girl who buried part of herself alive? How did I choose to save self? The Mama Bear inside of me has unrecognizable remains.

Living Spiritually BRAVE naturally comes to the forefront of "let's get it done."

" Out with it...

There isn't anything that can un-spill milk.

There isn't a street long enough for this conversation."

I told him I loved him and shared my story. No punches pulled, no excuses; the choice was mine to bear. Tears were spilling down my face and breaking words in my throat. Before the story ended, Joseph was holding me in his arms.
"Mom, I love you. I can't imagine this happened to you."
"Neither can I, son. Neither can I."

The fragile moment with each of my sons—Jace, Jacob, and Justin—the response was the same.
"Mom, I love you! I can't imagine this happened to you."
Humbled, you see your own brave self stare right back at you.

You are braver than the sum of your secrets.

My youngest, having the luxury of being raised by a little more transformed and heavenly-inspired Mom, spontaneously asked me this intuitive question: *"You mean I have two sisters in heaven?"*

He knew. Divinely he knew. Yes, son, you do.
• Fear was dismantled.
• Guilt was condemned.
• And Shame? We have never been introduced to her by name.

HEAVENLY GODIVA KANDY

"A coach is someone who tells you what you don't want to hear, who has you see what you don't want to see, so you can be who you have always known you could be."

— **Tom Landry**, Dallas Cowboys

The Kingdom of Heaven is like... your treasured 1873 farmhouse filled with the growing-up memories of your kids. Years later your adult child divinely returns, knocking on the door of its current owners. Graciously they invite him in; his heart bursting with stories, he tucks his head inside the pantry. Encapsulated in time, stories confirmed, his name "Jacob" is still pencil measure-marked on the inside lock stile of the door. Growing up remains in the heart, abides in the spirit.

In the Spirit: I would spend dedicated spiritual moments with my girls.

They appeared to grow as we spent time together. Can't say or explain, I wasn't always aware of the moments from diapers, to dance class or prom, yet pictures begin to develop in your understanding that make you wonder, who took the photo?

Heaven is filled with experiences of the living. Relationships continue to build and mature.

All earthly memory is cherished as a favorite chapter in a book.

I don't know about you, but I assumed it was two books until I experienced differently. "The Lamb's Book of Life"— One Book with every name written in it.

Spiritual growing: you flow in seasons, which brings forth fruit or pruning, which brings forth more fruit. Remaining fruit is what you come back to, to remind yourself what has been tasted and seen. It's an eternal book of remembrance still being written.

Jesus, Kandy, and I were walking on an ancient path. What makes it an ancient path? Your feet are not the only footprints that have walked on it; and yours aren't the only wisdoms hidden there.

Living Ancient Paths: For explanation purposes, we will frame it similarly to visiting a national trust site, or a wonder of the world. Sometimes God created the "site" and sometimes man did. We—Trinity, you and I—are walking on a paved path lined on both sides by tall, upright trees.

A tepid breeze is kissing the freshest of new spring leaves. Time has created a spiritual marker in every step. If you still your heart, ancient time—Heaven's time—will step out from a hidden place. People, instances, and unseen forces both good and evil can be discerned. Moses chose to turn aside, turn into the goodness of God, and realized that this "Ancient Path" was holy ground. Always turn into the goodness of God.

We were having a conversation. Kandy was a young woman now, the proverbial Heaven age, somewhere in her late twenties. How do I know its proverbial heaven age? Experience, time encountered. There are occasions that a person's spirit reflects the age in which you can relate to them. When I suggested Moses turning aside, you would imagine a man in his mid-life. Full of strength as he walked towards his destiny.

"It was at this time that Moses was born... But when he was approaching the age of forty, it entered his mind to visit his brethren... After forty years had passed, an angel appeared to him in the wilderness of Mount Sinai..." (Acts 7:20-31, condensed)

If we imagined him on our timetable, eighty would look different. Sometimes we meet members of the cloud of witnesses in the timeframe in which a family member remembers them.

If I were to turn aside and start thinking about my great-grandmother who stepped into heaven at ninety-nine: my spirit discerns and speaks with her as a young woman, beautiful and wise; my heart's understanding sees her as my very senior great-grandmother whom I loved, beautiful and wise. We are experiencing dual-seeing. Made in the image of our omnipresent Father.

Kandy was the same precocious child I was introduced to; the ability to command a room had matured and softened. As familiar as we recall that tepid breeze during our Ancient Path walk, from Kandy's perspective, mother and daughter have always been together. The entire conversation, word for word, is more of a feeling of what we were talking about than text.

We walked along the path, looking, admiring. I pulled a single leaf from a tree, running my fingers over creation's edge as unfolded origami in soft, tender green vinyl.

Jesus, walking just out of earshot as if to give us a moment. (As if Jesus is ever out of earshot...)

Kandy looked at me, intense brown eyes, her wavy ash blonde hair just below the shoulder, hair tucked back behind her ear. She grabbed both my hands, which halted our course. Her eyes in humble focus.

"Mom," she said to me, with the greatest of admiration, *"I knew that you would abort me!"*

Stunned by her direct comment, an instant waterfall of emotion flooded my spirit and burst its banks with tears.

She continued, *"Before, and beyond before, I was shown the verity of the gospel upon your life, how your relationship with Jesus would draw an important marker for your generation. I chose, before you chose."*

Vibrating at the same frequency as the cross: I chose before you chose... Selah.

Living Vision: The softest of thought pushed by the headwaters unveiled a portrait in my mind. Painted vividly in colors of gossamer pink, robin's egg blues, with a touch of baby chick yellow, consistent with the last light in the sky holding on to a summer's eve. The colors compressed, creating enormous pages of paper, bound in an immense opened book, bowed from the spine, laying smooth to the edge.

Jesus and Kandy now standing on top of the vast pages of the "Lamb's Book of Life". Bent on her knees, pen in hand, Kandy signed her name and within her name was her story. It was larger than life—her story or the book? Yes! The pen in her hand danced as a calligrapher moves the ink into the paper. Her signature, a ballet of grace, dancing into my understanding.

My spirit held firmly the portrait just arms length in front of me, a living dimension suspended so I could breathe. Hard tears and the weight of life moments wetting my face, wiped on my sleeves.

She chose before I chose.

She gave, so truth could abound.

Truth could be known, truth would heal, truth would restore, truth would speak and write. The ramifications mirror my Savior.

Mankind is in the same boat; their distorted behavior is proof of a lost blueprint. *"Sin is to live out of context with the blueprint of one's design; to behave out of tune with God's original harmony."*

"You have forgotten the Rock that begot you and have gotten out of step with the God who danced with you."
(Deuteronomy 32:18 / Romans 3:23 MTB)

She chose before you chose.

Beyond, before beyond: Jesus had shown Kandy my blueprint. Knowing His sacrifice, she also laid down her life for mine. She never walked out of tune.

"For God so LOVED the world that He gave His only begotten Son that whosoever believes in Him shall not perish but will have everlasting life." (John 3:16)

The entire cosmos is the object of God's affection. And He is not about to abandon His creation - the gift of His Son is for mankind to realize their origin in Him who mirrors their authentic birth - begotten not of flesh but of the Father. In this persuasion the life of the ages echoes within the individual and announces that the days of regret and sense of lost-ness are over. (John 3:16 Mirror Translation Bible)

COACHING...

"Football is an incredible game. Sometimes it's incredibly cruel. And that's the sport. If you can handle the pain, if you can handle the disappointment, then eventually you have to get up, and keep moving, and fight, and believe, and try to win."

— **Urban Meyer** | Celebrated American former college football coach.

Scan to listen to the first time I shared the story. Interviewing Jesus Podcast

ACTIVATION

"HELLO" SCARED, MAD, ANGRY, DONE
This chapter has called you to dismantle the power of the shame formula—secrecy, silence, and judgment—by revealing the truth of your eternal, blameless identity. Your history is not a residue; it is the Guarantor's Pledge that nothing can separate you from the love of God.

Now, let's step onto the Ancient Path and allow the questions of Jesus to open a personal conversation with Him, inviting you to exchange the heavy burden of "Scared, Mad, Angry, Done" for the light truth of complete Oneness.

A Direct Conversation with Jesus

1. The Dwelling Place *"Do you not know that you are God's temple and that God's Spirit dwells in you?"* (1 Corinthians 3:16)

Shame tells you that your past choices polluted your worth. This question confronts that lie directly, challenging you to see your body and soul as the Father's dwelling place. Bring the most painful detail of your past to Him and ask: *"Jesus, does Your Spirit truly dwell here, in this place of my greatest shame?"* Be still and listen to the truth of His immediate, non-conditional presence that removes the residue.

2. The Good Gift *"If you, then, being evil, know how to give good gifts to your children, how much more will your Father who is in heaven give good things to those who ask Him?"* (Matthew 7:11)

The author's capacity to love her four boys was never disqualified by her past choice. This question uses the foundational bond of parenthood to challenge your limiting belief about God's capacity to love and gift you.

Ask Him: *"Father, what good gifts are hindered from me because I am still believing the lie that I disqualified them?"* Listen for the promise of abundance.

3. **The Touch** *"Who touched me?"* (Luke 8:45) This question was asked in the midst of a crowd by Jesus, who felt a specific touch of faith that released power. Shame forces us into hiddenness (the girl who buried part of herself alive). This question invites you to come out of the crowd, out of the secret place, and approach Him with bold faith. Ask Him: *"Jesus, where is the most painful place I need to touch You with my faith today, to release the power to disarm my fear?"* Listen for the intuitive nudge to make a public or private declaration of your freedom.

Reflect and Respond

Take a moment to record what you received in this time of conversation with Jesus. What was the feeling of the Ancient Path? What truth did He illuminate about your inherent value? Let this be a record of your direct experience of freedom from the fearsome foursome of trauma.

____

____

____

____

Next Step

Carry the question that challenged your shame the most. Practice seeing your life through the lens of the Laborers in the Vineyard (Matthew 20:1-16)—knowing that the pay is generous and not dependent on your personal clock or your past failures.

Let that generosity fuel your courage.

Prayer and Contemplation

Father, thank You for the truth that I am braver than the sum of my secrets. I choose to lay down the Scared, Mad, Angry, Done and step fully into the assurance of Your Spirit, who is my Guarantor's Pledge. I believe there is no residue. I accept the freedom and life restoration You have already given. In Jesus' name, Amen.

PLAY SHEET | PROPHET

Prophet Edition
Redemptive Gifts Summary

THIS CHAPTER IS A DEEP FIELD PLAY that breaks the defensive line of shame and secrecy. It is a call to recognize that your past does not define your DNA. You are empowered to move past the "Scared, Mad, Angry, Done" cycle and step back into the liquid glory of your original design.

THE DNA WRISTBAND AUDIBLE: CHAPTER PLAY-CALL

   1. **The Green Dot Helmet** (*Individual Redemptive Gift*): **Prophet** The frequency for this play is set to the Prophet. This is your gift of "Design" and "Purpose." You are hardwired to see the Blueprint of your life, which means you have an internal intolerance for the "floating walls" of secrets and shame. The Prophet in you recognizes that while trauma may have cut a hole in your history, it was only to make room for a "light switch" of revelation.

   You are being called to stop managing the shadows of the "Fearsome Foursome" and to start employing the power of your pre-destined Design.

2. **The Coaches' Booth** (*Legacy Anchor*): *The Shack* by William Paul Young In the "Booths" of your spiritual legacy, The Shack (Prophet/Design) represents the deep, mystical meeting point where your "Great Sadness" is confronted by the Presence of God. You apply this by realizing that your story is not a tragedy, but a masterpiece of restoration. God is not afraid of the "shack" of your secrets; He is already there, waiting to show you that the Residue of your past has no legal claim on your future. Purpose is found when you are brave enough to walk back into the places you thought were lost.

3. **The Play-Call from God**

"Child, check your helmet—I am speaking over the noise of your yesterday. I see the pieces of your heart that you've swept under the carpet, trying to live like a snow globe that's constantly being shaken by fear and anger. I am calling an audible: There is No Residue! I watched My Son, Jesus, take every bit of that secret shame and nail it to the cross so that you could walk onto the field today with a clean jersey. I chose you before you ever chose Me. That is the C♡♡Lness of our Oneness. When the 'Scared, Mad, Angry, Done' voices start to shout, I want you to remember the 'Heavenly Nursery' of My grace. I am not a God who manages your mistakes; I am the Father who restores your Sonship. You are Spiritually BRAVE enough to tell the truth and disarm the fear. Your DNA is not a sum of your secrets; it is a symphony of My love. I have put My Spirit in your heart as a guaranteeing-pledge that the game is already won. Stop looking at your coping mechanisms and start looking at your Original Design. You aren't the last one in the vineyard; in My heart, you are the first. Run the play, Child. I am in your corner."

4. The Audible *The Timeline of Now* The enemy wants you to believe you are "buried alive" by the things you haven't said. The Audible is this: Your secrets have lost their power! Right now, on the timeline of today, I am removing the light-switch of shame from your mind. I am releasing the power to blow past the limits of your history. You are not a sum of your secrets; you are a King's Champion.
How Good is God!

REFORMATION DATA: THE ARCHITECTURE OF TRANSPARENCY

- To understand the "field" you are playing on, consider how to apply these principles of "Unveiling" to your own life:
- **The Anatomy of a Secret:** Research confirms that "Secrecy, Silence, and Judgment" are the fuel for shame. *Apply This:* By choosing to "Tell the Truth" to the Father—and eventually to a trusted witness—you are effectively dismantling the "Defensive Line" of the enemy. Transparency is the highest form of Prophetic Authority.
- **The "Sonship" Pay-Scale:** In the economy of the Kingdom, the "pay" (your righteousness) is a fixed asset. *Apply This*: Whether you came to the truth at 7:00 AM or 11:00 PM, you carry the full DNA Calling of a winner. Refuse to let "lost time" or "past mistakes" make you feel like a second-string player.
- **Division of Residue:** Your brain may have created "neural pathways" of regret. *Apply This*: Apply the Rhema Mind by declaring that the Cross has "bleached" the record. When you focus on your "New Identity" (Blueprint), you literally rewrite the physical structures of your brain.

HOW GOOD IS GOD!

THE QUIET LOVE

"The Lord your God in your midst, The Mighty One, will save; He will rejoice over you with gladness, He will quiet you with His love, He will rejoice over you with singing." — Zephaniah 3:17 (NKJV)

The storm has passed. The secret is told.

The song you threw away was not lost. He caught it.

He held the melody while you held the pain. And now, in the stillness after the scream, listen closely.

He is not silent. He is singing it back to you.

Chapter 12

Eight Days to Heaven

The Resurrection of I Love You

"It is easier to build strong children than to repair broken men."

— **Frederick Douglass** (1818–1895) | Social reformer, abolitionist, orator, and writer.

He was a quiet man, until he cussed. He wasn't demonstrative; he always came home, always went to work.

He wasn't going to make a spectacle of himself, except those mornings he would sneak across the front lawn in his boxer shorts to apprehend the newspaper. His acts of service were impeccable. Korean War, World War II, 11th Airborne, 127th Combat Engineers, Mascot "The Angels": They dropped from the sky to rescue people. The only paratroopers to jump into occupied Japan. He never drank coffee, smoked a cigarette, got a tattoo, or drank alcohol.

"I've said it before, but it's absolutely true: My mother gave me my drive, but my father gave me my dreams. Thanks to him, I could see a future."

— **Liza Minnelli**

We all have experienced in our lives measures of "hard," especially in the area of relationships. I use the word "hard" for its simplicity. The word "difficulties" is tangled in reasons. "Hard" is just what it is: four letters (the h↔d) that look like two chairs facing toward each other, with "ar" sandwiched between.

"HARD"

Him ar Daughter

h—ar—d

Her-ar-Dad

The chairs in this story have titles. Why titles and not names? A name is an identifier—what you answer to. It can be filled with affection, a story, distaste, lineage, or destiny. A title is a designation with ownership, power, authority, honor given, and an expected response to do something.

My four-letter description sounds more like a pirate's response: "Arrr." For reasons I may never understand, someone or some circumstance put the a & r between our chairs (My Dad and I).

My Dad: "a"lways there, but "r"eserved. That reserve withheld the most precious words and expressions that a child longs to hear: I love you. When you are little—maybe we are "little" more years than the size or age of our youth—gratitude hasn't matured yet to provide you with confidence and strength. I suppose many of us never work through the "whys" on the way to transformation.

I had to. It was imperative to know my name. It was necessitous to know my Heavenly Father and replace any lies of separation or unspoken words. God is not hard, quiet, reserved, or withholding.

Nothing can separate us from the LOVE of God, not even ar...

MY DAD

My Dad, 93, passed away from Alzheimer's on October 5th, 2020. His love escaped all obstacles when Alzheimer's erased the reasons that held him back.

I am honored to tell our story and reveal Jesus, who transformed the heart of an only daughter.

Dad's dementia was significantly "hard" for about three years. Bless my eighty-plus-year-old Mom for her sacrificial determination to care for my Dad in the home. Sixty-seven years married and loving him when "hard" challenged her beyond gratitude, just so he could be at home all the days of his life. As quoted above, I got my drive from my Mom.

Our Corvallis home is a quick twenty-minute drive away from the ninety-two-acre farm I have known since third grade. During this season of weekly visits—many times more— gratitude grew. Appreciation whispered at the sound of gravel crushing and popping out under the tire; this means home is 'round the corner.

Fortunate. My Mom's Iowa farmer-girl past persuaded my Los Angeles-raised Dad to plant his dreams and children in God's other Heaven: Oregon.

As I have coined before: It looks just like the English countryside without the hedgerows. Rolling grass hayfields, the captain of the Cascade mountain range, Mt. Jefferson, peeking over your backdoor. Daily, a lonely freight train echoes from the property's east boundary. Oak and fir trees line the meadows, rivers, and roads. Each acre is arrested with stories; my brothers (there are three), my four sons, and my husband all share in that earlier persuasion.

Decay of memory is an abominable disease. My Dad suffered from extreme sleep apnea, for which he refused to adhere to help. I attribute this as the root cause that stole his thoughts. In his latter days and with much weight loss— though he was never an overweight man—the sleep apnea disappeared. However, years of oxygen starvation to the brain took its ransom and left its scar.

My Dad softened in the final three years. Some of my most precious memories are the simplest attributes of habitual things he did throughout the years.

- Asking how much gas we had in our tank.
- Kicking the tires.

• Fanatical organization regarding his silverware and food on the plate.

• Rubbing the dry cuticle of his middle finger on his upper lip.

• Always, a perfectly tucked-in shirt.

• Long, animated ice rink stories from the days of Sonja Henie about how "My Dad" got to help the famous Freddie Trenkler (Ice Skating Clown) trip on ice and pour water on the audience. Tremendous audience slapstick humor.

• Grocery store customer stories over a lifetime as a grocery man.

• Jokes of "living California style" when real butter, orange juice, and fancy napkins were served.

• Feeding the family dog leftover pancakes or waffles with a fork. He would skewer the last pancake morsel, wipe round and round the sticky syrup plate as Champ (faithful Black Lab), Brutus (Great Dane), or Trinket (Fox Terrier) drooled in anticipation of one more sweet crumb.

We find ourselves overlooking the slightest of nuances until the nuances themselves are what remain of your loved one. Never did I imagine being a co-caretaker to the most private of men. Yet there abided an unspoken comfort Mom said I always bring. The days were spent mostly in bed. I'd arrive, open the back door, and Dash (my dog) would run across the house and leap onto the bed. (Unheard of to have a dog in bed!) Dad was always aware she was there.

I have a "live" photo taken—the animations only show on my phone—of my Dad turning his head, looking at Dash as she settled herself on the corner of his pillow.

Such treasures; you watch them again and again. The Why on so many levels? Because the obstacles that confine a human soul were gone. Decay had resurrected intimacy out of the ashes. I'd kiss him on the head, and he would say, "I love you." Words that took a lifetime to be spoken. Tenderness, pats, and physical touch restored. The humblest cognitive "thank you's" after cleaning and bathing the incontinence of a heartless disease.

Days ahead and behind, Mom would call me on the phone concerned that Dad was seeing (unseen) people inside and outside the home. He'd hear and see children singing and playing out on the lawn. Because I could "see in the spirit," I knew that the "atmosphere was getting thin." I said, "Mom, if the people he sees don't cause turmoil (that would be a different issue), I'd say Dad was experiencing more Heaven than earth." She never questioned me. Odd, the conversations in secret stress that were shared through this; Mom would tell me of past times Dad would leap out of bed, walk around the house concerned, sure he had seen somcone. The Lord explained that my Dad was also a "Seer." The gift never found relevance or development—unless you count passing it to me.

EIGHT DAYS IN MY JOURNAL Those days of normal nuances but countless irritations—Dad would haphazardly get on the floor to play and tease the cat, and my youngest brother, living only seven minutes away, would have to come help as Dad was unable to stand back up—they were gone. Dad's brain was no longer able to support the body. Gone was the cognitive. Arrival of the Spirit. Transition. Crop Circle Vision. Dad was sleeping. Hospice had been called. My brothers were notified of the changes. Mom, in an exhaling or exhausted blur, emailed and texted those who needed to know. Likewise, I called Don. Dash and I remained at the house for eight days. I sat on the edge of their bed, taking in the room: pretty floral and harvest plaid quilt, matching pillows piled in the corner on the old chestnut rocking chair.

Mom's antique jewelry boxes atop Great Grandma's oval mirrored vanity. Sheets that had been changed and washed what felt like a hundred thousand times. Listening to Dad breathe. The house quiet in a sad-welcome spirit. Stressful days of care were coming to an end.

How many times had I looked out their bedroom window over the fields, arrayed in conditions from seed to harvest? From where I sat, you could see the east end of the rabbit barn —one of my Mom's entrepreneurial adventures, the brilliant leftovers of my youngest brother Matt's 4-H rabbit project.

At one time I think she had some three thousand white New Zealand Rabbits.

Daily, her well-worn sweatshirt pockets were filled with white fur and wiggling pink babies. Hopping-kind-kittens destined for a warm Folgers coffee can perched next to the pilot lamp of our gas stovetop. The remains—bulbous plywood cooling fan covers protruding—only uncovered empty openings where buzzards and owls would find nesting in the stored grass hay. Behind the barn, burnt, bruised, and regrowing, a single huge black walnut tree stood stretching haunted-looking branches for the local winged predators' daily perch. Up-close in the yard, Mom's bird feeders bursting in hungry rummage. Her cement birdbath hosted the daily bath of the fattest robin. She dunked her red breast again and again in the cool afternoon water, washing late September dust from her feathers. My sight changed as a "Prophetic Screen" dropped like a jeweler's loupe over my eye. I saw a plethora of angels of all sizes, ascending and descending on the spent autumn field I just described. The angels' movement, comings, and goings laid the remaining long, bleached, calf-high grass stubble in circular wind rows. Crop Circles.

Days were now numbered in Heaven and on earth. I watched the wonder until only one large Guardian remained. The stage was set. What nobody had ever described was divinely laid ready. The Guardian remained in my seeing. Over the course of the next days, I continued to rise early and photograph my Mom's lovely garden.

Her landscape and the spiritual landscape before me provided a place to think, write, communicate, blog, and post glories that were otherwise hidden in the coming grief.

(Note: A couple of months later, my Mom sent my photographs to Fine Gardening Magazine; they were published the following month. Enjoy.)

JOURNAL NOTES I thanked Holy Spirit for helping my Dad transition, encouraging him to step to the other side. I asked: Help me to see, perceive, and sense what is going on...

1st Morning: My "Seer" Intercession: I see myself, much like the First Kiss of the morning, sitting in the spirit in the Garden of Eden planted for us east in God's garden. For the last few days, I have been sitting under a different tree. I think I'll name it Mercy. One of the trees God told Adam that he could eat from. I am passing out mercy to my family members.

2nd Morning: The same view described out my Mom and Dad's bedroom window: the back half of the rabbit barn, a few degrees west. So much to contemplate and muse.

3rd Morning: Texted to my family members: Good morning. Mom still resting. We both took shifts sitting up with Dad for the night. His heart beating strong, breathing deep slow breaths consistently, breaths stopping now and again.

Fingers and around mouth showing signs of blue. Giving morphine for his comfort about every three hours. Dad responded when I washed his face. He is resting peacefully.

My "Seer" Notes: Cloud of witnesses coming and going freely. Dad's family: His Mom (Gaga), his Dad, uncles, sister Jeanie (Aunt Jeanie). Two large angels on duty since yesterday morning. One holds Dad's book. One holds his crown, robe, and scepter; he will be well-dressed to meet up with the Lord. Dad's spirit has separated from his body. I see him watching himself (body & soul), talking with his family.

He came into my room last night as a young man, about thirty. (Note: When Dad came into the room last night he was wearing a turquoise check shirt.

The one Mom made him. She carries that black and white photo in her wallet still today—Dad in that shirt. How did I know it was turquoise check? (Amazing to have eyes that see. Love you Dad, Love you Lord.) Familiar to us:

"For the word of God is alive and active. Sharper than any double-edged sword, it penetrates even to dividing soul and spirit, joints and marrow; it judges the thoughts and attitudes of the heart." (NIV)

"The message God spoke to us in Christ, is the most life giving and dynamic influence in us, cutting like a surgeon's scalpel, sharper than a soldier's sword, piercing to the deepest core of human conscience, to the dividing of soul and spirit; ending the dominance of the sense realm and its neutralizing effect upon the human spirit. In this way a person's spirit is freed to become the ruling influence again in the thoughts and intentions of their heart. The scrutiny of this living Sword-Logos detects every possible disease, discerning the body's deepest secrets where joint and bone-marrow meet." (Hebrews 4:12 Mirror Study Bible)

I saw my Dad's spirit divide from his body before breath left him. We have each been given this grace. Our spirit is free to become the ruling influence in our lives, today, on the earth.

4th Morning: Journal Notes: Dad is still chugging along, which surprises me Lord. I heard three days when I asked him. Lord, is there any assistance I can offer Dad's transition into Your loving arms? I heard yes...

I will follow Your lead, what is on Your mind Lord?

While sending Mom each new day's morning photos, which greatly encouraged her, I meditated on my request to the Lord. I saw Dad's timeline, like a movie in the downloading process… you can see the straight download line across your device, moving ahead but the picture is behind and not clear.

Death and decay, Lord. *What would You have me to do?*

I wrote: Need a little beauty, time to switch fonts. I need a shower, desperately.

Poem: Life is just a moment of breaths,
Counting "hales" in and ex.
The days they number themselves,
The nights fall to slumber.
Regret a hard taskmaster,
Unforgiven thoughts you are buried.
East & West, as-far-as has no measure,
Tomorrow, what list do you have to do,
That today has not checked off?
Mercy, I only have one question,
I'll trade it, without due course.
By the dawn's early light,
Oh Say Can YOU see…
There are streets of gold & Seas of Glass,
Where angels trod revealed.
Emerald bows circle His glory,
His throne, there is no other.
In God we put our trust,
And trust regained all brothers.

5th Morning: On top of my Dad's "Chiffonet" (phonetically, I heard him say it for years). The sofa wasn't a sofa or a couch, but a davenport. His dresser, a "chiffonet." Dad, just a little google correction.

A Chiffonier is a tall and narrow chest of drawers that is commonly used for storing delicate items such as undergarments, lingerie, and other small clothing.

On top of my Dad's very organized chiffonier: a black and white photo of his Dad, a tire gauge, a pocket knife, the silver watch my Mom gave him when he made store manager, and a small green frame.

My Dad, not a crafty man in the least, had clipped a photo that caught his fancy. Inside the small green frame was a picture of two hat-wearing old men, arms crossed, sitting on a park bench.

The quote says:
My wife said, *"Watcha doin' today?"*
I said, *"Nothing."*
She said, *"You did that yesterday."*
I said, *"I wasn't finished."*

My Dad finished doing "nothing" today. October 5th, 2020, late morning, still at home. We witnessed the slow, held rattle breaths for about an hour: his wife of sixty-seven years, his three sons, and me, all beside his bed. With no rush, pain, or fear, my Dad gave up his last breath. His spirit stood as his soul left the body. A body who looked like my Dad, loved like my Dad, and gave me the ability to see dreams.

I saw the two angels who stood by his side. The book holder signed the page and closed the book. The second angel put Dad's robe over his shoulders and crown on his head.

My spirit felt a warm intuitive smile; my Dad knew I could see. They faded into another realm. The Regal Guardian who stood in my "seeing" for days at the edge of the crop circle also ascended out of sight.

That precious sound of gravel underneath tire or foot—just a few hours earlier that morning I had laid my body and phone landscape on the driveway to catch the morning's distant photo illusion. Moss growing rich amongst the stones, my car, and the blurred neighbor's house down the lane.

The rocks, I could hear their story...

Poem: It's not as we may have thought
or pulpit might expound.
There isn't a judgement, or questioning to be had,

No measurement or finger to point at our days.
Just glory how He covers His own,
In righteousness robes, our crown is awarded us,
To meet Him properly dressed in Himself.
His death finalized, every jot and every tittle
We just need to read between the lines.
Our spirits not contained, our soul no despair,
To see His salvation love so utterly sublime.

For the last few days, we had placed extra chairs around the hospital bed. He was gone in flesh; we sat around his quiet body and began to tell stories.

No tears or misunderstandings, but precious memories, oddities that make you laugh, and times that Dad had spent being there.

6th Morning: I wrote: Good morning Father, can't thank you enough for supporting us in this journey, my Dad is now in your company.

We filled the days till Saturday with end-of-life plans, military honors, took Mom to the coast, gathered around the table each evening, told stories that made us laugh until we cried, and prepared our thoughts.

CELEBRATING DAD

The swing set of my childhood: Generations of joy have squealed from this ol' swing set. This afternoon we will gather not fifty yards from this spot, looking over the pond and spreading the ashes of my Dad across his dearly loved farm.

Poem in the morning | Throne of Grace:
Lord I lift up my family today,
I remember that Jennifer is far from home.
Holy Spirit Your comfort and assistance is most desired.
Dad, I loved that you were chosen as my Dad,
Family within the Cloud of Witnesses, of course you are welcomed.
Angels minister in the secret places,
Family=Hearts, you need touching and strength,

I open a special window prepared for this day.
Elements, I ask a favor of you.
Hold the rain, Sun warm the air,
Earth breathe hope, Water reflect beauty.
Fire burn slowly the dross of sorrow,
Metal soften the hue of color into a gentle quilt,
Grace, I need an extra measure today.
Surely, Goodness and Mercy,
today instead of following
I invite you to lay a path.
Easy to see and walk on.
Jesus, thank you that
the kingdom of Heaven is at hand,
I lay hold of it, grasp tightly, with my right hand.
(Written by Kristen Wambach 10/10/20 For her family in Memory of George A. Richards, her Dad)

In the morning light, my spirit could see my Dad. He was dressed in light khaki/tan trousers bloused at the ankle of his boots with a cotton or canvas bomber jacket and helmet. Later that afternoon before the service commenced, Mike, Matt, and I were standing in the living room. The closeness of the days behind us had given me many unique opportunities to share and explain what I saw in the spirit. Grief has a way of softening the heart when at other times it's locked from logic. They already knew their sister was "special." Very normal from my experience to see the deceased amongst their family giving comfort.

I shared with them that I could see Dad in the spirit, and proceeded to describe my Dad's obvious military attire. My brother Matt, an avid WWII collector, was amazed that I detailed period utilities perfectly.

He knew that I had no idea what would have been worn. A little later I asked my eldest brother Mike, U.S. Army Chief Warrant Officer-Four (Retired), *"Why would Dad be wearing a helmet with his uniform today?"* Mike said, *"In wartime, that was always their cover."*

This little sister thought that was mystical coolness! The services were planned, family had arrived and gathered near the house at the top of the hayfield knoll, overlooking the pond. I sat shotgun in my youngest brother Matt's Jeep, the exact model jeep my Dad would have used during service. Mike the eldest, carrying Dad's remains, looked amongst us as to who would like to spread them. Then he turned to me and said, *"Since I was the last one to care for him, why don't I spread the ashes."* Honored, I did.

Mike and Mark secured the American flag between them in the backseat. We slowly rolled, hard-bounced over field-mice holes and clumps of grass around the perimeter of the property, still laid in autumn tones. Crossed old fence rows, swung north 'round the rabbit barn, passed the "bows" of the decrepit black walnut tree, up the backside of the farthest north field.

Soaring above a red-tailed hawk, as we rose over the highest viewpoint. Near the point of holding your breath, the billowy sky looked down as reflections skated on the pond, hemmed by poplar and cottonwoods. Our authentic "Jeep" ride bumped us just so, to keep the autumn chill from creeping down our necks as we descended to our last parade. The only heavy-bladed flat was across the dam of the pond my folks had built in the 1970s.

Many good distractions were pinching the moment for me as I held the earthly remains of my Father on my lap. Whoever fathoms that—I held the earthly remains of my Father on my lap? SELAH.

Turning my gaze into the spirit, behind us was the largest Rearview Spiritual Monitor imagined.

Parading behind our "Command Car" was my Dad, proudly, with head held high. Point-Man. Marching behind him was his battalion of comrades (same dress) carrying rifles, walking with him, in perfect V'd position, 3's, 5's, 7's.

Still in bouncing cadence riding roughshod over the field, I asked my brothers if I could tell them what I was seeing in the spirit. Our cheeks were wet in awe. We are reminded from the movie rolls of heaven above that the sacrifices of war are looked upon as holy. Honor in its company from the cloud of witnesses. How many sons and fathers from the handshake of war walked in the spirit on the fields of our farm that day?

"As we express our gratitude, we must never forget that the highest appreciation is not to utter words, but to live by them."

— **John F. Kennedy**

We call them remains. I opened the heavy square cardboard box, a little wider than a Kleenex box, and untethered the twist tie of an industrial-grade plastic bag. The contents inside were coarse multicolored purified sand, burnt without a trace of my Dad's DNA. Made aware of the direction of the wind, I began to tip the box. Its weight made me hold tighter for balance as I discharged the contents to descend onto our homestead. Since 1964 we have called these rolling hills, at the end of the Oregon Trail, home. The little Jeep, encapsulated with all my Dad's wartime memorabilia, chugged up the hayfield from the dip of the dam bank, passing my standing family like the Blue Angels flying overhead. I shook the last particles of an upended box, my assignment complete, tucked the plastic inside, closed each flap, and adjusted myself center back in the seat. We parked, leaving the American flag snapping its colors lightly in the wind. At attention, with gaze over the farm, my eldest brother Mike gave Dad his last salute. My family and I stood in silence as my nephew Thomas, Sergeant 234th Army Band (Active), lifted his uncle's bugle to his mouth.

The bugle commissioned, the first three notes G, G, and held the C, as it has since 1848 West Point.

He called precisely, all twenty-four notes which raised a palpable sense of immemorial call.

Day is done, gone the sun,
from the lakes, from the hills,
from the skies,
All is well, safely rest;
God is nigh.

The sound of honor, "Extinguishing Light." Its "TAPS" tapped us all. God was certainly nigh...
Back standing with my family, receiving half hugs of encouragement, my brother Mark stepped forward and shared his poem he wrote for Dad's last birthday:

Christmas lights at the Dunbarton house,
we could see the city from the roof,
If Mom knew we were up there,
I'd be in Big Trouble and feel like a goof!
4th of July Fireworks at the Mayfair parking lot,
As a young boy, I remember Rockets and The Spinners on the
power pole were ever so Hot!
So glad you and Mom agreed to move out of L.A.,
 A Family of six in a Ford Station Wagon
heading North, seems like yesterday.
You've shared stories about
customers young and old,
I always enjoyed them the way they were told.
How "You" handled those customers
and taught us right from wrong,
Is why "I know People" has been my life song.
My Dad said there was an opportunity
to make some Cash, on a Pre-Easter Day,
I knew it was a Bunny suit
"But" Pink, No Mask, Whiskers, he did not say!
Mayfair Markets Manager
was a position that you Earned,
When they went away,
So Sorry, a Life Lesson we all learned.

> If we Kids would spill a glass of Milk
> at the Dinner Table after you had a long day,
> you might Erupt,
> But the day I hit you with the post hole driver,
> you rubbed your head looked at me and said,
> we have more posts, What's Up?
> You taught us about guns with the Lever Action 22, Safety,
> Common Sense, Respect!
> And Never shoot into the sky blue!
> Sheep, Cows, Horse, Rabbits, is what Country Folks
> You and Mom taught us to do,
> Feed and Care, a Stallion, Newborns,
> Fence Repair, and scoop a lot of Poo!
> 92 Acres, Kids, School, Sports, Work,
> Church, always so much to do,
> Thank you Both for your Sacrifice,
> we All made it through.
> Happy Birthday Dad, we are Blessed You are here, Your
> Family is so Proud to give You a Great Big Cheer! — **Mark A.
> Richards** (July 20th, 2017)

A pause for breath to catch our emotions between each heartfelt eulogy. You are as close to the flap of the envelope called heaven and earth in moments like this. I'd say a "family thin place," much like the veil that pulled back that allowed my Dad to see things in the spirit.

From the disarming of Alzheimer's my Dad had experienced. It's not fear, it's reality's question. Thankfully my family has been well acquainted with the Gospel for generations. Jesus came and overcame sin and death. But the reality is: we need to consummate the revelation to eradicate decay, since death is that last enemy to fall for His kids. If any tear had been held back by this time, it was about to fall.

My eldest son (Retired Marine Corp, two tours Afghanistan) stepped out and turned to address his family. Nervously with confidence, saying to himself, *This is for Grandpa!*"

My Dad, their Grandpa, had the knack of telling a good story. And it was the "tellin'" that captured the hearts of our boys. Those idiosyncrasies that made you shake your head; He possessed a manner of consistency that we will never misplace. The day wasn't complete until the newspaper was read, cover to cover.

Dad always had a large coin jar, never overlooked picking up a penny; the empty pop cans were his retirement fund. He was always working on getting an "Image." For a kid who grew up on the southern shores of California, he never learned to swim. In card playin', he could withhold and bluff just long enough to make you question, and then crack his wrist to slap a trump card on the table setting it to spin.

This next story is the kind that opens the chambers to a daughter's heart. The memory can see a weathered ring on the inside leather of the man's wallet and in my opinion, thus the remains of his legacy. As shared earlier my Dad served in two Wars, the Korean and WWII. Not a man of many possessions but the few he had, had walked with him a mile or two. I have one: the linen-type suitcase, tortoise shell handle, that he carried his meager belongings in into both wars. And my son Joseph has the other: an 1800s silver dollar which wore a dollar-size ring on every leather wallet he ever owned. As Grandpas do, they give treasures that are familiar to the habits and likings they have gotten used to. So my Dad handed out a single silver dollar to his three boys and my four, his grand-boys. I'm not 100% sure it was across the board. But he handed them out none the same. Now each of my own had a silver dollar to also wear a ring on every wallet they carry.

See, therein lies the thinkin'. And my boys knew that. That's what made it a story.

Here's Joseph, our Marine and eldest, standing in front of our intimate family on that emotionally weary and wonderful day. In the official "Grandpa style tellin'," he reached around and took out his wallet. While opening the weathered piece of leather he began to share a military tale from his first tour in Afghanistan.

See, his troop had been marching in a compromised zone. Compromised: well he didn't go into much detail but you knew that there were armed bad guys (the shooting kind) aware of your location. His troop had arrived at a crossroads and a decision needed to be made whether to go left, or turn right. Joseph reached into his back pocket and pulled out his billfold with that silver dollar Grandpa had given him. The epitome of the one His Grandpa had carried into two wars. I can imagine him telling his buddies the extra-short version of the story in this uneasy location. But the Korean War & WWII veteran Grandpa-honor was obviously conveyed. He said with that coin in hand, why don't we flip for it? Flip for which direction to turn.

I'll assume it was heads because as he told it, his troop turned right.

Safe and Right! This Momma would say so!

Now you could call it luck, but then the story loses its divine intuition, and from my Dad's current residence in the Cloud of Witnesses that just wouldn't do!

Just a couple of months ago, my Mom gave Joseph Grandpa's official 1800s Silver Dollar. I would never glorify sickness or disease. Jesus paid the entire price and that is a deposit that needs enforcing and withdrawing. Scripture says that all things work together for good. All things aren't good, but for those who believe and believe and believe and ask and keep asking. Father God's heart moves the mountains of "hard."

As you can tell in the reading, redemption gave me a story of love. Nearly 5,000 words that lasted just about eight days.

My Dad found His words and the 'ar' that were caught in the chair of hard.

I heard my Dad tell me he loved me. Did he make up for time lost?

I guess maybe you need to re-read this chapter again. When you re-read, highlight the part that I had the privilege to witness the Lord as we in the church say "taking somebody home."

And please use the highlighter on my son Joseph's story. I call that a love response to the next generation.

I'd like to make note at the grace that appeared...
My Dad never transformed anything I'd hear.
He did the "Preacher Call" sinners prayer,
after I was out of the house.
Yet outside of this divine moment,
Jesus waited in his heart house.
I'm sure the Lord knocked on his soul,
asked him to re-think his life and love flow.
It remains in God's Goodness vault,
I'm sure to this day,
That the Lord clothed him and crowned him
because the blood washes it all away. —
Kristen Richards Wambach

ACTIVATION

The Resurrection of I love you.
This chapter invites you to look at the "hard" chairs in your own life—those relationships where words have been withheld or silence has grown cold. Kristen's journey with her father proves that God's Goodness can move the mountains of "hard" and that even in the decay of the mind, the spirit can be freed to its original design. A Direct Conversation with Jesus

1. **The Living Sword** "For the word of God is alive and active... piercing to the dividing of soul and spirit." (Hebrews 4:12) In the quiet of those eight days, the "Sword-Logos" divided the disease from the man, allowing the spirit to be the ruling influence. Ask Him: "Jesus, where is my 'sense realm' (my logic, my pain, my offense) currently neutralizing my spirit?

    Use Your living Sword to divide my soul from my spirit so I can see my 'hard' situations through Your eyes of mercy." Listen for the clarity of the spirit.

2. The Resurrection "I am the resurrection and the life." (John 11:25) Resurrection happened in the "nuances" before the breath left the body—the "I love you" that took a lifetime to arrive. Ask Jesus: "Lord, what 'dead' word or 'withheld' expression in my family needs to be resurrected today? Show me how to participate in the 'softening' of a heart, even if the person isn't ready or able to change on their own." Listen for a gesture of tenderness you can offer.

3. The Point-Man "Who do you say that I am?" (Matthew 16:15) The guardian angel at the crop circle and the battalion of comrades in the "spiritual monitor" revealed the Dad as a "Point-Man" and a "Seer." Identity was restored in the spirit even as it faded in the flesh. Ask Jesus: "Who do You say [Name of a loved one] is, beyond their current struggle or 'hard' exterior? Show me their 'robe and crown' so I can honor the spirit of who they truly are, rather than the title they have struggled to carry." Listen for His word of honor.

Reflect and Respond

• The Hard Chairs: Visualize the "h↔d" chairs. Who is sitting in the other chair? Ask the Lord to help you "read between the lines" and see if there is any "ar" (agreement or resentment) that can be traded for mercy.

• The Nuances: What are the small "nuances" of your loved ones that you may be overlooking? Take a moment to thank God for the habitual things—the tucked-in shirt or the organized silverware—that represent the person's unique soul.

• The Transition: Reflect on the "guardian" and the "robe & crown." How does the reality of an "unseen atmosphere" change your perspective on the end of life? Or how Life should be Lived!

____

____

____

____

Next Step

Identify one "hard" relationship. This week, consciously "trade" a question of "Why?" for a prayer of Mercy. Like Kristen passing out mercy in the garden of Eden, release mercy to that family member, trusting that nothing can separate them from the love of God.

Prayer and Contemplation
Father, I thank You that the kingdom of Heaven is at hand and that the atmosphere is thin between Your heart and mine. I lay hold of Your goodness today. I choose to see the dreams You have given me through my heritage and to trust that even in the 'hard' places, You are making all things new. Clothe my loved ones in Your righteousness and help me to see them properly dressed in You. Amen.

____

PLAY SHEET | MERCY

Mercy Edition
Redemptive Gifts Summary

THIS CHAPTER IS A HEAVYWEIGHT PLAY for the restoration of the "h↔d" chairs in your own life—the distance between you and those you love. It is a revelation that even when the mind or the relationship feels like it is decaying, your spirit can be liberated to its original design, allowing for the Resurrection of I Love You.

THE DNA WRISTBAND AUDIBLE: CHAPTER PLAY-CALL

1. The Green Dot Helmet (*Individual Redemptive Gift*): **Mercy** The frequency for this play is set to Mercy. This is your gift of the "Atmosphere Shifter" and the "Internal Healer." You are hardwired to navigate the "hard" places in your family without the heavy armor of judgment. When you feel the weight of "ar" (agreement or resentment) standing between your chair and another's, your Mercy gift allows you to sit under the "Tree of Life" and release the pressure. You have the unique ability to see the "Robe and Crown" on a person even when their current behavior or disease has hidden them from the world.

2. The Coaches' Booth (*Legacy Anchor*): *The Five Love Languages* by Gary Chapman In the "Booths" of your spiritual legacy, *The Five Love Languages* (Mercy/ Healing) serves as your ultimate guide to the Healing of the Heart. This anchor proves that when words fail or the mind is clouded, "Acts of Service" become a language that can be heard by the spirit.

You apply this by realizing that love is the primary language that bridges the chasm between years of silence and a final moment of peace. It reminds you that how you serve in the "hard" seasons is a declaration of the Father's heart.

3. The Play-Call from God

"Child, tune your heart into the frequency of My Mercy. I see you sitting in the 'hard' chair, feeling the sting of words withheld and the frustration of a relationship that feels out of reach. I am calling an audible: Nothing can separate you from My love—not even the 'ar' between the chairs. I have given you the power to divide the soul from the spirit so that the ruling influence of your heart can be restored. That is the C♡♡Lness of our Oneness. When you look at

the 'spent fields' of your history, I want you to see the 'Guardian' standing there, making a way for a homecoming. You don't have to wait for the other person to change to start passing out Mercy in the garden. Stop wrestling with the 'Why' of the distance. Your DNA is hardwired for dreams and restoration, not just for the 'drive' to survive the tension. Be Spiritually BRAVE enough to see the 'Point-Man' in your lineage—the version of your loved ones that I am currently clothing in light. I am so good that I can use the smallest nuances to tell a story of redemption. The love you are looking for was never lost; it was just waiting for you to thin the atmosphere with My grace. Run the play, Child. I am the God of the Resurrection, and I am making all things new in your house."

4. The Audible (*The Timeline of Now*) The enemy wants you to focus on the "Decay of the Relationship" as a sign of final defeat. The Audible is this: Your spirit is the ruling influence! Right now, on the timeline of today, I am bypassing the "logic of your history" to show you the Resurrection of Identity. The "ar" is being dissolved. The chairs are being turned toward each other. The words are being released in the spirit. How Good is God!

REFORMATION DATA: THE ARCHITECTURE OF YOUR TRANSITION

To understand the "field" you are playing on, consider how to apply these "Transition" principles to your own life:

• **The 4th Dimension of Honor**: When you choose to honor a parent or a child—even if it's just in the secret place of your heart—you are sounding a spiritual "TAPS." *Apply This*: This frequency signals to the Cloud of Witnesses that the "war" in your family is over, and it invites the Restoration of All Things to settle on your home.

• **Identity-Based Resilience:** Like the Silver Dollar story, you have a spiritual inheritance that is meant to be a physical anchor. *Apply This*: By choosing to "flip the coin" and move in the direction of grace, you increase the "will to win" for your children and your children's children. Reclaiming a "heirloom of honor" from a messy past increases your breakthrough success by over 55%.

• **The Division of Soul and Spirit**: Hebrews 4:12 is your "Special Teams" tool. *Apply This*: When a relationship feels "hard," ask the Lord to use His living Sword to divide your offense (soul) from your identity (spirit). This allows your spirit to override your brain's logic of "it's too late," leading to a moment of "lucidity" where love finally finds its voice.

Chapter 13

God's Favorite Charity:

The Currency of the Hall of Fame

"... go to the sea, and cast in a hook: and that fish which shall first come up, take: and when thou hast opened its mouth, thou shalt find a stater [coin]: take that, and give it to them for me and thee." (Words of Our Lord to St. Peter.) — Matthew 17:26

"To have the kind of year you want to have,

something has to happen that you can't explain why it happened.

Something has to happen that you can't coach."

— **Bobby Bowden**, Legendary College Football Coach

Sometimes, God provides in ways that defy all human logic and expectation. Only God can expand the tipping point where we teeter up and down, right smack into a face-to-face question: "How Good is God, really?" We have a choice: do we move into new considerations and ask questions that defy our own human logic?

From the Schools of Jesus' Humanity:

Where did the gold coin come from, and how did He/Jesus know and learn that He could create it or move it?

I think we can agree, we have all had a "Temple Tax Mindset" within different seasons of our life. We shake our "now" faith to apprehend hope's substance on a journey of evidence that will eventually be seen. Much as a search engine crawls through text, my heart has crawled through many perspectives of the "Gold Coin in the Fish's Mouth" passage.

"You never really understand a person until you consider things from his point of view… until you climb into his skin and walk around in it."
— **Atticus Finch** in Harper Lee's novel To Kill a Mockingbird.

Consider the different "skin or shoes" perspectives within Jesus' Humanity in this living story. Doctrinal TRUTH story!

• Son "Shoes": On His Rabbi journey, He is aware (living life on our behalf) of His former divinity and earthly Sonship. Jesus had to develop a relationship with God the Father from 100% humanity. Law is still the framework of the hour, and Grace isn't yet uploaded. Just fully human Jesus. Always gives me great hope, more questions, and the honor that I can stand in His shoes of experience.

• Teacher "Shoes": Teaching a student. Add Peter's Shoes: impetuous, kinetic learner, over-eager, confident hard worker, undeveloped leader. Bobby Bowden's snippet in the quote above: "Something has to happen that you can't coach!" Peter, before the betrayal (modern-day imposter syndrome fallout). Scripture gives us an advantage when standing in Peter's shoes. We are allowed to read the entire story from the witness's pen, the Perfecter of Peter's faith. We know the coin will be there, we know why Jesus didn't want to offend in this instance, and we know the sifting that will take place with Peter's name on it. Stand in Peter's shoes! And this "something" that has to happen—no earthly playbook can compute "talent" on Peter's draft ticket because Jesus' faith in him is what is being extracted.

"The NFL Draft measures potential in a moment; greatness is measured in decades. History is littered with first-round projections that vanished, and Hall of Famers who proved that a low draft number is just a louder reason to become undeniable." — Kristen Wambach

In Sonship, the King instructs His heir in the doings and dominions of the Kingdom. Oorah!

Thank you very much; I choose to stand in those Sonship-shoes! Join me!

MY STORIES

The Year 1873: Before the railroad tracks were laid by the backs of pioneering men to follow the old stagecoach and pony express route of Highway 99E, stretching from Canada to Mexico, the land itself was an untamed testament to distance —a vast, rugged corridor traversable only by grit, dust, and the fading memory of a hoofbeat.

Her design and Dutch architecture had been carried in the hearts of those families who traversed the Oregon Trail. She was built by the children who walked hand-in-hand with their parents' faith across a nation for the personal freedoms to love God. We called her the "Train House," the switch track just fifty yards from our front door. She is second-generation Aurora Colony, still standing, surrounded by filbert orchards, nursery stock, and the worn dreams of generations past.

Open the back door, take two steps over and inside the "Kitchen" threshold, turn left, and peek 'round to the backside of the scrubby, mish-mash-and-missed painted pantry door. You'll notice two things at some time in the train-house history:

- Somebody's shotgun had gone off indoors, and
- Scratched in #2 lead are the lines, names, and pencil marks of our four boys' growing chart.

Our list of life and family stories would fill the conversations around many campfires: Eve our beautiful Jersey milk cow (best prayer partner I've ever had). Don churning butter till 3 AM. Roosters in the apple trees. BB-guns on parade.

How far will an arrow go through a hay bale or come out the other side? Ouch! 52-recumbent-bike-speeds. Myrtle the turtle. Go-carts and motorcycles. Ministry to Vietnam Vets riding the rails—"Cobra." What name did your mother give you? Clarence. (Listen: Episode 233 Beyond Reaction: Don't Underestimate the Kindness of God). Nike the rat. Cowboy hats and black eyes. Jana the little roan POA pony and Dolly the oversized Clydesdale. We loved the life those twelve acres allowed us to dream on. I met and was baptized in Holy Spirit within the walls of this house. The UnFinished Book unpacks that story brilliantly. The Lord remembers every offering we give Him. Whether tear, toil, giving, time, in loss or through gain, it is His delight to remind you that His word is not finished yet.

"And it is His delight to remind you and I, that His word is not finished yet!"

I water-fasted for forty days when she, the "Train House," was under the threat of foreclosure. He, the Lord, has returned with me (in the spirit) to keep in my remembrance that over-stuffed plum chintz love-seat where my prayers were heard. He never tires of reminding me of my meal-offering more times than my digital journal's search bar can account for. "His word is not finished yet!" We lost everything... thus the riches entrusted in this collection of supernatural stories. Encounters are living and learning metaphors filed in the libraries of your life book in Heaven. Hebrew is a pictorial language, but it isn't a still life; it's a language of action. In the Bible, a metaphor isn't a subtle description or a religious "shroud"—it is a Rhema revelation of an active purpose. Actually, even that sounds too "Greek" and clinical.

Let's be real: metaphors in the Spirit aren't just clever poetry. They are symbols of a true reality vibrating right under the surface of our world. They don't just tell you what something is; they reveal what it is doing. It's the "In-With-in" momentum of God caught in a picture.

"Over the course of four years, Jesus signed me up for a divine classroom experience—a deep dive into a realm where 'In-With-in' reality is as tangible as the gold coin appearing in a fish's mouth."

LESSON #1: THRONE OF GRACE ENCOUNTER
(One encounter with months of Rhema work)
"Let us then fearlessly and confidently and boldly draw near to the throne of grace the throne of God's unmerited favor to us sinners, that we may receive mercy for our failures and find grace to help in good time for every need appropriate help and well-timed help, coming just when we need it."
(Hebrews 4:16 Amplified Translation)
I prefer it written from the Mirror Translation:
"For this reason we can approach the authoritative throne of grace with bold utterance. We are welcome there in his embrace, and are reinforced with immediate effect in times of trouble."

Thrones in Heaven and on earth = Dominion.
It is a very important aspect to know who is sitting in power, rightfully or usurped.
Word Search Count (All context, the Bible)
Context Related to Believers/Us:
• Throne (singular) ~176 times: 1 reference directly related to our access: Hebrews 4:16 (The Throne of Grace).
• Thrones (plural) ~9 to 19 times: 4-5 references directly related to our co-reign and authority: Revelation 3:21, Matthew 19:28, Luke 22:30, Revelation 4:4, and Revelation 20:4.

As I have stated from a podcaster's mic, some items are worthy to repeat and make note of, and this is one: It is a very important aspect to know who is sitting in power, rightfully or usurped.

We all know "technically" that there is a Throne of Grace, and just as in the schools of Jesus' humanity, the kingdom needs to be experienced and learned on our journey of faith.

I had just returned from a conference where the speaker had walked us through an activation of "Lifting the Veil" and stepping through to access the Throne of Grace firsthand.

It was as simple as pulling back curtains, opening the window, and climbing out onto the Portico of OMG!

My first encounter showed a massive amphitheater with marble floors and the familiar faces of the people who were also at the conference with me. From the floor perspective, you could see upper balconies that contained seating for more people and entrances to other rooms. It "felt" like the hospital of hospitality for God's heart, a well-trafficked place. The wonderful thing about ascension is that it leaves a living open door within you to return again and again to discover the purposes and plans. As Jesus describes in John 10:9, "going in and out and find pasture." Heaven is a vast pasture of restoration, the court systems of governance, and the infrastructure of creation. It is the mirror and face-to-face for the earth below.

I couldn't wait to get alone with God to extract its riches. Later, alone with God. Reality tears. I need help. Can't talk about this with others. "Intimacy and Passage" in a Widow's type season of prayer looking for the how-to faith, Jars of Oil. My journal notes begin with slim pickings in my checking account, no pastoral payroll in the church checking account, and a mass of people on my intercession list. There are tears because you can "See in the Spirit," and there are tears because the worries of life are poking holes in your ability to rest in Him.

Yes, I am not alone by any means in this discussion, amen. I'm on the twenty-yard line and need to be stepping into the End Zone, 10 x 53 1/3 yards. Help me Jesus! Alone in my living room, sitting on my prayer pillow on the floor, leaning back against the couch in the quiet before the sun rises. Open my spirit and followed the same path to the Throne of Grace...

Hmm, there isn't an amphitheater here. Waiting. Feels like I am standing before a solid mountain. Stairs appear, and I ascend before my understanding climbs them.

My first sight: the largest set of hands and fingers, draped over the arm cap of an immense chair. Solid chair. Throne! It's God; the massive divine Papa. In that moment, you want to be that huge! Imagine standing on the ocean shore, looking twelve miles across a flat sea to the horizon. The beachfront becomes a hinge and the ocean face tips up creating a twelve-mile high wall. King-size Abba. Once again, my spirit, which has a mind of its own, ascends (without asking) and squeezes right next to the Man in Charge. Can't tell the story even today without a teary-eyed exhale—that's my Dad! Now when the conversation continues between Dad and daughter, the power of who He is remains, and love makes Him Abba, who I can talk to about anything. And my "anything & everything" has already reached His ears. Father places a brown kraft paper wrapped shoebox with pink grosgrain ribbon into my hands. Wrapped such that I could just lift the lid without unwrapping the paper. Inside was a small bird, a Sparrow, that looked asleep. Lifting my sight to share a smile with Papa, and with His approval, I reached into the uncovered box to touch the sweet bird. She awoke, startled me, flew out of the box, and circled back to sit on my shoulder.

"For this reason I say to you, do not be worried about your life, as to what you will eat or what you will drink; nor for your body, as to what you will put on. Is not life more than food, and the body more than clothing? Look at the birds of the air, that they do not sow, nor reap nor gather into barns,

and yet your heavenly Father feeds them. Are you not worth much more than they?" (Matthew 6:25-26)

"Papa," I asked, "what do I do with this...?" Before I finished my question, she, the sparrow, flew away and my spirit quickly followed. Not having noticed Him in our company, Jesus, my spirit, and the sparrow flew high up over the top of this massive throne. Following Her, she led us to a set of white double doors. So much was happening, my fingers typing what the spirit revealed, I continued to ask Jesus to go with me.

He opened the doorway and we walked down a long, echoey hall/corridor much like the access tunnel football teams use in a stadium. And that is what it was: a textbook stadium, with lush green grass. I'm with Jesus, and He is showing me the contents of the box and sparrow that Papa gave me while sitting on the Throne of Grace together.

The oval-shaped stadium, so easy to see, so well-lit, full of people cheering, joy in the air. We kept walking out onto the "field" right in the middle. In the moving commotion, I was trying to get Jesus' attention to ask Him about this place when I noticed the people start passing around those velvet burgundy-colored wood-handle offering sacks. (Google says: most commonly referred to as Offering Bags or Collection Bags. In more traditional or liturgical settings, they are often called Alms Bags.)

Trying to take it all in, find my purpose and thought in the situation, Jesus finally gives me His attention. We are standing on the fifty-yard line by now. And the ah-ha of the ah-ha moment was blue-toothed into my understanding: The entire stadium was taking an offering for ME!!!!

Composure blasted and gone. I'm bawling in heaven and on earth at this point. My spirit eyes witnessed the putting in of all kinds of currency, and some white pieces of paper with handwritten notes on them. A delegate from the stadium gathered and dumped the bags in the middle of the grass field. The entire stadium in a roar of cheers and clapping in the giving to me. I was undone, undone, undone... that the cloud of witnesses would take an offering for me...

I saw Kathryn Kuhlman smiling from ear to ear. I knew King David was there but didn't see him directly. Faces so familiar from the stories I have read about them.

I asked Jesus what this place was and He said, "The Hall of Fame."

Can the heart possibly expand in being poured out, transfixed, melted, totally undone?

I am so thankful for our relationship and to have Him to follow and be shown the way. When I asked what I was to do with it all, He simply told me to put them into my spirit. Can your spirit hold such a bounty? I asked where I was to take it, wondering if I should trade it, and He said, "Yes, to the trading floor." I thanked everyone with many waves, blessing them as I stepped in the spirit over to the Sea of Glass to present this offering to Melchizedek. I gave it to him and waited...

Do you recall the movie Miracle on 34th Street (the original with Maureen O'Hara and child star Natalie Wood)? Remember the scene when they were trying to "prove" if Kris Kringle, the kindly old gentleman who played Macy's Santa Claus, was the "Real" Santa Claus? By sheer luck and nail-biting eleventh hour, the United Postal Service decided to forward their backlog of "Letters to Santa Claus" directly to the New York State courtroom.

This is my "then": Seven large grey mail carts rolled out onto the Glassy Sea, each one overflowing with currency for me. I gathered them into my spirit and stepped out, decreeing them into the earth, framed by Mercy and Grace (original Gift box given at the Throne of Grace).

But before I went to trade, I returned to the Father just to say, "Thank you, thank you, thank you." It was a most excellent and encouraging way for Him to provide for my need —both inside of me and out.

THE BOLDNESS OF THE PORTICO: HEBREWS 4:16 "So, don't just stand there at the curtain, peering through the cracks of your own 'slim pickings'—climb out! Step onto the Portico of OMG and walk right up to that massive Throne of Grace with the boldness of a daughter who knows the Dad in the chair.

We aren't going there to beg; we are going there to obtain. It's the place where the Beachfront of Mercy meets the Ocean of His Face, and everything you need—inside and out—is waiting for you. Come face-to-face with the Mirror of His Heart, so you can catch the currency of His Mercy and find the 'Seven Mail Carts' of Grace that arrive exactly when you need them most."

Thinking... So, here is the wrestle. Can they do that? Is it legal? How does this work? Time-warp miracles, frequency and faith? Jesus is a very faithful Rabbi, and I am one of those students that walks so closely behind Him, the dust from His sandals flies up and covers me. Hall of Fame learning...

I do not doubt that Holy Spirit is revealing so many types and shadows to you. Heaven is alive as words within words on the paper. This divine technology is not new; Saints, Mystics, and such miracles have been scrutinized and recorded for thousands of years.

Remember our wisdom thought for note-taking: write down the thoughts you think.

LESSON #2: ONE OF MY FAVORITE CHARITIES
(One encounter with months of Rhema work)
Not a big space. Reminds me of a small eclectic shop hidden from the beaten path on the side aisles of a large shopping mall.

She had a bell that tinkled if someone walked through the front door. A counter to greet and exchange with the customers, but her largest square footage was hidden in the backroom: organized stacks, in rows of large canvases. God introduced me to her that day and specifically said that it was one of His Favorite Charities. That perked my ears up. A great place to learn the heart of the Father. Her name was Gina. A bitty thing with so much energy. She wore black-rimmed glasses and covered her street clothes with a sea-green painter's smock. Gina? Short for Virginia, Eugenia, Regina, a version of Georgina. Her sandy brown hair was wispy, shoulder-length, and a bit unkempt. She was a creative for sure. My spirit was nudged to ask her, "May I look at your artwork?" Gina said, "With pleasure."

(Still running through my thoughts: God's FAV, huh?)

The canvases were all the same size, orderly, hundreds of them. I asked her as I rifled lightly through the frames, "Are you an angel?"

She replied, "No!" "

Are you a spirit being?"

She said, "Yes."

"What about 'men in white linen'?"

"No!"

Very matter-of-factly, she offered me her mission statement: *"I paint spines with gold, to heal people."*

The spine is a living, vertical bridge that functions as the central pillar of the human body. It is a masterpiece of both strength and flexibility, acting as the structural "50-yard line" that holds the entire person together.

My curious looking moved deeper as I pondered her artwork. Flipping through the paintings, noticing I was being watched. No color, just gold leaf brushed as paintings of the different size rungs on the ladder of the human body. Prompted in my pondering over the days of the encounter (1 John 2:5-8 Mirror), with prophetic inspiration:

Whoever treasures the "Logos"—the logic of God's authentic thought—is standing in the place where Agape love is fully realized in its most complete context. This isn't just a theological idea; this is what our association and this union in Christ is all about.

It's like the process of refining gold. In the natural, gold is put into the crucible and heated until it melts. The heat doesn't change the nature of the gold; it simply releases the dross— the "thinking text" of the old self—so it can rise to the surface and be skimmed away. When the gold is pure and refined, it becomes a liquid mirror. The Refiner knows the process is complete when He can look down into the crucible and see His own face perfectly reflected back. It is in this place of consciously abiding in the awareness of your oneness that your conversation unveils the same fellowship with the Father that Jesus enjoys. It results in a daily walk that mirrors His—one where you are "riding the bike" in the full benefit of His strength, with His hand forever on the seat. My beloved family, the words I write to you here may not immediately sound like the heavy stone precepts of Moses, but don't let that fool you into thinking this is some "new" doctrine. This is the Ancient Conversation—the prophetic echo of God's voice that has been bouncing back and forth in the Mirror since before the clock even started. It is the very conclusion of the Word you've heard from the beginning; it is the absolute Finish Work realized in the now. And yet, there is a glorious newness to this message. You might ask, "How can something so old be so fresh and new?" Here is the secret: Whatever is true of Jesus is equally true of you. The days of darkness being the "scout report" for your life are over. The true light doesn't just flicker; it shines with bold certainty. It illuminates your life as it is unveiled in Christ, because you aren't just looking at the Light—you are the portal, the living gateway, where that Light breaks into the earth.

And Gina is painting with that kind of Gold Leaf paint—oh my!

I like the details: Gina is a popular feminine name, primarily of Italian and Latin origin, meaning "queen" (from Regina) or "well-born" (from Eugenia), also linked to "farmer" (Georgina) and potentially Hebrew for "garden." Yes, I finally asked if I had a painting in her collection. Previously, I had sketched out her store in my journal, the rows of simple framed stretched canvas. I knew where mine was exactly.

How would you respond (God's Favorite Charity) to a canvas painting of you or your spine; the masterpiece that supports your entire body, painted purposely as a message of healing over your life with the frequency of the words from above? Whatever is true of Jesus is equally true of you. In gold leaf? Selah.

LESSON #3: GOD'S FAVORITE CHARITY
(One encounter with months of Rhema work)
God is into details. This encounter, I have no need to re-read it. I've read it a thousand times. Played in its glory and wrestled the permissions of old thought and new thought.

Jesus held my hand the entire day, or at least four hours on the clock of wonderment. He said, "Come with me, I have something to share with you."

Yup, I so treasured the stillness of my morning. Husband off to work, I cleared my entrepreneurial schedule. Saying, "I'm all yours Lord." Life and business will run themselves in the capable hands of Angels. In the spirit on the Lord's Day (every day is the Lord's Day).

"Well hello Gina." As the Lord gave her a big hug, I followed suit as an avid friend of her artwork by now. Curious and excited to finally be shown His purpose in (Gods Favorite Charity "Paintings"), at least particulars written on my blueprint. The Lord didn't have to ask where my "Canvas" was; He walked right to the aisle on the front right and picked out my gold leaf painting. Gina just sat on her bar stool, grinning the toothiest grin. He handed it to me and said, "Here, put this on."

I cocked my head a bit, and thought, put this on? Accepted the canvas painting of my "Gold Leaf Painted" spine.

The spirit realm is a conduit of wave thought. You think it and, "it" becomes. Authority and dominion has something to do with it for sure. Telekinetic thoughts are an energy-fluid conversation without the need of cell phones.

For your note-taking: Divine Knowledge/Happenstance of Jesus

- John 1:47-48 - Jesus saw Nathanael under the fig tree before they met.
- John 4:16-18 - Jesus knew the Samaritan woman had five husbands.
- Matthew 17:24-27 - Jesus knew about the temple tax question and the coin in the fish's mouth.
- Luke 5:4-6 - Jesus knew where the fish were in the water.
- Mark 14:13-15 - Jesus knew a man carrying a jar of water would meet the disciples.
- Matthew 21:2-3 - Jesus knew exactly where the donkey and colt would be tied.
- John 11:11-14 - Jesus knew Lazarus had died before the news reached Him.
- Mark 2:8 - Jesus perceived in His spirit that the scribes were reasoning in their hearts.
- John 6:64 - Jesus knew from the beginning who did not believe.
- Luke 22:10-12 - Jesus knew the specific details of the man and the house for the Passover meal.

We all have the capability but have forgotten the blueprint of our identity. Hello lessons of Jesus' humanity (Doctrines of Christ) teaching this writer. In the realm of spiritual and supernatural experiences, there are several "manifestation nouns" used to describe specific types of divine or extrasensory interaction. These often fall under the category of spiritual gifts or metaphysical phenomena, describing how the spirit influences the physical world.

Before anybody gets *freaked* out by a mere collection of letters that form a list of words; words that were confiscated, polluted and literally burned at the stake of religious ignorance a couple of hundred years ago... How Supernaturally Big is Your God? How Good is He? And how much God is inside of you? And who said that learning the doctrines of Christ and how He manifested God's goodness to us was unholy?

Can we please grow up?

Physical & Spatial Manifestations

• Apportation: The supernatural appearance or transport of an object from one place to another (often associated with the "gold coin" or "mail cart" experiences).

• Bilocation: Being physically present in two different locations at the exact same time. (Jesus Mt. of Transfiguration in Mt. 17, Mk 9, Luke 9).

• Translocation: The instantaneous movement of a person from one geographical point to another (like Philip in Acts 8).

• Levitation: The rising of a human body or objects into the air by spiritual or supernatural means. (Please google Saints that levitated).

• Invisibility: The state of being obscured from physical sight, often described in scripture when Jesus "passed through the midst" of a crowd unnoticed. Sensory & Cognitive Manifestations (Luke 4, John 8).

• Clairvoyance: "Clear seeing"—the ability to perceive events or objects that are not visible to the natural eye (like Jesus seeing Nathanael under the fig tree).

• Clairaudience: "Clear hearing"—the ability to hear sounds or voices from the spiritual realm.

• Clairsentience: "Clear feeling"—the ability to sense the emotional or physical state of others or the "vibration" of an environment.

• Precognition: "Fore-knowledge"—the divine knowing of an event before it happens.

• Retrocognition: The knowledge of a past event that could not have been learned or known through normal means. Manifestations of Substance

• Materialization: The process of a spiritual entity or object taking on physical, tangible form (like the "sparrow" in the box appearing in a physical-feeling space).

• Transmutation: The supernatural change of one substance into another (like water into wine).

• Emanation: A visible or felt "flowing out" of power, light, or scent from a person or object (often called the "fragrance of Christ").

Yup, I got my "preach on!"

Back to trying or putting on a Canvas??? Jesus said, "Here, put this on." I cocked my head a bit, and thought, put this on? Accepted the canvas painting of my "Gold Leaf Painted" spine. Prior lessons in the kingdom have taught me: don't over think it, what would a kindergartener do?

Holding the rigid canvas in both hands I "pretended" to put it on and hugged the painting to my chest. Now what do you think happened? You're getting good at this! Welcome white, screen-printed T-Shirt with Gold Leaf painting of my spine. Jesus, a bit more concerned about where we were off to on our spirit travels, waved me to hurry up. Kristen you can think on it later. He was right. I waved to Gina as we stepped out of her perfectly appointed divine art shop into what I had perceived felt like a decade ago: a large Mall. Jesus a stride ahead of me, as I was gawking at the atmosphere, pinging the familiar Mall layout, and the people who didn't appear to return my smile as we walked south down the main mall walkway. Above, at a four-corners section, was an outdated light fixture; people sitting in the courtyard eating ice cream. Jesus and I kept walking toward the Big-Box end cap store. Sears? JC Penney's? Not sure, though familiar within malls, shopping and such. Inside the large department store, we caught the escalator to the second floor and arrived in the southwest corner department: the Lingerie Section.

Odd, I know. When was the last time you stood in the "lingerie department" with Jesus? Never-mind wearing a supernatural screen-print T-shirt. My kinda strange, amen. I kept looking around to gather details for my journaling. Why were we here? Yet, Jesus seemed to finally rest and be content to wait in the lingerie department with me. Like a clap of lightning my spiritual sight split. I am in three places at the same time:

• Sitting on my prayer pillow typing the encounter just as it happens.

• Standing in the lingerie department with Jesus.

• Able to see a young lady descend from her car in the parking lot. She walked through the rotating glass doors, side entrance of the large department store, hopped on the elevator system, switchback twice, taking it to the third floor and entered into what appeared to be an employee locker room.

She opened her personal locker, took out an envelope, closed the door and next thing I knew she was standing next to Jesus and I in the intimate apparel department. Now to get a better look at this: she is late 20s, early 30s, dark hair brushed up meticulously into what I would call a bouffant hairdo.

She is sporting a perfect Jackie O rose-colored tweed straight skirt and jacket suit. "Dorothy" (sassing myself with a Wizard of Oz quote), we are not in Kansas-timeline-2018 anymore. Must be late 1950s, early 1960s. I was born in 1959??? Jesus introduced me to Charlotte. We said our hellos. Nothing seemed amiss, her countenance totally expecting this rendezvous. The energy sphere calm with generous expectation. I am clueless. Between Jesus and Charlotte was a "Knowing" and a very long dialog charted before I arrived. She smiled at me, reached into the lining of her cute tweed jacket and pulled out the same envelope I had just witnessed her retrieving.

Charlotte handed it to me. All stop. I opened it... Inside was her thousand-dollar paycheck, and she handed it to me. More words caught in my throat, an unspoken melt came over me in the atmosphere of God's goodness.

Money. Lessons in supernatural money... Since it appeared I was behind in the conversation, I thanked her with tears running down my face and crossing dimensions to drip on my iPad. How does God do that? They are brilliantly in cahoots! With a small amount of lessons clipped to my belt thus far, I looked at Jesus and asked Him, "What do you want me to do with Charlotte's paycheck?" Too easy, right! What does one do in the year 2018 with a check?

He said, "Deposit it using your phone." So strange. And yes, somehow my red iPhone Max just happened to be on site? With her 1960s check in hand, my iPhone at that present time, I walked over to the slant-open wall of the escalator to a convenient bench, sat down and looked up at Jesus saying, "I need a pen, please."

Who can think this stuff up? Oh, I'm laughing at myself telling the story to you. Faith comes by hearing and hearing the "Living" Word of God. I signed the check, Jesus handed the pen back to Charlotte and positioned my phone camera directly over the signed check. Lost in the translation, I assume I opened the application to my bank... and snapped the camera. Nonetheless, if Jesus tells you to deposit it using your phone, you deposit it with your phone. I can feel the spiritual high and exhaustion of being stretched beyond reason. End of encounter.

Is this my test from Lesson Two? Again, thinking... caught in the wrestle. Can they do that? Is it legal? How does this work? Time-warp miracles, frequency and faith? My brain was a blur with legalism for days. I knew that I knew Jesus had relocated me supernaturally and my tenacity of heart would not let it go. I knew Charlotte Cummings was a real person, a very giving person walking a supernatural journey with the Master. Imagine the Cloud of Witnesses at the Stadium of the Throne of Grace cheering me on!

Yes, I can hear you ask! Did I check my checking account to see if it showed up? Our question: Did a check from the 1960s deposit supernaturally into an account in 2018? You read that quickly didn't you? I did check my bank account via my phone, and no, it did not show up. My head racked with the encounter, the tangible "GOODNESS" residue still present in the memory bodily. Now what? Like a crocodile rolling and gripping its prey between its teeth, I'm not letting my Lord or Charlotte down!

We 'house' the miraculous and need to learn how to host His goodness and immense trust in us. I've read stories of when Smith Wigglesworth prayed, the atmosphere was so weighty people who joined in this prayer meeting could barely crawl out of the room. We do live in a modern age. It's time to encourage yourself in the Lord and find a testimony.

I googled supernatural money miracles and was drawn to the Saints of old. Their testimonies have gone through a rigorous authorizing system by the Catholic church to verify them. And yes, there is a host of testimonies.

And what was the text we started this very long journey on?

"... go to the sea, and cast in a hook: and that fish which shall first come up, take: and when thou hast opened its mouth, thou shalt find a stater [coin]: take that, and give it to them for me and thee." (Matthew 17:26)

"To have the kind of year you want to have, something has to happen that you can't explain why it happened. Something has to happen that you can't coach." — Bobby Bowden

This is my Something!

LESSON #4: MOVING MONEY, IS IT LEGAL? God knows the way we think and why we think the way we do. We have all been constipated with religious dogma. I invite you to read my voyage in The UnFinished Book. It is so important to know a person's story, how we didn't fall off the *turnip truck the same day.

(*A classic American idiom that basically means "I am not a naive country bumpkin" or "I wasn't born yesterday.") The testament of how Jesus grew our faith, to look like the faith He so willingly vowed to authenticate as the author.

Another learning story from the Master.

The proof is sewn in my heart; nothing can rip it from its dwelling. Now I have a testimony in both hands, so I am encouraged. Mountains have to be spoken to for any movement! About now you have figured out I have a large cozy floor pillow. It's tucked behind my Grandmother's enclosed bookshelf, the one that holds the miracle of my Great Grandmother's dishes.

The days are full of query and questions. I'm taking up my normal morning residence, in my bathrobe, slippers and favorite coffee cup, which rests on a seasonal cocktail napkin laid in the dish or bend of a large saucer. Steaming cup of coffee, with cream and a "sshh" dollop of whipped cream on top. Atmosphere people, setting the atmosphere.

I'm going to hang out with a King.

Distracting to hush your thoughts, quiet your ego and get your feelers tuned into the unseen. Talking to God, iPad note ready, sipping my coffee, hugging the moment. My legs are ankle-crossed in front of me, back leaning against the mushroom color, tufted-back couch.

Rattan coffee table holds my "Cup of Java Gold," the useful hospitality coffee table decor; contents of white wooden scrolled tray, candle in crystal dish, cool old book, personalized "W" marble coasters, silk eucalyptus do-dad and a snow globe from Mount Vernon, Virginia—the home of George Washington's Estate.

I picked up the snow globe and gave it a shake, set it down and watched the snow float to the enclosed bottom. It's a treasure with a powerful story; years back, My folks and I were visiting my eldest brother and his wife who at that time lived in Virginia. Mom and I visited the famous George Washington Estate and Museum of our Nation's first President.

I purchased the hand-size tourist snow globe just a day before I was to fly back to Oregon. Mom and Dad would continue their RV adventure without me.

Arriving at the airport in plenty of time to check in, partially disrobed and go through security, I placed my one piece of luggage on the conveyor belt, large purse strapped to my shoulder and followed my belongings through the security checkpoint. The attendant pulled me aside with my luggage and asked me to open it. Kinda gets you a little off guard, but I followed instructions, opened my suitcase and gave them permission to lightly rummage around my belongings.

The surgical gloved hands found it and pulled it out from its safe nestle spot amongst my clothes.

"Ma'am," they said, "you cannot carry this container (Snow Globe) on the flight with you!"

"What?" I said.

"The Snow Globe, Ma'am! It is against regulations for the amount of liquid size allowed to travel. You have to remove it to make your way through security."

Rats. Nothing to do but kiss it goodbye into the bins of non-collected travel items. I was saddened but made it home to Oregon without anymore glitches.

Days later a package arrived in the mail for me, postmark return, from my brother Mike, Virginia. I opened the well-tissued packed box to the same "Snow Globe" from Mt. Vernon. See, it's a treasure with a story.

Back to my morning moment with the Master Teacher. The snowflakes are still settling on the floor of the enclosed snow globe.

I pick it up again, happy thoughts from the memories it bestows, and I took a much closer notice. The snow globe is divided in half: one side is the Estate Picture of Mt. Vernon, Home of George Washington. The other side is the United States Capitol white round dome building. Upon closer investigation, I toyed with the idea: Am I able to "move" the entirety of the snowflakes floating in glycerol, from one side of the snow globe (home site) to the other side (government building) of the snow globe? So, in curiosity, I played with it, turned it upside down, waited for all the flakes to rest on the top, inside of the snow globe dome.

Very patiently I turned the upside-down globe, rotated ever so slightly, focused on the slow glycerol movement of the snowflakes, until the snow slid in unison back and forth to either side. And, you guessed it, another lightning moment in the spirit. I'm sure thunder cracked and pealed somewhere when Rhema thunder-bolted logic! Yes, I could move "snow" (money/resources) in the spirit between "home" and over the "government" of time!

Didn't I say He was a Master at His job?

So excited, I even captured a video of the story I just shared on my phone to record my revelation.

St. Teresa of Avila (the "Doctor of Prayer") often used the imagery of a royal court or a Great Castle to describe our access to God. She famously taught that we do not receive more because we do not ask for more: "You pay God a compliment by asking great things of Him." She described the "Interior Castle" as a place of immense riches where God dwells as a King. Her perspective was that most people stand outside the gates, begging for crumbs, unaware that they have a "royal account" in the inner rooms. She believed that our small thinking is the only thing that "locks" the door to these provisions.

One may wonder where St. Teresa obtained the bank notes, since currency is not used in Heaven. One author quotes a bank employee as saying that, There are a good many bank notes issued that never come back. They are lost, and thus become res nullius, no man's property. Some are so effectively hidden away by misers that they are never found by their heirs; others are dropped and blown away by the wind; others are burned when houses catch fire; others go down with foundering ships. The lost notes give a supply exceeding all demands that miracles will ever make. — **Cruz, Joan Carroll.** Mysteries, Marvels and Miracles: In the Lives of the Saints

To my right, on the office window wall, is a cork-board next to my desk and computer, where I speak these testimonies with you today; pinned is a deposit slip from Charlotte Cummings' gracious gift. I wrote almost 6 years ago. Like Mary the Mother of Jesus, I have hid many things in my heart.

"... go to the sea, and cast in a hook: and that fish which shall first come up, take: and when thou hast opened its mouth, thou shalt find a stater [coin]: take that, and give it to them for me and thee." (Matthew 17:26)
"To have the kind of year you want to have, something has to happen that you can't explain why it happened. Something has to happen that you can't coach." — Bobby Bowden

Surrender of self, surrender to what has been experienced, is a powerful mechanism of faith. When we finally concede to the contenders presented on the war of life. We lift the white flag of surrender and with our last strength carry it waving across the field of failure, trials of self, transitions of grace. Money, currency, resources—this is a different nut some are called to wrestle with, like Jacob who wrestled with the Angel of the Lord.

Found in Genesis 32:22-32, is a pivotal and symbolic moment in his life. The event is not a simple physical brawl, but a deep, multi-layered spiritual struggle that leads to a profound transformation. These stories of faith belong to all of us.

• A Confrontation with His Past: Jacob is on his way to meet his estranged brother, Esau, whom he famously tricked out of his birthright and blessing years earlier. Jacob is filled with fear and anxiety, so he sends his family and possessions ahead, leaving himself alone. The wrestling match takes place in the dark, symbolizing Jacob's confrontation with his fears, his past deception, and his own self-reliance.

• He is forced to grapple with the consequences of his actions before he can face his brother.

• A Test of His Faith: Jacob's life had been one of cunning and manipulation. He had always relied on his own wits to get what he wanted. The wrestling match is a test of his resolve and his faith in God's promises. He refuses to let go of his opponent until he receives a blessing, showing his determination to seek God's favor.

• A Transformation of Identity: The climax of the struggle is when the mysterious figure—referred to as a "man," "God," and an "angel"—asks Jacob for his name. When Jacob truthfully answers "Jacob" (a name that means "deceiver" or "supplanter"), he is acknowledging his past identity. In response, the figure gives him a new name: Israel, which means "he struggles with God" or "God struggles." This name change signifies a new identity and purpose for Jacob and the nation that will descend from him.

• A Physical and Spiritual Wound: The wrestling match is not without cost. The figure touches Jacob's hip socket, causing him to limp for the rest of his life. This permanent physical injury serves as a constant reminder of his encounter with the divine and the change it brought about in him.

It shows that his transformation was real and had a lasting impact. In essence, Jacob's wrestling match is a powerful story about surrendering one's self-reliance, confronting one's flaws, and finding a new identity and purpose through a direct, intimate, and challenging encounter with God. It represents the struggle of faith and the transformative power of perseverance in seeking God's blessing. God's blessing may be experienced in a new way, and the old root of earthly limitations must be pulled up and burned.

"The real glory is being knocked to your knees and then coming back. That's real glory. That's the essence of it."
— **Vince Lombardi**

"Each of us could fill out a lifetime of battles and breaking points with such a story. You remember laying in spiritual sweat, surrendered flag flown, and you lay exhausted covered in your paratrooper's parachute rests, laying on your adversary's soil. Surrender always walks in the footsteps of grace."

ACTIVATION

THE CURRENCY OF THE HALL OF FAME
In the "Schools of Jesus' Humanity," we often find ourselves stuck in the "Temple Tax Mindset," trying to coach our way out of a deficit that only a miracle can solve.

This chapter takes us beyond the 20-yard line of our need and into the End Zone of Heaven's infrastructure. From Charlotte's 1960s paycheck to the gold-leaf spines in Gina's shop, we are learning that the "In-With-in" reality is as tangible as the coin in the fish's mouth. It is a relocation from "begging at the gate" to "sitting on the arm cap" of the Throne.

A Direct Conversation with Jesus

   1. The Shoes of the Son Jesus, what "skin" am I standing in today? Am I in Peter's kinetic, over-eager shoes, or am I ready to step into the "Sonship-shoes" that recognize the King's dominion over every fish in the sea?

   2. The Gold Leaf Spine Lord, show me the "Gold Leaf" on my own spine. How have You already painted my structure with Your frequency of healing, and what "thinking-text" dross needs to be skimmed away in the Refiner's fire?

   3. The Royal Deposit Master, where is my "Snow Globe" moment? Show me how to move the resources of Heaven—the "lost notes" and unclaimed bank notes—into my current earthly timeline. What are You asking me to "deposit" using the phone of my faith?

Reflect and Respond

   • **Reflect on your "Train House"**—the place where you have fasted, toiled, and offered up your "meal-offerings." Do you believe that the Lord has filed those encounters in the library of your life book in Heaven?

   • **Consider the "Hall of Fame"** taking an offering for you. Does your heart expand or shrink at the thought of the cloud of witnesses actively cheering for your provision?

   • **Aha! Moment**: The "Something that can't be coached" is often the very thing God uses to move you from self-reliance to a "Portico of OMG" boldness.

———————————————————————

———————————————————————

———————————————————————

———————————————————————

Next Step

Find a physical object that represents a "memory of provision" (like a snow globe, a specific photo, or a journal entry). Hold it while sitting on your "prayer pillow." Ask Jesus to help you "put the bounty into your spirit" and decree that currency into your earth, framed by Mercy and Grace.

Prayer and Contemplation

Papa, I thank You for being the King-Size Abba who lets me squeeze right next to You on the Throne. I surrender my self-reliance and the "deceiver" identity of Jacob. I receive my new name and my new provision. I believe that whatever is true of Jesus is equally true of me. I thank You for the seven mail carts rolling out onto the sea of glass with my name on them. I am undone by Your goodness. Amen.

PLAY SHEET | SERVANT

Servant Edition
Redemptive Gifts Summary

THIS CHAPTER IS A "PAYDAY" REVELATION for the Servant heart. It shifts the focus from the "toil" of the Train House to the "Trust" of the Hall of Fame. It is a declaration that you are not a hireling working for a paycheck; you are a Son/Daughter stewarding the Family Business, where the gold coin is always waiting in the fish's mouth.

THE DNA WRISTBAND AUDIBLE: CHAPTER PLAY-CALL

1. **The Green Dot Helmet** (*Individual Redemptive Gift*): **Servant** The frequency for this play is set to the Servant.

This is your gift of "Authority through Obedience" and "Platform Builder." You are hardwired to see the need (the Temple Tax) and often feel the pressure to fix it with your own sweat. But the Servant in you is being activated to stop "working" the problem and start "fishing" for the promise. You are being called to the "Portico of OMG," realizing that your act of service (like Gina painting spines or Charlotte giving her check) is actually a supernatural key that unlocks the Treasury of Heaven.

2. **The Coaches' Booth** (*Legacy Anchor*): *The Purpose Driven Life* by Rick Warren In the "Booths" of your spiritual legacy, The Purpose Driven Life (Servant/ Foundation) represents the "Why" behind the provision. You apply this by realizing that God doesn't fund "projects"; He funds Purpose. This anchor reminds you that the "Gold Coin" wasn't just about paying a tax; it was about validating Peter's Sonship. You apply this by understanding that your "daily grind" (your Train House) is actually the training ground for a kingdom assignment that Heaven is eager to bankroll.

3. **The Play-Call from God**

"Child, check your helmet—I am releasing the 'Logistics of Heaven' into your hands. I see you standing in the 'Temple Tax' line, worrying about the cost of living and the price of ministry. I am calling an audible: The Supply is in the Assignment! I watched My servant Peter trust Me enough to go fishing for money. I want you to have that same 'In-Within' confidence. I am not looking for you to burn out for Me; I am looking for you to cash in on Who I AM. That is the C♡♡Lness of our Oneness.

Stop measuring your worth by how much you can endure. Your DNA is designed to host 'God's Favorite Charity'—which is My goodness flowing through you, not just to you. Be Spiritually BRAVE enough to deposit the 'invisible check' and put on the 'Gold Leaf Spine.'
You are My trusted Servant, but more importantly, you are My Beloved Heir. Run the play, Child. The Hall of Fame has already taken the offering for you.''

4. The Audible (*The Timeline of Now*) The enemy wants you to focus on the "Temple Tax"—the demands of the world that drain you. The Audible is this: Divine Apportation! Right now, on the timeline of today, I am authorizing the movement of resources from the "Government of Heaven" to the "Home of Your Heart." The snow globe is shifting. The coin is in the mouth. The provision is present. How Good is God!

REFORMATION DATA: THE ARCHITECTURE OF YOUR SUPPLY

To understand the "field" you are playing on, consider how to apply these "Servant" principles to your own resources:

- **The Hall of Fame Offering**: The Servant often feels alone in the work. *Apply This*: Recognize that the Cloud of Witnesses is your "Support Staff." You are not funding the vision alone; you are the ground-operator for a heavenly campaign.

- **The "Gold Leaf" Spine:** The Servant carries the weight of others. *Apply This:* Let the Father paint your spine with Gold Leaf (Healing). You cannot carry the kingdom if your structure is broken. Service requires supernatural strength, not just human effort.

- **The "Peter" Protocol**: Peter didn't argue logic; he went to the sea. *Apply This*: When God gives you a "ridiculous" instruction (like depositing a 1960s check with your phone), obey the Who, not the How. Authority is released in the act of obedience.

Section V

Gates of Time

How Good is God!

THE LONG TABLE

"And he shall turn the heart of the fathers to the children, and the heart of the children to their fathers..." — Malachi 4:6 (KJV)

The table of the Lord is long. It stretches through the kitchen of your childhood, past the dining rooms of your ancestors, all the way to the feast of the Lamb.

We are not just healing a memory. We are resetting the place settings.

Where there was silence, let there be conversation. Where there was a curse, let there be a Cup.

Pull up a chair. The family is waiting to be made whole.

Chapter 14

Reclaiming the Table: Disowning the Curse,

EMBRACING the Blessings |Amelia

"Today I will do what others WON'T,

so tomorrow I can accomplish what others CAN'T."

— **Jerry Rice** | Widely regarded as the greatest wide receiver in NFL history, known for winning three Super Bowls with the San Francisco 49ers.

Have you noticed that many families have "maladies" or negative oddities which seem to mark a person or persons into the next generation? We probably all have a well-endowed, squishy-around-the-middle, cheek-kissin', Aunt Ruth or the like. As sure as Monday follows Sunday, she brings her upside-down "Spiced" Plum Cake to EVERY family outing or church social. A baker she is not. With mastery, we would politely and cunningly avoid it like the plague.

Holiday get-togethers showcasing the beloved legacy of culinary dishes, and there was Aunt Ruth's Plum Cake caught in those awful food pictures Grandma had to take before we could devour the bounty. Odd how, in our life, we can't imagine a gathering without that Malady donning our family table.

The jokes, Uncle Pete's eye rolls, gesturing to look out—the "spice cake" is being doled out. We would fake smiles, make expressions of "yum," and say "thank you" for making this, Aunt Ruth. We are silently comfortable with the horrid upside-down recipe, and nobody ever knew *why* Aunt Ruth was so attached to the making.

The big WHY: how well we stretch ignorant white lies from the tips of our taste buds, literally.

In my family, the horrid "Malady-recipe" was passed from one maternal apron string to the next. As if crippling arthritis in the hands had a category section in Great Grandma's recipe box.

Unthinkably, the generational "Malady's" Tab was well-worn and discolored from use, nestled inside its tin walls.

In writing: each life-ingredient bulleted, directions *mix thoroughly with tears, bake until the dough twists and cracks*, all on a familiar splattered recipe card, uniquely titled with our name ______________________ upside-down "Spiced Plum Cake" of our era.

How did that nasty "recipe" card get inside of my Grandmother's circa 1940s black and white metal recipe box? Why were we okay with it being a part of our family body history, expectantly showing up even if "Aunt Ruth" wasn't there to make it? Somebody did.

Isn't it time to "tell Aunt Ruth's" Spiced Plum Cake recipe the truth! You taste awful and I pull your memoirs from showing up on the communion table of family.

Aunt Ruth's "Spiced Plum Cake"
- **3/4 cup butter:** Pain softened at room temperature.
- **3 eggs:** Laid fresh in your joints every morning.
- **6 to 8 dumb plums:** Grandma used to say her fingers were dumb, forgetting their use.
- **1/2 cup brown sugar:** To contort the thumbs, disfigure and enlarge joints.
- **1 tsp vanilla:** Ring Finger curved, trapping wedding rings behind oversized knuckles.

- **1/4 tsp salt:** Across all the nails, ridged and splitting.
- **1 tsp baking powder:** Rising pain and stiffness.
- **1/2 tsp cinnamon guilt:** What did I do to deserve this?
- **3/4 cup milking it:** And removal of self-worth.
- **2 cups sifted shame flour:** Hiding your hands, making excuses, losing their grip.

Cream and attempt to mix thoroughly, do not overbeat.
Pour into prepared pan-out-your-day.
Bake at 365° every day of the year.
Serve at parties and family get-togethers, infamous.

If I were to ask you to take a moment to ponder stories from your Great Grands to your children's children, wherever the "time marker" road rises to meet you today. Have you noticed that in every generation a certain person within the family is divinely called to draw a line in the sand with the blood of Jesus? They also draw a line under John 3:16 and question the faith that our Father's father believed.

That "certain person"—whose life is set apart through personal struggles and life-saving victories—might be you. Perhaps you are shaking your head with agreement. Jesus walked into your life, again and again. At times you wondered who invited Him, but nonetheless, the line was drawn until you finally followed Him into His Life.

Because of you, that divinely chosen "certain person," *"Aunt Ruth's Spiced Plum Cake" is no longer welcomed at your table.*

The traditions of men often offend, and no amount of sugar-coating can hide the truth: Uncle Pete's eye-rolling practices turn as sour and quick as a drop of vinegar in milk. Faced with these family-shaking realities, you take your stand. Like Jacob under the thumb of Laban, you are declaring at the water trough: *"My family and I will be free!"*

This is more than curiosity; it's a matter of personal integrity between you and your Lord—a question demanding an answer, even many years later.

THE MEMORY

I was about twelve; old enough to stay with my aging Great Grandmother while my maternal Grandparents went on road trips with their travel trailer. Old enough to remember when divinely reminded of the exact moment "Aunt Ruth's Spiced Plum Cake" (arthritis in the hands) was copied and pasted into the epigenetic computer disk of my recall and filed within my recipe box.

I'll give you the good news and then I'll finish the story: *Christ redeemed us from the curse as consequence of our failure to keep the law. In his cross he concentrated the total curse of the human race upon himself. In his abandoning himself to death, he absorbed and dissolved the horror of the curse in his own person. Scripture declares that anyone hanging on a tree embodies the curse. (Deut 21:23.) This act of Christ released the blessing of Abraham upon the Gentiles. Now we are free to receive the blessing of the Spirit.* (Galatians 3:13 Mirror translation)

He then looked everyone in the eye and said to them, "Joining me in close companionship in your daily walk, involves perceiving my mission as fully representing you. Get over and done with any idea of "self" that contradicts your true I-am-ness. Here is how you do it: lift up your cross once and for all, by seeing it mirrored in mine. My cross is your cross." (Luke 9:23 Mirror translation)

If this were a podcast episode I'd state it again:

"Here is how you do it: lift up your cross once and for all, by seeing it mirrored in mine. My cross is your cross." And pause...

THE BLACK AND WHITE RECIPE BOX

Of course, my Grandma's tin box was filled with her Grandmother's recipe cards, including her Aunts', neighbors from the Iowa farm, and ladies from church as well.

It's not a negative, but the "Recipe Box" is a powerful metaphor to help us grasp generational Maladies in our own life. Family is priceless; God forbid, we never want to lessen the price of Jesus' offering at the comfort of our own traditions of men.

Handwriting Treasures on display: I'll post a picture in the blog so you can see it. Festively, every year on my Gingerbread man-themed kitchen Christmas tree, precious recipe cards are attached with mini clothespins. Those tiny wood clips hold a display of card-potpourri spanning more than five generations of culinary literature. Each bearing love-familiar cursive, crooked print handwriting, and for the working woman, the typewriter keyed. Included is one shopping list, scribbled on the back of a narrow and aged grocery receipt, circa 1953 Roth's grocery store ad. What the apron strings represent—that uniquely recognizable handwriting—has blossomed into a treasured story. I am fortunate enough to know, share, and remember every distinct pencil flair.

On one of those family gatherings, after our bellies were stuffed with traditional tastes, and before the *"Oh Hell"* cards were brought to the table, I reached into my country pine cabinet, grabbed my Grandma's still-well-in-use recipe box, and set it on the table. We were transported back in time, like kids in the candy store. The penny candy stories flew; how much gas or a loaf of bread cost.

Thumbing through: we were holding the daily bread of kitchens and historic times, each card worn. They had been handled by beloved family members thousands of times, through tears, wars, weddings, holidays, harvests, and Sunday go-to-meetings.

My family picked and sorted through the recipe box like a *Go Fish* game. Different notations: We found "short" telephone numbers (era 1940-1967) from Iowa to California, food items that only an Iowa farm shelf could stock, friends' names and addresses.

Martha from the Baptist church choir, notes in Great Grandma's pen, honorable mentions of the author of the recipe: "this was given to me by," whether it was good, easy to make, and to call next Tuesday. The romance and nostalgia we love remembering in our traditions?

Back to the "Spice Cake" metaphor

Huge question mark here; how, and where, and why, did "Aunt Ruth's Spiced Plum cake" crippling arthritis arrive in the hands of the women I love to remember? The little things...

- Always a delicate hanky in pocket, apron, or purse.
- Worn little black bibles with the smallest of text.
- Sugared cereals and soda pop (treats not afforded in our house).
- Angel figurines in the hundreds, with names, stories, and the dime store they purchased them at.
- The sweetest of pink climbing rose bushes, arched, canopied, and spidered, in the front walkway.
- Cribbage games around a grey and white marbled laminate and chrome-legged kitchen table.

How, and where, and why, did it get there? And why the hands?

Our good news (Galatians 3:13) kissed my understanding during my years of calling the "Faith Movement" my church family; it tempered fire and brimstone to meet FAITH.

You can't live on little girl salvation prayers. What do I mean *live*? I am now a wife, mother of four sons, and officially graduated into the "Being drawn by Holy Spirit Camp." Let's call it what it is: the Cavalry has come to help! I seriously needed a savior to save me from myself and divine assistance for the responsibilities life hands us as parents and e-spoused.

Hello a new baptism with signs, wonders, and the prophetic. This baptism "Sign" wasn't listed as the First Church in the phone book either.

A thought to suggest: just because a *something-new-recipe-card*, or a *change-recipe-card*, is not in your family "Recipe Box," doesn't mean it's wrong, of the devil, witchcraft, or false.

It simply means the people who you love, and who love you, don't have an experience-story to tell you.

From above: **That "certain person"—whose life is set apart through personal struggles and life-saving victories—might be you.** Perhaps you are shaking your head with agreement. Jesus walked into your life, again and again. At times you wondered who invited Him, but nonetheless, the line was drawn until you finally followed Him into His Life.

By dying our death as fully God and fully man, once and for all (not for a "select few"), death became the doorway, whereby Jesus would enter into our hell and deepest darkness and sense of lostness and loneliness as a result of the lies we believed about ourselves - to triumphantly lead us out as his trophies and relocate us face to face with the Father of the universe. Eph 4:7,8 and 9 See Mirror Bible. All this happened while we were still dead in our trespasses and sins. Eph 2:5,6 Co-quickened, co-raised, co-seated in his Executive authority [his right hand] Now ponder Colossians 3:1-3 and engage your thoughts with throne room realities.) (Ephesians 1:4 Mirror)

Curse, that dreaded word.

• "Then the LORD God said to the serpent, 'Because you have done this, you are cursed more than all animals, domestic and wild. You will crawl on your belly, groveling in the dust as long as you live.'" (Genesis 3:14 NLT - The fate of the Serpent)

• "And to the man he said, 'Since you listened to your wife and ate from the tree whose fruit I commanded you not to eat, the ground is cursed because of you. All your life you will struggle to scratch a living from it.'" (Genesis 3:17 NLT - The punishment of mankind)

• "Now you are cursed and banished from the ground, which has swallowed your brother's blood." (Genesis 4:11 - Cain murders Abel)

Our definition, Curse: Having some sort of divine harm, malady, or other curse.

Malady:

1. Any ailment or disease of the body; especially, a lingering or deep-seated disorder.

2. A moral or mental defect or disorder.

"Don't give up at half time.

Concentrate on winning the second half."

— Paul "Bear" Bryant

Now that the recipe box is laid before us, it's time to take a look at the game file to assess team performance, develop strategies, and improve players' techniques.

Holy Highlighter: Learn from mistakes, Improve performance, Uncover tendencies.

Here are some tips for watching football film (in the spirit):

• *Watch without notes first:* Get an overview of the game and players before taking notes.

• *Watch a second time:* On the second viewing, focus on position specifics and critical factors.

• *Analyze specific moments:* Look at moments like why and how an offensive play breaks down, or where and how the opponent beat your defense.

• Just a thought: there is nothing wrong with the fresh baking ingredients used in "Aunt Ruth's Spiced Plum Cake." There is more to a recipe than the ingredients.

BACK TO MY STORY

We are here: I was about twelve; old enough to stay with my aging Great Grandmother when my Grandparents went on camper travel trips and old enough to remember when divinely reminded the exact moment "Aunt Ruth's Spiced Plum Cake" (arthritis in the hands) was copied and pasted into my epigenetic computer disk of my recall DNA and filed within my recipe box.

My grandmother's living room is so clear to me; memories are powerful imprints within the library of the mind. The wallpaper, a grey-green base, large white flowered floral print on the far wall, where Grandpa built their bedroom addition. Great Grandma's spinning wheel sitting in front of one of two large bay windows, looking out on the walk with the "spidery" pink rose-covered arbor, kissing the edges of Boones Ferry Rd, filled with miles of farmland, lazily stretching from south of Woodburn to the busy overpasses and bridge bearing the same name in Wilsonville, Oregon.

Have you ever seen a Grandparent's living room that didn't have "his and hers" recliners? Ugly, oversized fake leather recliners. Grandpa's had cracks on the arm and headrest, which Grandma tried to cover with doilies and throws.

That day, in the memory of a twelve-year-old, this room was filled with the most valuable people in my life: four generations of my maternal line. An infamous day. Grandma Coffman, the family matriarch, was seated in the extra recliner chair marked as hers. My Mom and her Mom (my Grandma) each at rest with our well-endowed hips on the arm of the easy chair. Me, I was squeezed in on the side next to Great Grandma's knees. My hands warmly held in Great Grandma's crooked hands, as we were reminiscing the day's activities. Truly in my comfort zone, surrounded by love.

You know how relatives like to *ooh, aah*, compare and the like. One would say, *"She has her father's hair," "her mother's eyes," "high cheekbones like Dad's sister," "a temper like you-know-who."* We have all enjoyed recognizing the familiar wealth of our family DNA.

I remember someone was stroking my hands; they were warm in the clasp of Great Grandma's hands. All admiring my long fingers that were just like my Dad's; and here comes the copy and paste. I don't know who said it—that's not the point, because three of them had the evidence of it in their crooked hands. *"Ignorant agreement."* While stroking and admiring my long fingers, she said: *"Isn't it too bad that they will be curved and crippled someday!"*

The weights were pulled and calibrated on an epigenetic Grandfather clock. Aunt Ruth's Spiced Plum Cake recipe is mentally transferred into the maternal DNA recipe box, verbally and with ignorant agreement.

Scary, isn't it? In a mindset and positive growth-conscious society, I am sure we all have shared "season tickets" by the unconscious efforts of those around us. And even scarier... we may have invested in the same seats!

"Faith is the bird that feels the light when the dawn is still dark."
– **Rabindranath Tagore** | Philosopher, poet, and Nobel laureate.

In the "spirit" is a mind-altering and unlimited quest in His love. Moments of silence make an hour pass in the blink of an eye, while the peace that passes understanding races at Mach speed or easily rests in the comfort of being in His darkness. Breathe in, breathe out; as Dorothy said to Toto: *I don't think we are in Kansas anymore.* Experiences from subatomic level into the cells of the body, to the tables of heavenly government.

I am so utterly grateful that I believed where "Love" led me, through the veil.

As His children, we have permission to discover the Alpha and Omega of His brilliance. Time is just a small measurement that reaches across ages; ages are ideas acted on within His omnipresence. Available, far-reaching, and as near as the breath you just exhaled.

How did arthritis develop, and where did it come from, and why did it attach to the hands of women in my family? Galatians 3:13 clearly says: *"In his abandoning himself to death, he absorbed and dissolved the horror of the curse in his own person."* My faith made a transaction at the revelation, and the arthritis was dissolved, but identity and destiny asked the questions. Graciously, He showed me the steps of the abandonment He walked for me.

THROUGH THE VEIL - ON THE TIMELINE OF FAITH

The room was more than large, musty, and dimly lit by several wall sconce candle flames fighting to burn above the heavy drip of wax. It took several moments for the eyes of my spirit to focus, get accustomed that we weren't in "Kansas" anymore, and my "feelers" to activate. Your spirit responds similarly to sonar reaching out and returning on a submarine monitor, pinging the ocean it is submerged in. Your senses—some are naturally stronger than others—develop with practice and create a library through Jesus-led experiences.

The mass of the room, height, depth, and circumference dictated that my spiritual feet were standing in a cathedral-type sanctuary. The wheel of time turned to a darkened age; one only has likeness of memory from history books or the round tables of Hollywood. Under my feet are carved stones laid into the patchwork floor. You'd assume rows and rows of seating, but those didn't look like pews! I didn't understand. Relaxing, expanding my spirit to decode the consistent dark rectangle shapes filling the room. The atmosphere was heavy, broken, and deathly quiet.

Then I heard a higher-pitched muffled sound of crying, barely carried past the sound of candle flames breaking from a draft. I followed the sound, walking up the center aisle, looking down the erratic rows of multi-sized black boxes. Stopping about ten yards back when I caught sight of the back of her. She was small, frail, and on her knees sobbing. The shallow cold gust whisked up the back of my neck as if shuddering me to understanding: they were coffins. Rows and rows of small, medium, and mostly large rough-cut blackened coffins.

Again, only in the recesses of history did I know; plagues would crawl through towns choosing their weakest victims until the overworked caretakers also succumbed to its tallies. Entire towns and villages wiped out. Churches would house the mass memorial site in their sanctuaries, creating an altar of death until means and the weather would allow for burial services.

My breath held, as reality choked me by the hair standing up on the back of my neck. Her sobs turned into whimpers as she curled into her tartan shawl and melted down the side of the casket that was holding her on her knees. Caught off guard, her head turned and looked over her shoulder, as if she heard me exhale in horror. We both gasped as she saw me watching her.

Eyes meeting. My gasp. She saw me! Too exhausted to display much fear but enough caution, she rose to her feet in slow motion turning to face me. She couldn't have been more than twelve or thirteen. Her dark swollen eyes staring at me in fearful wonderment. Internally I asked: *How did she see me?* As big of a miracle question as me seeing her on the timeline of my questions.

How, and where, and why, did arthritis get there? And why the hands?

In slow motion, this frail dark-haired girl continued to turn and rise to her feet facing me. This little bairn from another time adjusting her stance, pinning her shawl under her elbow to keep it from falling. Divine knowledge filled my understanding like the quick paper roll of an old-fashioned flip book. My eyes aghast at the story shared in my spirit and the story before me.

She, Amelia, had no hands.

Anger! The atmosphere full of rage towards God. His rules, leadership, and establishment. The last place on earth she would have come to; but it held the diseased remains of the only kin she had. The deception: this isn't a house built for peace, the evidence was death and judgment.

Broken and in lamentation, my spirit could hear Amelia's screams behind every tear she had shed. Distrust wailed in the air as her reality screamed at God: *"Now how am I supposed to take care of myself? First You judge me for the crimes of my family and removed my hands, and now You have taken away any source of my survival."* Selah...

There isn't enough paper to pause for the *ah-ha* of the moment.

How, and where, and why, did arthritis get there? And why the hands?

The picture isn't pretty.

• *How:* The attempt to rid the sins (thievery) of a family, therefore ridding the community of the offending tool (hands) of the offense. Laws were often judged and executed by the church, in whom God was deemed responsible for the actions within.

• *Where:* During a Medieval time of great darkness in the church, where plagues cleared villages and the word "Sanctuary" could save your life.

• *Why:* Wrath, even justifiable.

Arthritis is a disease that causes inflammation or degeneration in one or more joints. It can be acute or chronic, and there are many different types of arthritis with different causes and treatments. Symptoms include: Pain, Stiffness, Decreased range of motion, Joint deformities, Redness, Heat, Swelling in your joints. In some types of arthritis, other organs, such as your eyes, heart, or skin, can also be affected.

Scriptures where sin is described with consequences:

• *Fear:* Psalm 6:2 NLT - Have compassion on me, LORD, for I am weak. Heal me, LORD, for my bones are in agony.

• *Terror:* Habakkuk 3:16 NLT - I trembled inside when I heard this; my lips quivered with fear. My legs gave way beneath me, and I shook in terror.

• *Depression:* Proverbs 17:22 KJV - A merry heart doeth good like a medicine: but a broken spirit drieth the bones.

• *Taunting:* Psalm 42:10 NASB - As a shattering of my bones, my adversaries taunt me...

• *Grief:* Psalm 31:10 NASB - For my life is spent with sorrow... My strength has failed because of my guilt, And my body has wasted away.

• *Shame:* Proverbs 12:4 NLT - ...a disgraceful woman is like cancer in his bones.

- *Sin & Sickness:* Psalm 38:3 NLT - Because of your anger, my whole body is sick; my health is broken because of my sins.
- *Discipline:* Job 33:19 NLT - Or God disciplines people with pain on their sickbeds, with ceaseless aching in their bones.
- *Envy/Anger:* Proverbs 14:30 NLT - ...jealousy is like cancer in the bones.
- *Bitterness:* Jeremiah 20:9 NLT - ...It's like a fire in my bones! I am worn out trying to hold it in! / Lamentations 3:4 NLT - ...He has broken my bones.
- *Unconfessed Sin:* Psalm 32:3 NLT - When I refused to confess my sin, my body wasted away...
- *Cursing:* Psalm 109:18 NIV - He wore cursing as his garment; it entered into his body like water, into his bones like oil.

I wanted to know. I had asked the Lord what could possibly have hindered and crippled the women whose only testament before me today was that they loved and cared for me.

And the Good News

Like any coach or player watching a game film, "Aunt Ruth's Spiced Plum Cake" can either be avoided, ignored, eaten, trashed, declared a mistake, bad ingredients, the fault of the cook, oven, overbeating, or the like. We can't get rid of Aunt Ruth, but she can learn, practice, and experience a new revelation about baking.

Graciously He has showed me His own steps of the surrender, His cross of suffering, and that Sin's consequences have been paid for Amelia and I.

I tell myself in the story, that in Amelia's understanding, I am perceived as an Angel. In that day and age who would have believed her if she said that a distant relative traveled in the spirit to visit her? On her behalf, we can agree that she has struggled = "burned at the stake" of life for more than a couple of lifetimes. Angel it is.

(To be moved in the inward parts, i.e., to feel compassion).

I am more than moved by the person (my own flesh and blood relative) standing before me.

Amelia, I'm sure, is a cheerful industrious person in the cloud of witnesses. But today, Jesus has come to not only change my life, but hers.

Back to the experience: Without thinking about my actions, I moved towards her. She didn't back away or frighten. Brave little soul. As tenacious as the Virgin Mary, when an angel visited her with the most outlandish news. *"Be it unto me according to thy word..."*

My western oorah acknowledges - *Git-R-Done!* (Popularized and made a national catchphrase by comedian Larry the Cable Guy in the 1990s.)

My hands reached gently towards her to pray. Symbiotic in the spirit, fluid in compassion, I do not recall either of us ever saying a word. My hands softly resting, one on the back of her right shoulder, the other ever so lightly, laying all my fingers just over her heart.

And Amen.

What else can one say or write?

Amelia's hands, wrists, fingers re-grew—more like they popped out!

No time for our surprise! And I was gone.

This is the story Jesus tells me about her. The miracle so profound, she has been justified before God, her family, and town. It made her famous. She married a member of a royal family. I know, I know—a bit of a Cinderella ending. But truly, haven't we all?

Now what about "Aunt Ruth's Spiced Plum Cake?"

Yes, I have an Aunt Ruth, but there isn't a said recipe.

We had many a family potluck and picnic when I was a kid. I would assume she was a very good cook because she and her Pastor husband, my Uncle Scott, were always the hosts.

The encounter is true. My hands still have beautifully long straight fingers. The metaphor is true. The recipe box is true and still sitting inside my country pine cabinet.

There are reasons Jesus knowingly takes us down the back stairs and shows us our hell.

Today I can tell you about the keys of the kingdom He retrieved and then handed them to me.

I love to unlock TRUTH! Go Team!

"There's always something in the game you wish you would have done different. That's why players improve, because they learn from what they did before. They might have been guessing before, but now they know."

– **Gordie Howe** | Known as "Mr. Hockey," iconic Canadian professional ice hockey player and one of the greatest players in NHL history (Detroit Red Wings).

ACTIVATION

EMBRACING THE BLESSING

This chapter invited you to confront the profound connection between your generational identity and the redemptive work of Christ.

It encourages you to find your freedom by confronting the "recipes" that have been passed down and choosing to embrace the blessing. Now, let's allow the questions of Jesus to lead you into a deeper conversation about your own journey and the words He is speaking to you.

A Direct Conversation with Jesus
1. The Request
"What do you want me to do for you?" (Mark 10:51)

Jesus asked this of a blind beggar named Bartimaeus, putting the power of his healing request directly into his own hands.

Bartimaeus had the courage to ask for exactly what he needed: to see. As you've been reading about the generational "maladies" or "recipes" in your own life, ask Jesus: *"What is the specific change or healing I am asking for from You today?"* Be bold and clear, just like Bartimaeus, and listen for His loving response.

2. The Touch

"Who touched me?" (Mark 5:30)

A woman suffering for twelve years with a chronic condition touched Jesus's garment (the hem, the cords, of his garment which represented the law that forced her separation) and was instantly healed.

He knew power had gone out from Him and wanted to acknowledge her faith. This story reminds us that our faith can bring about miraculous healing, even in hidden struggles. Ask Jesus: *"Where have I been afraid to reach out and touch Your power to heal? What is the secret pain or generational 'recipe' in my life that I am ready for You to heal?"* He is waiting to acknowledge your faith and your breakthrough.

3. The Lack

"What do you lack?" (Mark 10:21)

Jesus asked this of the rich young ruler, who believed he had followed all the laws but still felt a spiritual emptiness. The "lack" in this chapter may not be material wealth, but spiritual freedom from a generational curse. We may believe we are doing everything right but still feel bound by the traditions and beliefs of our past. Ask Jesus: *"What am I still lacking in my pursuit of spiritual freedom and personal integrity? Show me where I have accepted a curse in my life that You have already dissolved."* Listen for His gentle guidance that leads to your total liberation.

Reflect and Respond

Take a moment to write down what you heard from Jesus in this conversation. What did you learn about your ability to receive healing and break free from generational patterns? What is one step you can take today to act on what He has revealed?

____

____

____

____

Next Step

Over the coming week, pay close attention to the stories and beliefs you tell yourself about your family history. Every time a negative thought or "ignorant agreement" about a family "malady" comes to mind, replace it with the truth from Galatians 3:13 and declare, *"In Christ, I have disowned the curse and embraced the blessing."*

Prayer and Contemplation

Father, thank You for the divine inheritance You have for me in Christ. I ask for the courage to confront the generational recipes that have been passed down and to stop making excuses for them.

I believe that You have absorbed every curse and made me free. Show me how to walk in that freedom and to be the generation that draws a line in the sand for all who come after me. In Jesus' name, Amen.

PLAY SHEET | RULER

Ruler Edition
Redemptive Gifts Summary

THIS CHAPTER IS A HIGH-STAKES LEGISLATIVE MANEUVER in the Courts of Heaven, designed to move you from the "inherited hunger" of a family curse to the "extravagant feast" of your true inheritance. It is a call for you to stop eating the bread of sorrow and to realize that your seat at the Table of Blessing has been legally secured by the Sonship Authority of Jesus.

THE DNA WRISTBAND AUDIBLE: CHAPTER PLAY-CALL

1. **The Green Dot Helmet** *(Individual Redemptive Gift)*: **Ruler** The frequency for this play is set to the Ruler. This is your gift of the "Architect of Authority" and the "Legitimate Heir."

You arc hardwired to recognize when a "Counterfeit Decree"—like a generational curse of scarcity or early death—is trying to govern your territory.

The Ruler in you is being activated to serve a *Restraining Order* against the "Amelia" spirits of your past. You have the inherent capacity to realize that the "Power of the Curse" is broken the moment you stand in the Inherent Truth of your blamelessness. You are being called to stop managing the symptoms of the curse and to start enforcing the Blessing of the New Covenant.

2. **The Coaches' Booth** *(Legacy Anchor)*: *More Than a Carpenter* by Josh McDowell In the "Booths" of your spiritual legacy, *More Than a Carpenter* (Ruler/Architecture) represents the investigation into the solid, structural reality of the Resurrection. You apply this by moving beyond "wishful thinking" and into a *"Structural" confidence* that the "Legal Debt" of your ancestors has been paid in full.

This anchor reminds you that the Table is not a "religious suggestion" but a "Legislative Reality." Just as this anchor book provides the evidence for Christ, you are applying it to the evidence of your own freedom. It proves that the "Curse" has no architectural support in the New Creation.

3. The Play-Call from God

"Child, check your helmet—I am speaking a 'New Decree' into your ears. I see you feeling the 'inherited hunger' of a family line that has struggled to lay hold of My goodness. I am calling an audible: *The Table is reclaimed!* I watched My Son, Jesus, become the 'Curse' on the tree so that you would never have to eat its fruit again.

You aren't a 'beggar' trying to earn a crumb; you are the 'Guest of Honor' whose seat has been prepared from the foundation of the world. That is the C♡♡Lness of our

Oneness. When you feel the 'weight' of the old family patterns trying to pull you back into the shadows, I want you to remember that I have given you the Master Key. I have authorized you to disown every lie that says you are 'unworthy' or 'limited.'

Stop believing the lie that the 'Amelia' in your history has the final word. Your DNA is hardwired for Abundance and Blessing. Be Spiritually BRAVE enough to take your place at the Table and eat the 'Best Wine' I've saved for you. I am so good that I have removed the 'Restraining Order' of the law and replaced it with the 'Freedom of the Son.' Run the play, Child. The feast is ready and your name is on the card."

4. The Audible *(The Timeline of Now)* The enemy wants you to remain "curse-conscious," stuck in a loop of trying to break what has already been shattered. The Audible is this: *The Blessing is in effect!* Right now, on the timeline of today, I am removing the "Scarcity Mindset" from your brain. I am releasing the power of Generational Restoration. You are not a victim of your bloodline; you are a King's Champion in the lineage of Light. How Good is God!

REFORMATION DATA: THE ARCHITECTURE OF YOUR RECLAMATION

To understand the "field" you are playing on, consider how to apply these "Ruler" principles to your own "Table":

• **Disowning the Decree:** In spiritual law, a decree is only valid if it is not contested by a Higher Law. *Apply This:* Consciously "disown" the words of the curse (e.g., *"we are always sick," "we never have enough"*). By speaking the Higher Law of Blessing, you are legally evicting the "squatter" spirits from your family territory.

• **The Communion Audit:** You apply the Higher Law by treating Communion as a "Legal Audit." *Apply This:* Every time you take the bread and the wine, you are auditing the "accounts" of your life and realizing that the debt is zero. Refuse to carry the "emotional debt" of your ancestors' mistakes.

• **Seating Authority:** You apply this by "Seating yourself" in heavenly places. This isn't a future hope; it's a Present Reality. *Apply This:* When you face a "hard" situation, visualize yourself at the Table of the King. This perspective shifts your "Tactics" from fighting *for* victory to fighting *from* victory.

HOW GOOD IS GOD!

THE UNBROKEN LINE

> *"Surely goodness and mercy shall follow me All the days of my life; And I will dwell in the house of the Lord Forever." — Psalm 23:6 (NKJV)*

Immortality is not a puzzle to solve. It is a Goodness you cannot escape.

We often view eternity as a distant destination. But the Father views it as a continuous presence.

He is not just good for a lifetime. He is good for a timeline that has no end.

Death is not a period that stops the sentence of your life. It is merely a comma in the story of His love.

Do not worry about the "how." Just follow the "Who." His Goodness is the bridge that carries you over.

Chapter 15

NDE · PDE =

Past Death EXPERIENCES Immortality

"In this lifetime, you don't have to prove nothin' to nobody - except yourself. And after what you've gone through, if you haven't done that by now, it ain't gonna never happen. Now go on back."

— **Fortune** | The head groundskeeper at Notre Dame Stadium in the movie *Rudy* (1993), who served as the mentor to Rudy when he was ready to quit.

Let's re-cue the scene: Rudy was contemplating quitting the Notre Dame football team and leaving his beloved university when Fortune gave his famous speech.

Rudy was distraught because the new coach, Dan Devine, would not allow him to dress for the final home game of his senior year, despite the previous coach, Ara Parseghian, having promised him he would get to suit up for one game.

After years of struggling just to get on the team's scout squad, this final rejection caused Rudy to lose faith in his dream and feel he had nothing left to prove.

THE RUDY RUETTIGER PRINCIPLE

The story of Rudy Ruettiger resonates deeply with our own lives. He was told he was *"5 feet nothin', a 100 and nothin', and you got hardly a speck of athletic ability."*

The Surrender and the Challenge

• *A Divine Spark:* Christ's gift of surrender sparks our own received surrender to and in Him.

• *Defying the World:* When we fully dedicate ourselves (poured out to Christ), our actions start to defy the logic of worldly systems.

• *Defiance or Determination?* Does this dedication require us to defy the systems, determine a new path, or both?

Rudy's Victory

Rudy's perseverance was met with two contrasting reactions:

1. *To Supporters:* It became a sweet savor of inspiration and possibility.

2. *To Critics:* It was a declaration of failure to every voice that told him his dreams were impossible.

3. *The Ultimate Outcome:* His victory was not just personal. It was a public, resounding declaration of the defeat of limitation and cynicism. Fortune found a distraught Rudy after he had quit and used the motivational speech—and the confession of his own regret about quitting the team years earlier—to convince Rudy to return.

Now go on back! Go back to the voice of the Lord in your life.

And ask: *How much Life did Christ provide for your Life?*

THE CHECKLIST OF LIFE

Tick every check box that He overcame and, in-our-favor, gave us Life:

☐ *Freedom:* "Christ has set us free to live a free life. So take your stand! Never again let anyone put a harness of slavery on you." (Galatians 5:1 MTB)

☐ *Saved/Salvation:* "If you openly declare that Jesus is Lord and believe in your heart that God raised Him from the dead, you will be saved." (Romans 10:9 LBT)

☐ *Eternal Life:* "For God so loved the world, that He gave His only begotten Son, that whoever believes in Him shall not perish, but have eternal life." (John 3:16 NASB)

☐ *Forgiven:* "You were dead in sins, with no hope at all, but God gave you new life with Christ! (He forgave you all your sins!) He took away the list of sins and shortcomings we had failed to keep, and nailed it to the cross." (Colossians 2:13-14 LBT)

☐ *Sickness, Disease, Decay:* "But if the Spirit of Him who raised Jesus from the dead dwells in you, He who raised Christ Jesus from the dead will also give Life to your mortal bodies through His Spirit who dwells in you." (Romans 8:11 NASB)

☐ *Healed:* "He personally carried our sins in His own body on the cross so that we would be dead to sin and alive to righteousness. Our healing flows from His wounds, for by His stripes we were healed." (1 Peter 2:24 TPT)

☐ *Wholeness:* "Through the action of baptism we were immersed into His death; so that just as Christ was raised from the dead by the Father's glory, we also should live in a new dimension of Life." (Romans 6:4 TMT)

☐ *Delivered:* "Much more then, having now been justified by His blood, we shall be saved from the wrath of God through Him. For if while we were enemies we were reconciled to God through the death of His Son, much more having been reconciled, we shall be saved by His Life." (Romans 5:9-10 NASB)

☐ *Law of Works:* "For Christ is the end of the law for righteousness, so that everyone who believes will be justified." (Romans 10:4 NASB)

☐ *Sin and Death:* "Therefore there is now no condemnation for those who are in Christ Jesus. For the law of the Spirit of Life in Christ Jesus has set you free from the law of sin and death." (Romans 8:1-2 NASB)

☐ *Grace:* "For it was by grace you were saved. It was not the result of your own actions, but God's gift to you. And you were not saved by the works of the Law, so there is nothing for you to boast about." (Ephesians 2:8-9 TPT)

☐ *Peace:* "and through Him to reconcile all things to Himself, having made peace through the blood of His cross; through Him, I say, whether things on earth or things in heaven." (Colossians 1:20 NASB)

☐ *Communion (Bread of Life):* "Jesus replied, 'I am the Bread of Life. Come every day and you will never be hungry. Believe in me and you will never be thirsty... I am the living Bread that has come down from heaven. If anyone eats this Living Bread, he will live forever. And the Bread that I will offer is my own flesh, given for the Life of the world." (John 6:35, 48, 51 TPT)

☐ *Rivers of Living Waters:* "On the last and greatest day of the feast, Jesus stood and spoke in a loud voice to the crowds: 'All you thirsty ones, come to me! Believe in me and drink! For out of your innermost being will flow continually rivers of living water!'" (John 7:37-39 TPT)

☐ *The Ability to Walk in Abundant Life:* "The thief comes only to steal and kill and destroy; I came that they may have Life, and have it abundantly." (John 10:10 TPT)

IS YOUR LIFE A PERFUME OR A PUNCH?

Does the fragrant message communicated by Christ, in and through our life, follow the playbook—the "death of death?" First to us, then to those around us.

Sweet Savor of Christ to God Evident in Everyone.
"All the every, All the ones!"

Rudy's unwavering commitment and eventual victory—even a single play—was a public announcement that inspired everyone who witnessed his journey (to life) and shamed those who doubted him (the odor of death to the religious systems and structures of "the law of works," or in his case, the rules and limitations).

Fortune's words confront Rudy with the truth that his internal transformation and perseverance is the proof—the sweet savor—that speaks for itself, regardless of external validation (proving to nobody else).

I am overwhelmed with gratitude. Wherever my travels take me I am so aware that God leads us as trophies in his victory parade. What he knows to be true about us diffuses through us like a perfume of sweet aroma everywhere we go, celebrating the success of the cross. (In ancient triumphs, abundance of perfumes and wreaths of sweet smelling flowers were used in victory celebrations.)

We are a sweet savor of Christ to God evident in everyone we meet. (All the every's, All the One's) The fragrance of Christ is recognized in all to salvation. The same gospel that announces the fragrant victory of Christ declares the odor of death; the defeat of destruction in everyone. (This parade of victory is a public announcement of the defeat of the religious systems and structures based on the law of works. Just like it is in any public game where the victory celebration of the winning team is an embarrassment for the losing team. The death of evil, [the death of death] is announced in resurrection life.)
The message we communicate is a fragrance with an immediate association; to darkness, it is the smell of doom [the death of death]; to life it is the familiar fragrance of life itself.

We are not competing with those who have added their price tag to the gospel. Our conversation has its source in Christ; we communicate from the transparent innocence of a face to

face encounter with God. (Face to face encounter = the story that He continually reveals in us.)
(2 Corinthians 2:14-17 Mirror Study Bible)

STORIES THAT BEAR WITNESS

By now you understand the power of experience. My favorite transformation in the Bible is shared through Nicodemus.

Now amongst them there was a man who was a prominent leader among the Jews, a Pharisee named Nicodemus. He came to see Jesus under the cover of the night and said to him, "Rabbi, it is clear for all of us to see that you come from God as a Teacher - the signs you perform are proof that God is with you. No one is able to do these signs you do if they are not in union with God."
Jesus answered him emphatically; no one would even be able to recognize anything as coming from God's domain unless they are born from above to begin with. The very fact that it is possible to perceive that I am in union with God, as a human being, reveals mankind's genesis from above.
Nicodemus did not understand this answer at all and said to him, "How can a person be born if they are already grown-up? Surely one cannot re-enter your mother's womb and be born a second time?"
Jesus answered, you have to get this, unless someone is born out of water (the womb) and Spirit, there would be no possible connection with the realm of God. Whatever originates out of flesh is flesh; but what is sourced in Spirit is spirit. Don't be so surprised when I say to you [humanity - plural.] You couldn't get here in the flesh unless you got here from above.
(John 3:1-7 Mirror Study Bible)

"Seeing the kingdom of Heaven."

Jesus faithfully takes us into Himself and shows us a preview of text written about Him (his humanity) and view in Him.

Nicodemus Transformation

To know Him is a daily privilege, but to ask Him, *How Good is God?* is to be known by Him as a story experiencer and teller.

Then Joseph of Arimathea asked Pilate permission to remove the body of Jesus which Pilate was pleased to do. Joseph was a prominent leader, and a secret follower of Jesus, (but here, while most of his close friends and followers forsook him, Joseph fearlessly offers to bury Jesus in his own rock-hewn tomb.)
Also Nicodemus, who was the one who approached Jesus in the shelter of the night in order not to be publicly associated with him, made a very bold announcement of his love for Jesus and brought expensive sweet-smelling spices; a mixture of myrrh and aloes which weighed about a hundred pounds. Then Joseph and Nicodemus took Jesus' body and prepared it for burial. And according to Jewish custom they wrapped the body in linen cloths together with the spices.
(John 19:38-40 Mirror Study Bible)

How will I truly know my co-inclusion in Him if I do not have an experience of what occurred behind and or before the stone rolled away?

Inquiring minds... the grave/tomb.

It was dark, but my spiritual eyes could see clearly... my senses said it was a cool, unwavering ground temperature, the air stagnant and lifeless. My first moments I viewed His wrapped body laying on a stone surface. The next moment I was bodily standing next to Him; together we were looking at that same *no-body-on-the-table.*

He finished folding His head napkin. In the same body, He had walked the miles of His mission. The same flesh, broken for many and I knew Him. Just as one would be familiar with their husband's hand holding yours under the covers in the darkness of night. Firm, warm, calloused from work, yet knowing without thinking, more than half asleep, I just wrapped my small hand around his large pinky and ring finger. Familiar; that is how we hold hands. I knew Him, Jesus, and He looked no different than the thousands of times He talked with me on the road of my transformation.

Jesus did the oddest thing! He bent over, grabbed a handful of dirt, the kind that never sees the light of day or mist of the earth; gray pulverized dirt. In the same motion of bending, He straightened up, full hand, palm lifted—*bam!* Jesus hit His left shoulder, and the dirt exploded over His shoulder. Like violently throwing salt for luck.

Childlike, I mirrored His odd, dirt gathering and bursting over the shoulder movement, just like Him. Odd went to *Oh, My!* Authority, restoration, and dust of the earth stuff.

"Then the Lord God formed man of dust from the ground, and breathed into his nostrils the breath of life; and man became a Living Being." (Genesis 2:7 NASB)

Or "the breath of lives." To breathe into someone's nostrils is what happens when two people kiss. God kissed life into Adam. The dust of earth and the breath of Deity mingled as one, so that Adam could interact in both realms (physical and spiritual). *{Immortal}*. This breath or "Spirit of Life" was more than air; it brought intelligence, wisdom, light, and the image of God into Adam.

I was dressed just like Him, typical Jesus Savior white linen with belt and sandals. He smiled at me, and watched, as I folded the remaining messy linen. *What changed?* We were restored to our original design, Living Beings! Death had died and so did the shroud that clothed us.

The grave is a window to the soul... I could see through multiple monitors into the lower realms of the earth. With the same "husband-like" familiarity, I always let Jesus choose the channel, or fiddle with the key ring, to find the right key. Haven't met a man that didn't have a mastery over the remote control.

The stories from here... limitless, but my favorite is sitting with the "Marys." Badass women who believed, broke community rules, and were rewarded with the first of the firsts. We are cut from the same cloth.

Appearings: Jesus never changed His clothes (appearance), though the accounts they shared, you would derive He wore many hats, had many duties, with a large closet.

Today, since the messy linen that represented my burial, the body, is folded, and we are restored as *Living Beings,* intimacy is focused on discovering and experiencing what being like Him really means. How do we Live, learning Our resurrected humanity, walking between heaven and earth as per our original design? Death has died, along with you and I. Decay, and everything that defiles a resurrected body, is breaking the folded napkin rules. Life and breath belong to us.

I know there are masses of "Marys" out there joining the first of the firsts party. Peters are more than welcome.

How many times in this book have we declared: *How Good is God!*

Today, is our **PDE...**
PAST DEATH EXPERIENCE

In the movie: What was Rudy's ultimate line drawn in the sand, fueled on faith and identity, doing his dream, line?

"I've been ready for this my whole life."

— *Rudy* | *Rudy* (film)

ACTIVATION

NDE · PDE = PAST DEATH EXPERIENCES: IMMORTALITY

This story invites us to stop thinking from a perspective of death being the gateway to Heaven. Instead, step fully into our "Past Death Experience"—the reality that we died, were buried, and rose with Christ. It challenges us to stop trying to "make the team" like a frantic underdog and realize we have already been suited up in the finished work of the Cross. Now, let's allow the questions of Jesus to cut through the noise of religious striving and open a conversation with your heart. We are not proving anything to the world; we are walking and learning to live as Living Beings who know the tomb is empty.

A Direct Conversation with Jesus

1. The Belief

"I am the resurrection and the life... And whoever lives and believes in Me shall never die. Do you believe this?" (John 11:25-26)

We often check the boxes of doctrine without letting the reality of Life change our biology and our mindset. In the chapter, we listed the victories Christ provided—Freedom, Wholeness, No Condemnation. Yet, like Rudy, we sometimes struggle just to get on the "scout squad" of faith. Before you strive for the next spiritual milestone, look at the finished work of the "folded napkin." Ask Him: *"Jesus, do I really believe this? Show me the specific area of my life where I am still acting like I am 'waiting' for Heaven, rather than living from Your resurrection life right now."* Listen for His assurance that death has indeed died.

2. The Logic

"If I have told you earthly things and you do not believe, how will you believe if I tell you heavenly things?" (John 3:12)

Nicodemus came at night, trying to understand the logic of the kingdom with a mind built for earthly systems. But Jesus invites us into "Quantum thinking"—where dirt and breath mingle to create a Living Being. You are designed to interact in both realms, physical and spiritual. In a quiet moment, ask Jesus: *"Lord, where is my logic limiting Your 'breath of life' in me? Open my spiritual eyes to see the heavenly things—the 'folded linens'—that reveal my restoration."* Listen for Him to breathe new understanding into your identity as a New Creation.

3. The Identity

"But who do you say that I am?" (Mark 8:29)

Rudy had to decide if he believed the critics who said he was "5 feet nothin'," or the dream inside him. Ultimately, your identity is anchored in who you believe Jesus is.

If He is the Living Bread and the Resurrection, then you are a co-heir and a participant in His victory. You don't have to prove nothin' to nobody—except to align with who He is. Ask Jesus: *"Who do You say that I am in light of Your resurrection? How does Your victory parade change the way I walk into a room today?"* Listen for the "sweet savor" of His affirmation over your life.

Reflect and Respond

Take a moment to record what you received in this time of conversation with Jesus. What did you hear? What did you feel? Let this be a record of your direct experience of His living presence.

____

____

____

____

Next Step

Over the next few days, carry the question that resonated with you the most. As you go about your day, whether you are "folding linens" or facing a challenge, practice listening for Jesus' voice reminding you of your Past Death Experience. Let the fragrance of His life be the only proof you need.

Prayer and Contemplation

Father, thank You for the "death of death." Thank You that I do not have to strive to earn my place on the team; Thank You for revealing how good You are and that You have already suited me up in righteousness. I choose to be filled with the breath of Your Spirit of Life today. I am ready for this—because You have made me ready. In Jesus' name, Amen.

____

PLAY SHEET | PROPHET

Prophet Edition
Redemptive Gifts Summary

THIS CHAPTER IS A HIGH-VELOCITY OFFENSIVE PLAY against the "Spirit of Death." It is a call for you to stop viewing your life through the lens of a finite timeline and to start living from the perspective of Immortality. It shifts the focus from a Near-Death Experience (NDE) to a Past Death Experience (PDE)—the reality that in Christ, you have already passed through death and are now playing from a position of eternal victory.

THE DNA WRISTBAND AUDIBLE: CHAPTER PLAY-CALL

1. **1. The Green Dot Helmet** *(Individual Redemptive Gift)*: **Prophet**

The frequency for this play is set to the Prophet. This is your gift of "Design and Eternal Perspective." You are hardwired to see the "end from the beginning." While the world is terrified of the "Final Whistle," the Prophet in you recognizes that you are already living in the "Post-Game" glory. You are being called to be Spiritually BRAVE enough to acknowledge that your "Old Self" is a Past Death Experience. You apply this gift by refusing to be managed by the fear of "running out of time," instead operating from the timeless "Blueprint" of your original design.

2. **The Coaches' Booth** *(Legacy Anchor)*: *The Shack* by William Paul Young

In the "Booths" of your spiritual legacy, *The Shack* (Prophet/Design) represents the intersection where your deepest trauma meets the "Great Resurrection." You apply this by realizing that the "Garden" of your heart isn't just a place for healing; it's a place of Immortality. This anchor reminds you that the Father, Son, and Spirit are not bound by your "earthly clock." Just as Mackenzie had to realize that his daughter wasn't "lost" but "present" in a different realm, you are applying this to your own grief. It proves that the "Chasm" of death has been bridged by a Relationship that never ends.

3. The Play-Call from God

"Child, check your helmet—I am speaking a 'Forever Frequency' into your spirit. I see you looking at the graveyard of your past mistakes, feeling the 'decay' of missed opportunities and the fear of the unknown. I am calling an audible: You are a PDE—a Past Death Experience! I watched My Son, Jesus, swallow up death in victory so that you would never have to 'near' it again.

You aren't a mortal trying to reach immortality; you are an immortal being, currently navigating a mortal field under transformation within the 'Restoration of All Things.' That is the C♡♡Lness of our Oneness. When you feel the

'anxiety of the end,' I want you to remember that the 'Spirit of Life' is your current atmosphere. Stop believing the lie that you are 'running out of time.' Your DNA is hardwired for Eternal Continuity. Be Spiritually BRAVE enough to walk through the 'veil' of your daily routine and realize that the kingdom is at hand. I am so good that I have removed the 'Sting' from the game. You are playing with house money now because the debt has been paid and life has been given. Run the play, Child. You aren't headed toward a sunset; you are living in an eternal dawn."

4. The Audible (The Timeline of Now)

The enemy wants you to remain "death-conscious," stuck in a loop of self-preservation. The Audible is this: *Death is a thing of the past!* Right now, on the timeline of today, I am removing the "Mortality Mindset" from your brain. I am releasing the power of Resurrection Awareness. You are not a victim of time; you are a King's Champion in the realm of the eternal. How Good is God!

REFORMATION DATA: THE ARCHITECTURE OF YOUR IMMORTALITY

• To understand the "field" you are playing on, consider how to apply these "PDE" principles to your own "Game Clock":

• **The PDE Reality:** In spiritual law, Romans 6:8 states, *"If we died with Christ, we believe we will also live with Him." Apply This:* Treat your "Old Man" (the scared, mad, angry version of you) as a historical casualty. You are the "New Creation" playing in the Post-Death Era.

• **Bypassing the "Near" Fear:** Most people live in "NDE" mode—scared of what happens when they get "near" failure or death. *Apply This:* Realize you are already on the other side. This removes the "Performance Anxiety" from your life because you cannot lose a game that has already been won.

• **Liquid Glory Continuity:** You apply this by practicing "Heavenly Consciousness." This isn't about "going to heaven" when you die; it's about bringing the Immortality of Heaven into your Monday morning. *Apply This:* When you realize the "Atmosphere is Thin," begin to see "Miracles" as simple "Native Tactics" of your true home.

HOW GOOD IS GOD!

Mercy does not just forgive the past; it remembers the beginning.

When the fear of the end is finally swallowed by the victory of the cross, the Father does not just hand you a trophy. He hands you a mirror.

He invites you to take a breath, step off the battlefield, and see what He has seen all along: your original design, perfectly intact, held safely in the quiet love of His Oneness.

Chapter 16

I Love It, Too!

The Blueprint to the First Estate

"The best way to predict your future is to create it."

— **Abraham Lincoln** | The 16th President of the United States, who led the nation through the Civil War and paved the way for the abolition of slavery.

> *For the creation waits with eager longing for the revealing of the sons of God. For the creation was subjected to futility, not willingly, but because of him who subjected it, in hope that the creation itself will be set free from its bondage to corruption and obtain the freedom of the glory of the children of God. (Romans 8:19-21 ESV)*

Does this mean the "devil" will be restored? Can you imagine anything more infuriating to the enemy than the Love of God? The simple way to look at it is in his original state: he was beautiful and highly trusted.

Ezekiel 28:12b-15 (God saying):
*'You were once the consummate model of perfection.
You were full of great wisdom, and your beauty seemed perfect.*

You lived in Eden, in the very garden of God.
Every precious jewel formed your mantle.
You were dressed in splendor with diamonds, carnelian, topaz, chrysolite, beryl, onyx, sapphire, turquoise, and emeralds; each gem engraved in settings of gold.
I, Yahweh, made them for you on the day I created you.
I placed you with an anointed guardian cherub.
You were on the holy mountain of God where you walked among the fiery stones.
Your ways were blameless from the day I created you.'

AN "*INSPIRED*" CANVAS FOR THINKING

In the profound geometry of the beginning, before time wore a shroud, We, Trinity, stood as the Divine Artists before the blank canvas of the cosmos. Think of Us as the Masters stretching the heavens like a ceiling, Our fingers poised in that Sistine moment of intentional touch.

Before We drew the blueprint of your DNA, We fashioned a masterpiece of light and reflection—Lucifer, the "Seal of Perfection." He was Our most intricate "Defensive Play" of beauty, a twin amplifier of sound and light, encrusted with every precious stone that had a few mirror tiles of Our own brilliance. We didn't just make him; We composed him. He was the Heavenly Tabernacle's first melody, a walking liturgy of glory, designed to be the guardian of the "active participation" in the heights of holiness.

But Our heart was not seeking a collection of mirror tiles that only reflected—We were seeking a Body that could respond.

Lucifer was the fresco, magnificent and fixed, but he became enamored with the "Logos" of his own splendor. He mistook the reflection for the Source. He settled into the pride of his own "Pew," forgetting that he was but a tuning fork for Our light. Even as his heart hardened into a "black sack" of self-will, Our gaze was already beyond him.

I was looking at you.

Before the foundation of the world, Trinity saw the cross-section of your life. We saw you not as a finished painting on a wall, but as a living, breathing extension of Our own Spirit. While the "anointed cherub" chose the isolation of his own imagined throne, We chose the Oneness of our shared breath. We knew that even if the light painted fell, We would descend to lay in the altar of your humanity, to unwrap you from the grave clothes of the fall, and to invite you into the "Tomorrowland" of Our eternal Goodness.

You are the masterpiece We were reaching for when We first stretched out Our hand.

Selah...

You can't tell me that God didn't have some form of affection for His original ornate design—a stunning being created specifically to spend his existence in a prominent position close to God.

We might as well add to the restoration list: Judas, war villains, creatures that have spirit, and maybe a member of your family? Just think, if people actually went to hell every time we (angry humans) said in haste, *"Go to hell..."*

Beings of light in all their marvelous forms—Angels, animals, mankind—have spirits.

What if God forgot your original or first estate?

Again, it's the behavior we choose that separates us from communion with God. He gives us the freedom to hold Him at arm's length.

- We don't acknowledge Him.
- We don't talk to Him.
- We don't believe in Him.

Now, the Son of God is revealed...

But the one who indulges in a sinful life is of the devil, because the devil has been sinning from the beginning. The reason the Son of God was revealed was to undo and destroy the works of the devil. (1 John 3:8 TPT)

In simple terms, the results of sinful works or sinful life were undone and destroyed.

Then what remains? The Restoration of All Things.

The choice to accept restoration... or bring forth restoration, for which the LOVE of God is patient and long in suffering.

I'm getting to my stories, but let's imagine and set a benchmark. Contend against death, decay, disease, and its infiltration within the fabrics we call life. Yes, seen and unseen, All Things—Mankind, including earth/creation/cosmos—just for a moment. Allow the imagination to see portions of life's tapestry restored.

Possible scenarios of your natural comings and goings, to stir the Goodness of God on the end of your "Sonship" paintbrush:

1. Camping Trips: You take your family on a well-deserved vacation camping into a national forest. Fathom no disease hanging off the trees. No more nasty "blooms" in green-blue water. Prior to the Restoration of All things, the forest was a patchwork of disease-laden trees fighting for light, stifled in the debris of slash piles. Now, it is a lush canopy above and below. And God saw that it was good.

2. Spot, Lassie, Lady, and Rex: Your faithful companions are not allergic to the earth. No dysplasia or chronic diseases. Take away the injections and edible chemicals we use to ward off pestilence and unending itching. Imagine no reason to inoculate your beloved pet from the ravages of pestilence. Ponder "man's" best friend, flourishing upon the earth according to its kind. And God saw that it was good.

3. Organic Divinely: The vegetable seeds you plant in the garden have not been chemically altered; the soil is full and fertile. Resulting in: No allergens or allergies to contend with. You can eat a crisp, sweet, and golden-yellow delicious apple right off the tree. The aquifers and ground waters are filled consistently by original weather patterns. Children and adults can literally enjoy bread in spirit and bread on their table.

The earth produces vegetation: seed-bearing plants according to their kinds and trees bearing fruit with seed according to their kinds. And God saw that it was good.

And what was our original divine to-do list?

What did Queen Adelaide say to a newly married Queen Victoria, from the movie *The Young Victoria*... "A man that has no work is ridiculous. Let him share your work!"

And God blessed them in his love, saying, "Reproduce and be fruitful! Populate the earth and subdue it! Reign over the fish of the sea, the birds of the air, and every creature that lives on earth." And God said, "I give you every seed-bearing plant growing throughout the earth, vegetables, and every fruit-bearing tree with its seed within itself. They will be your food. They will also be food for every animal and bird, and every creature that moves on the ground—every creature with the breath of life." And so it happened.

God surveyed all he had made and said, "I love it!" For it pleased him greatly. Evening gave way to morning—day six. (Genesis 1:28-31 TPT)

Maybe God is waiting for His kids to say, **"I love it, too!"**

On the other side of the veil, the first thing perceived for transformation is *you*. It is impossible to step through Christ as a door and not be altered by the threshold of the-WAY, the door named the-TRUTH (Himself), and the mystery of the-LIFE (Love has no timepiece).

You are transformed by the perception of your (has-always-been-perfect-spirit) "in God," and now you are on a cognitive quest with the Lord to bring truth into every portion of your being. In short, John 3:16 gets a little bit larger.

...that if you confess with your mouth the Lord Jesus and believe in your heart that God has raised Him from the dead, you will be saved. (Romans 10:9)

And *saving* takes on an unfathomable confession when we have taken off our grave clothes, honored the folded head linen of His Lordship, and begin to use the keys to the kingdom.

A BRIEF PEEK: TARTARUS AND THE AUTHOR'S INITIAL ENCOUNTER WITH THE GATES OF HELL

There is a well-respected book I talk about within our pages. A coined phrase: *Lunatic, Liar or Lord?* He is the King of Kings, Lord of Lords, lunatics, and liars. Whether our perceptions fall at any given time under His Kingship, it should be more than a crap game of parroted truth.

For God did not spare angels when they had sinned, but hurling them down to Tartarus consigned them to caves of darkness, keeping them in readiness for judgement. (2 Peter 2:4 Weymouth New Testament)

Other translations use the words: to the lower parts of hell, and committed them to chains of darkness.

I trust that in our prior chapters we have established a testament that the keys to the kingdom Jesus gave to us (You and I) open up inexhaustible wonders.

The first time the Lord held my hand and we descended to "lower realms," my understanding gathered it like a vintage black and white spooky movie. We walked down a circular flight of creepy stone stairs as if we were going down to a dungeon in a castle. It is a kingdom, and rightly so, there are "castles" (points of authority and rule). I'm with Jesus, so "spooky" or fearful feels empowered in faith, similar to a valiant David and vanquished Goliath.

Yes, it is arid; that seems to be consistent in my Sheol encounters. We bring the light into darkness. The gates of hell looked like a tall, man-made weathered wood ranch gate entry— On each side, connected to a weathered and falling-down split rail fence. The fence was so flimsy it wouldn't restrain any type of livestock. You can see desert for miles and miles; no one was there or guarding said entrance.

I'll let you just think on that for a bit...

In the moments of getting my spiritual bearings, as I shared earlier, the word picture of submarine sonar pinging is an extremely insightful metaphor. The gates of Hell encompass many different topographies and territories. In this instance, the horizon was made of misty shadows of hills, like looking across a valley on a foggy day. In a nanosecond, my spirit was allowed to see into the horizon, ever so briefly. My journal notes say: *a row of barred iron cages with snarling tigers or striped beings—beasts with massive teeth, quarreling and gnashing.*

That was it! I didn't recognize the place as Tartarus by scripture text for some time. But it stuck in my knowing for another day. That "knowing" has gathered a tremendous amount of "hours." Much like a pilot would accrue to master a Captain's wings and fly valuable cargo.

My "ah-ha" to share: *if Jesus has shared and revealed it, then we are commissioned at some point to restore it!*

A huge future day of heart transformation, where All Things are destined to be restored by the LOVE of God.

HERMAN: ETERNAL MOMENTS
You and I are curious sorts.
"It is the glory of God to conceal a matter; to search out a matter is the glory of kings."
— Proverbs 25:2

"I was merely thinking God's thoughts after Him. Since we astronomers are priests of the highest God in regard to the book of nature, it benefits us to be thoughtful, not of the glory of our minds, but rather, above all else, of the glory of God."

— Johannes Kepler | Mathematician and Astronomer who discovered the laws of planetary motion.

I will add to both these quotes: *God expects we will catch Him in the act.* He invites us to think His thoughts and find the matters He has concealed for us.

We all have threads in the same color scheme that stretch over the breastplate of our lives. Our struggles, our life lessons. The miraculous to tragic, a reoccurring bent that bends us. Life stories, intimate treasures like the skin of the heart, in the telling make one feel vulnerable as you expose the conversations in the spirit.

And this Author's story of "thinking His thoughts" and catching God in the act?

"You cannot hope to sweep someone else away by the force of your writing until it has been done to you."

— **Stephen King** | On Writing: A Memoir of the Craft

Now persuasion and every pleasurable expectation is completed in agape. (Here, in agape, my soul remembers who I am. Psalm 23). Faith, hope, and love are in seamless union. Agape is the superlative of everything faith and hope always knew to be true about me. Love defines my eternal moment. (1 Corinthians 13:13 TMT)

How would you respond if you caught someone standing in your way?

A million years ago, in the struggle of raising a young family, founding faith, and discovering the crazy hopes God has for you. What began in victories of faith turned round as we lost our auto repair business and our beloved second-generation Aurora Colony farm and farmhouse. A house that truly looked like me and my likes, with acres outstretched to teach the curiosities of life to a house full of testosterone. All my loves of British period yumminess with historic American pilgrimage—gone, lost, loved. We moved to Corvallis, Oregon, with our tails between our legs and a mess to re-establish ourselves financially. The wind had been knocked out of us.

Our challenge is not foreign to any of us. Each unique faith promise, once up in lights, is now a collection of half-blinking neon letters on a vintage marquee sign. Our trauma and our trust electrocuted. Our faith wires were broken and frayed. Shame and unworthiness on constant illumination as neon-faith, listless electrical cracking of insufficient power, and poor connection to the power source: God.

The Restoration of All Things is, a restoration of *All Things.*
He promises to restore: Lost Years, Health, Joy after suffering, Blessings, Prosperity through repentance, restoration of heart, restoration in the church, in family. Nehemiah (restoration of the wall), Isaiah (restoration of the foundations, ancient ruins). Restoration of relationships, after discipline, of the soul, renewal of strength, fortunes through confession, creation, property, prodigal sons restored, and the healing of the nations.

We have the "Choice" to partner with His promise, and allow curiosity to think His thoughts and finding matters to search out.

The first prophetic word given me from my husband Don... pretty HUGE for a Lutheran altar boy:

It shall be, if you will listen to all that I command you, and will walk in my ways, and do that which is right in my eyes, to keep my statutes and my commandments, as David my servant did; that I will be with you, and will build you a sure house, as I built for David, and will give Israel to you. (1 Kings 11:38 New Heart English Bible)

Sure House = The Hebrew word *bayith* primarily refers to a physical structure or dwelling place, such as a house or temple. It can also denote a household, including the family or lineage associated with a particular house. In a broader sense, "bayith" can symbolize a place of refuge, community, or worship. *(Berean Strongs 1004)*

You can never replace or augment a first. God sets principles from firsts.

As people of faith, we learn, continue to grow, and get familiar with the supernatural ways God orchestrates happenings. I never spoke or gave a prophetic word until one had been given to me.

The impact opened a door for learning. Laying on of hands was non-existent until healing was established in the doctrines of relationship with Him. Dreams were sleeping movies from eating too much pizza, or hauntings after an ugly argument with my husband. When I hungered for His voice, the instruments of conversation revealed their parts of the symphony's score. The unseen continues to unfold on an everlasting scroll.

A SHOPPING ENCOUNTER:
An early December day, delightfully alone, and doing some well-needed emotional shopping to detach from my computer. The OSU thrift store (college town) is an off-and-on charity shop haunt on my path of emotional enjoyment.

Their store hours aren't as copacetic with mine, like the Cat's Meow, Furniture Exchange, and Goodwill, which catch my attention on a regular basis. Who doesn't love the conquest thrill of a bargain? For me: Glass pretties, serving dishes, hardback books, and designer clothing—an easy find.

That day, I was snooping the lower shelves in the dish and glassware department. Moving bulbous serving dishes to see the hidden treasure stacked beneath, or opening the flap of clunky cardboard boxes which usually held the unwanted grocery store patterned china. Before moving on, I checked just one more box. Full stop! That looks familiar, hmm?

Down on my knees to pull the weighty box gingerly off the shelf and into the "light." It can't be? It is. I don't believe it. I start digging into the box: a gravy boat, eight dinner plates, three soup bowls, seven coffee cup saucers, and four coffee cups. Scalloped white edges with delicate 24-carat gold trim. I flipped over a dish to read the stamp: my Great Grandmother's Haviland China from France. The box said $35.00.

The rag-tag collection of dishes currently in my possession had been lovingly carried from our three-hundred-year-old family Iowa farm to the California shores after the depression. I have a handful of beloved pieces stored in Grandma's dark oak curio.

The box said $35.00 and so the firm conversation began. "But God, but God, I know this is a miracle just for me." But God and what about this: it is December. Christmas is just around the corner and I'm supposed to spend $35.00 on me and lower my checking account to less than ten bucks!

I have had this "faith" argument before; it's a bit futile. The miracle won out. Half-heartedly, I shared my find with the cashier, a mature alumni volunteer, as she zipped my debit card through the machine while wrapping the loose dishes in tissue.

In the backseat of our trusty white Subaru wagon, I secured the box safely, strapped myself into the driver's seat, and breathed a huge exhale! With the same release of long-suffering breath, I asked: "Father, why do I need a twelve-piece place setting of my Great Grandmother's China when I live in a humble 1964 ranch house?"

He responded, *"Kristen, you are going to need them."*

The word was need, not want, or to bless you—*need!*

Two weeks later, the charity shop encounter repeated itself at the Cat's Meow, the local Humane Society Thrift Store. I'm thinking that particular estate sale shared the community wealth. How many people have a turn-of-the-century china set from France, intact? And the same pattern! This time the box was $30.00 and I didn't hesitate.
Several Months had gone by.

I had a dream. Valiantly I kicked out a slimy, short Mario-car-guy entity that had set up house in something that God said was mine. In the dream, we had just moved in. I could feel it. The aah, Oh, the *mine*. I remember that sensation, just the same way I described the second-generation farm house a paragraph ago. It looked like me, it smelled like me, and it was God making me smile. Catching Him in the act so to speak, He was healing a place in my heart by reminding me that He had not forgotten our conversation of why?
He used words in the dream to describe the house that were secret *double 007* words, hidden between Him and I. Curiosity in action, I got out of bed, journaled the encounter, and the next morning I googled the *"double 007"* words. God uses Google, love it. And there she was. In the nanoseconds it takes Google to gather said search, she poked her pretty head with a smiling real-estate listing. *Mum is the word.*

For the curious ones, yes I have that story written in book form with all the juicy and detailed lovelies. But this book is about what you believe, helping you live Spiritually BRAVE. God wants you to see yourself written in the nuances and truth stories of this epistle.

He has *double 007* words hidden here for you. Secret words from you to Him, and the "hidden-in-your-heart" response from Him to you.

Mum's the word; we weren't even looking, not in the market. I'll give you a hint: God's restoration is *always* on the market.

So, with a secret on my lips, telling no one, I carried it in my heart for thirty days.

Bam, *a dream avalanche;* other people dreaming about and for you, avalanche. The dearest of friends' spirits are seeing God's prophetic word about you; in this instance, they were inside our "Sure" house, describing the rooms. A dream landslide. The glass pane from this open window of heaven was dripping her essence.

My turn again: During that morning's devotion time with the Lord, He took my spirit on a journey. This time into the realms of the earth, the here and now, or should I say, within your own timeline of seeing the "Possibilities" of your future.

P.S. on seeing your future: your footsteps and choices have to be moving on the same Oneness path.

Catching Him in the act: This was not the first time I had been inside this particular house—another divine real estate showing from the Lord. This will make you laugh. The first time the Lord and I met in the kitchen for communion, I remember saying, "Lord, aren't we in somebody's house? If they discover us, isn't this going to creep them out?" Jesus just laughed at me. If anybody knows about covenants and ownership graces, it's Jesus. He said, *"Kristen, we just stepped in ahead of time; you are the owner."*

But today, we are visiting a particularly special room. OMG. We stepped into a large warm light, a long room decorated for an occasion. Daylight shined through a north-looking, large diamond-leaded glass paned picture window.

The ceiling was high, lit by two twinkling crystal chandeliers, decorated with garlands, hanging over an extended dining room table laid with beautiful white linens, vases filled with flowers, and room for at least twelve chairs.

I could feel the Lord's smile warming from behind me as my spirit paid attention. Honing in on the exquisite table decor, which, by the way, is just my cup of tea, when emotion kissed recognition...

Like the front cover of my favorite *Victoria Magazine,* there lay in all her glory my Great Grandmother's Haviland China. Laid, ready, just as if I had prepared the table for guests myself. Perfect. I think I cried off and on throughout the entire day, and I am feeling a bit misty-eyed telling you.

Just a hint: encountering the kingdom of Heaven is not necessarily chronological; that is what journaling is for. Just like Genesis, there is an account of how God made it and then there is an account of how God shared it with man.

Do you remember my question at the beginning of this story?

How would you respond if you caught someone standing in your way?

Just hold onto that thought, as the story begins to put weight on certain "Promises" in your own heart and you understand how much this means between God and me.

Pièce de résistance: the best part of the meal.

Up to now, Mum has been the word. It's my Mary moment; she hid these crazy, impossible things in her heart.

It's time for a little solo drive to the countryside of faith. Address in hand, beyond excited, shaking in my boots, with the big HOW Lord?

That morning we had a light dusting of snow. Trees were silver-lined and country roads had single-tire mark definitions. The real-estate sign made it an easy find. I slowed my speed and pulled into the driveway at a snail's crawl. Prior curiosity training had educated me on the signs of a vacant house. Parked a bit out of the way, still moving slow, keeping an ear open for a holler, "You're trespassing!" Felt at peace, that it was just the Lord and I.

Now I could enjoy her beauty: three stories, British period yummies dripping in her architecture. It was quite evident that she had been sitting neglected for some time.

The English flower garden tipped in the morning silver temperatures, overgrown; unkempt fruit trees with long, long limbs and the bless-ed wild Oregon blackberry stretching at great lengths, slowly covering her crown. She was in desperate need of love, elbow grease, and a family who expressed a wee bit of hospitality. Glad I wore my rubber boots and wool socks, which made it easier to step into the jungle-like flower beds and stand tip-toe to peek into the windows. My breath-out misted the diamond-shaped glass as I peeked through a single pane inside the northern window.

Once again emotion kissed recognition when I spotted two crystal chandeliers. The dining room floor plan was exactly as I had encountered in the spirit, directionally and architecturally. More tears. What I can say at this moment is, I love the Lord's attention to detail.

Now, I have to get to the point of this chapter and the rest of the story will have to wait. Over the course of the adventure, God wrapped His supernatural around people we invited to see her: real estate agents, "same named" young adults from the surrounding community, odd happenstance. Every time we stepped foot on the property, something amazing happened. We made two offers on her, both turned down. Yes, persuasive and on-bent-knee letters written to the owner. God even orchestrated a crazy one-on-one meeting with the owner, and still, face-to-face, the answer was no. Her agent was fit to be tied. Our house sold a few months later for less than we had offered for her.

Take heart, God's not done yet and neither am I. He Guarantees there is a "rest of the story."

THE GIANT ON THE ROAD
Now what about that question: totally the reason for our Restoration of All Things story.

How would you respond if you caught someone standing in your way?
Having discovered how thoroughly God sanctified us in Christ, we now represent the principle of righteous judgment wherewith the whole world is to be judged; how can we possibly shrink from deciding trivial matters within our own ranks? If the judgment we are entrusted with extends even into the spiritual realm where we are to judge celestial messengers, how much more relevant is our judgment now in deciding on day-to-day matters. (1 Corinthians 6:2-3 Message)

Herein lies the shaking of my heart: *ALL Things!*

I set a reminder in my phone of the day the sale recorded at the county assessors. Annually the reminder triggers the best of the best. The best of God and best of me. I Am growing in Oneness. An early Saturday morning rise to write these words; His divine screen dropped into my spirit while tidying the kitchen, waiting for the coffee to brew. On my notations, I found 166 search tags in my digital journal as of today. One hundred and sixty-six times God has revealed us living life within her walls. Tag 11/23/24 in case you ask me when we meet.

Reader and writer share a universal experience of a ticker-tape parade of thoughts: *"I don't understand"* printed on each shredded strand, falling from the firmaments above. The pain is easier dealt with when framed like this: *measurement of understanding from the school of life has not yet educated me on. The "Fault" line is blurred.*

I've dusted myself off on a few occasions, and in the spirit, set up a blue camping chair on the road, centered in front of the driveway. Determined, there I sat and began to read back to the Lord my one hundred sixty and counting "Sure House" encounters.

Time marched on and eventually my spirit didn't wake up sitting in the camping chair. It became a sticky note on the upper corner of my computer and a battle-board collage, hanging front and center from the room divider (podcasting sound dampener) directly in front of my desk. A year has passed, my spirit is wrestling, and God consistently fuels my determination. Don and I are dreaming in tandem, learning to "Rule & Reign 101." Seated in "Heavenly Places 101!"

Now for those compassionate souls that say, "What about the Current Owner? How does his story layout in the matter?" Blessings, dear one, blessings. It's all part of trusting God's plan and speaking blessing that the windows of heaven are moving on their behalf... they have no idea that God invited them or blessed them to be on my prayer card. Restoration of All Things!

That morning, I must have asked the question differently, or maybe my "surrender screen" was laying prostrate on the floor of less-self. Father, with question mark tone, stationed in my blue camping chair: "Tell me what You see?"
Clear as a bell I heard: *GIANT!*
My surrender-screen still in focusing mode. Out loud I say, "I see Us, God. That's odd." I'm looking at a large, Eiffel Tower-sized being, facing west (towards the coast), feet straddled over the country road. Standing in front of our "Sure House." The day is clear, sky bright blue. Is the mass Us? What am I perceiving?

I pushed it on its shoulder. Nope, not us. *It snarled at me.*

My spiritual ears tuned in. The cloaked being. Suited in armor, he has a javelin (scepter) in his hands. Snakes in his hair, with papers stabbed on the point of his javelin-spear, which he proceeded to eat in front of me. Ugly, ugly, ugly. I think he has a side job of acting in those sci-fi horror movies. Racking my brain library of heavenly experiences...
Can't say that I have encountered a giant on the earth? Dragons and demons, but a Giant? In the spirit on my mountain, yes, and why straddled here, at my "Sure House?"
Thank you, Father, for clueing me in. *What is the course for removal?*

Before we step before the Courts of Heaven, we receive counsel from God, make sure we have clear permission, and then discuss strategies. There is always a legal right (like those papers consumed) why any being/entity can freely enter, obstruct, torment, or usurp authority. Restoration includes de-throning the usurper and establishing the kingdom.

This particular heavenly court case had roots (two missing pages) in the Heavenly Book of Oregon. Our "Sure House" has roots on the historic Oregon Trail and land deeds. Agreements were established between the government, development of infrastructure, waterways, railroads and the like, Church and State. I found a School Bill 1920 separating church and state and the presence of the Ku Klux Klan in Oregon.

Legislation in the Kingdom is fascinating, enlightening, and empowering. Every son and daughter has legal authority to represent their sphere of influence. The kingdom of Heaven is a King's dominion! Giants steal inheritance. Dragons pollute thrones. Principalities are false princes. Powers usurp authority.

For we wrestle not against flesh and blood, but against principalities, against powers, against the rulers of the darkness of this world, against spiritual wickedness in high places. (Ephesians 6:12 KJV)

Time to contend, Church!

It took a few days in the spirit to sleuth the violations, hold the court case, and get a judgment to uproot this Giant. I remember one morning, both of us—Big bad guy and me—had been hunkered in, in roughly the same location, and he "un-straddled the road" like a person dismounts a horse.

I didn't want him to escape before I had the opportunity to get to the bottom of what exactly he was doing there. I threw spiritual chains around him and gagged him. That ought to hold him!

In prior spiritual wrestling applications, or at least how I was taught to deal with the "dark-side": cut off the head of a Giant and draw and quarter a dragon, retrieving what "she" (never encountered a male dragon???) had consumed.

Sounds like a video game, doesn't it? Encounter first, then ask questions has served me well. The unseen isn't a dimension of gases and floating mist.

Processes of the Heart.

For every "Accusation" there is an "Exoneration" exchange of "Self." In plain English, to be exonerated is to be declared innocent. It is different from a "pardon" (which forgives a crime) or an "acquittal" (which says there wasn't enough evidence to convict). Exoneration says: *"The accusation was wrong from the start. You or the whomever didn't do it."*

Jesus' blood is the best "magic eraser" in the kingdom. Forgiveness is a powerful force in the Kingdom. As a legislator of "His" dominion, your heart is an "instrument" before a "Righteous Judge" or mercy seat of the Lord and His Witness. A Legal "Communion," removing errors of the flesh and giving justice to the voice of blood. Self is a defense mechanism for both sides. The courts of heaven have proven the most humbling witness of, How Good is God!

He, the "ugly being," is shackled and chained at my doing. I now have papers in my hands that say his rights, in this instance, are dismantled. *Here is a hint for curiosity:* the spiritual history mirrors the broken history of every previous owner. Rightfully, isn't this the part where we pull the trigger and rid ourselves of him ever doing this again to anyone?

Sword... or savior?

Logos, extracted logic, or Rhema, the frequency of love? "Self" is not the same "Self" that wrestled for right-standing. Haven't I been sitting under the tutelage of a King in the classroom of the Restoration of ALL Things?

One hundred and sixty-six "Sure House" subject tags (and counting)—words, notations, dreams, visions, real happenstances with real people, encounter stories. *Either I believe and begin to respond or sign up for the same class again.*

You can feel me rolling my eyes at the futility of the situation. Dreams and desires versus the verses!!! Unfathomable, fictional, video game story.

In the spirit, after brilliant days of spiritual surrender over a house—a promise of personal restoration that looks like me —I kicked that blue camping chair aside. I looked into the eyes of this nasty principality. I knew I had his number. With nothing but a "gut instinct" full of love... I considered my original response and behavior: to chain, bind, punish, threaten, manipulate. He could spit in my eye, get off scot-free, begone and be bad, and all this would be for naught.

What do you want to happen? How Good is God?

I reached out and unlocked the chains that held him—the rigid shackles I had forged out of my own need to "deal" with what he had done. For so long, I had held the key "of my RIGHTS," using it to punish, bind, and manipulate. I had treated him like a principality in the army of darkness, a captive to be threatened rather than a glorious being to be restored.

But this was a first of firsts on the intercessor's restoration roster.

It would take ten thousand words to describe the transformation. It was as if the "ugly" melted like wax in a furnace, and the "snake-hair" lies of the accuser vanished to reveal a face that always sees God. I watched as his hardened body was zapped by a lightning strike of the Grace I shared; his armor was re-forged in the fires of love, and the internal tattoos of the "wrong team" were lasered away by the sheer brilliance of the Light.

In an instant, the creature bound by the false promises of the enemy, enlistment papers of doom, my own hard bindings —gone. In his place stood the being God created for a noble cause and royal service—fully arrived back into his "First-Estate." If I could truly capture the weight of that restoration, the words would explode right off this page. *Selah!*

For days I grinned, laughed, and pondered the magnitude of God's plan. The sheer grace revealed to me, the How Good is God kind of love, that actually can make headway in the sound of creation's groan.

Herman, in the months that followed, returned to me the influences that he had stolen. He continues to partner on assignments, with a strong blueprint on the heavenly lives of aborted children. He shows up when I am struggling and treats me like an admiral in a royal army.

Yes God, we Love it Too!

Together we have multiplied this First!

"To do things you've never done before,
you have to do things you've never done before."

— **Sean Payton** | A Super Bowl-winning NFL head coach, widely recognized for his offensive brilliance and for transforming the New Orleans Saints into a championship franchise.

THE ANATOMY OF AN UNFETTERED HEART
In the "Schools of Jesus' Humanity," we often start by learning how to defend ourselves. We learn to bind, to rebuke, and to build walls against the "ugly giants" that straddle our path. But there is a higher classroom—a place where the Restoration of All Things becomes more than a doctrine. It becomes a decision.

I found myself in a "blue camping chair" moment, staring at a principality that had been consuming the "papers" of my inheritance. He was armored, snarling, and entrenched. My first instinct—the one we've all been coached in—was to chain him. I threw spiritual shackles around him, gagged him, and held the key of my "rights" firmly in my hand. I wanted him to pay for the "slim pickings" and the lost years.

The Pivot: From Jailer to Restorer
But here is the heart-evaluation for every intercessor: Are you holding a sword or a Savior? Are you extracting logic (Logos) to prove you are right, or are you releasing the frequency of love (Rhema) to make things new?

For days, I wrestled with the futility of the chains. Then, I caught God in the act. I looked past the "snake-hair" lies and the sci-fi horror of the giant's appearance and asked, "Papa, tell me what You see?"

He showed me the First-Estate. He showed me the "Seal of Perfection" that had been obscured by eons of rebellion.

The Moment of Exoneration
The transformation of my own heart had to happen before the transformation of the unseen could begin. I had to surrender my need to punish. I reached out and unlocked those rigid shackles—the ones I had forged out of my own fear and self-defense.

As I turned the key, a *"first of firsts"* occurred on my restoration roster.

It was as if the "ugly" melted like wax in a furnace. A lightning strike of Grace zapped the hardened exterior, re-forging his armor in the fires of Love. I watched as the "wrong team" tattoos were lasered away by the sheer brilliance of the Light. In an instant, the creature I had feared was gone, and in his place stood a being of noble cause and royal service.

Your testimony is not a spectator sport. Every struggle you face is a "divine classroom" designed to educate your Captain's wings. If you find yourself holding a key today, evaluate the weight of it in your hand.
- Is your heart a "Jailhouse" or a "Garden"?
- Are you willing to believe that the "Restoration of All Things" includes the very thing that is currently standing in your way?

When you choose Exoneration over Accusation, you unlock a dimension of the Kingdom where the "ugly" is just a veil waiting to be melted. You move from the 20-yard line of survival to the place where you can finally say to the Father, **"I love it, too!"**

ACTIVATION

The First Estate
REFLECT & RESPOND
We often spend our prayer life asking God to fix what is broken. But the First Estate is not about fixing; it is about remembering what was perfect.

- **Reflect:** If God designed you before the foundations of the earth, that means there is a version of you that exists *outside* of your trauma, your mistakes, and your history.
- **Respond:** Take a moment to stop "fixing" yourself. Instead, imagine sitting with the Father looking at the original blueprints of your life. Can you agree with Him? Can you look at His design for you and say, *"I love it, too"*?

DIRECT CONVERSATION WITH JESUS

- **The Question:** *"Jesus, take me back to the beginning. Show me what You saw when You first made me, before the world touched me. What did You love about me then, and how is that present now?"*
- **The Listening:** (Wait for a memory, a feeling, or a word that affirms your original design.)

THE PRAYER

"Father, I align myself with the Blueprint. I step out of the timeline of my mistakes and into the First Estate of Your design. I agree with what You wrote about me in Your book. You said it was good, and today, I choose to agree. I love it, too. Amen."

PLAY SHEET | PROPHET

Prophet Edition
Redemptive Gifts Summary

This final surge is designed to move you from the "Red Zone" of skepticism into the high-frequency momentum of the **Exhorter**.

It is a call for you to stop trying to out-think the mysteries of your life and to start leaning into the *Quantum Reality* that your victory is already a finished work.

THE DNA WRISTBAND AUDIBLE: CHAPTER PLAY-CALL

1. **The Green Dot Helmet** (*Individual Redemptive Gift*): **Prophet** The frequency for this play is set to the Prophet. This is your gift of "Design and Blueprint." You are hardwired to see the "Seal of Perfection" in every creature and situation, even when they are covered in "snake-hair" lies and "ugly" armor. The Prophet in you is being activated to look past the current "behavior" and see the original First-Estate canvas. You are being called to be Spiritually BRAVE enough to "catch God in the act" of restoration, moving beyond the 20-yard line of defense into the offensive strike of Agape Love.

2. **The Coaches' Booth** (*Legacy Anchor*): *The Shack* by William Paul Young In the "Booths" of your spiritual legacy, The Shack (Prophet/Design) represents the Logic of the Garden. You apply this anchor by realizing that, like Mackenzie, your "Great Sadness" often frames God as a "Jailer" who merely manages the mess.

However, the reasoning for this chapter is found in the pivot: God isn't seeking "mirror tiles" that just reflect His glory, but a Body that can respond with its own love. This anchor proves that the "Restoration of All Things" isn't a theological debate; it's the choice to stop mistaking the reflection of your pain for the Source of your Light.

By seeing from the Trinity's perspective, you realize that if God can restore the Garden in Mack's heart, He can restore the "Sure House" and the "First-Estate" in yours.

3. The Play-Call from God

"Child, check your helmet—I am speaking the 'Frequency of the First-Estate' into your spirit. I see you sitting in your 'blue camping chair' on the road of your future, staring at the 'Giants' that are straddling your path and eating your inheritance. I am calling an audible: Unlock the chains! I watched My Son, Jesus, descend into the lower parts of hell not to join the gnarling and quarreling, but to retrieve the keys and restore the captives. You aren't a 'Jailer' meant to bind and punish; you are a Restorer of the Breach. That is the C♡♡Lness of our Oneness. When you feel the

'stuttering electrical wires' of your frayed faith, I want you to remember the 'Haviland China' I hid in the thrift store just for you. Stop believing the lie that the 'ugly' in your life is permanent. Your DNA is a symphony of Our shared breath. Be Spiritually BRAVE enough to choose Exoneration over Accusation. I am so good that I can melt the armor of a principality with a single lightning strike of My Grace. I am waiting for you to look at the lush canopy of My restored creation and say, 'I love it, too!' Run the play, Child. The 'Sure House' is built, the table is laid with your Great Grandmother's dishes, and the guest list is ready."

4. The Audible (The Timeline of Now) The enemy wants you to remain "shadow-conscious," stuck in a loop of binding and rebuking what I have already destined for renewal. The Audible is this: Radical Restoration! Right now, on the timeline of today, I am removing the "Thinking Text" of judgment from your mind. I am releasing the power of Agape Transformation. You are not just looking at the Light; you are the Portal where the Light breaks into the earth. How Good is God!

REFORMATION DATA: THE ARCHITECTURE OF YOUR UNFETTERED HEART

To understand the "field" you are playing on, consider how to apply these "First-Estate" principles to your own "Sure House":

The Blue Chair Strategy: You apply this by "Taking a Seat" in front of your promises and reading back your "Sure House" encounters to the Lord. *Apply This:* This builds the Momentum of your faith and shifts your "Ticker-tape" thoughts from "I don't understand" to "I am catching Him in the act."

Exoneration vs. Pardon: You apply the Higher Law by realizing that the Blood of Jesus doesn't just "forgive" the accusation—it says the accusation was wrong from the start. *Apply This:* to your own *"Double 007"* secret words, allowing the "Magic Eraser" of the Kingdom to clear your history.

Restoring the "Giant": You apply this by looking at the thing standing in your way and asking, "Papa, what do You see?" *Apply This*: By releasing the Rhema frequency of Love, you move from a "Lesser Law" of binding to a "Higher Law" of restoring the original design.

HOW GOOD IS GOD!

THE HOLY HUDDLE

"Finally, my brethren, be strong in the Lord and in the power of His might... having done all, to stand." — Ephesians 6:10, 13 (NKJV)

We have seen the Blueprint. We have tasted the Goodness. Now, we gather our strength.

The journey has been long, but the destination is clear. This is the moment where the "First Estate" meets the final drive.

Do not let the urgency of the clock distract you from the peace of the plan. We do not run with panic. We run with **Purpose**.

Lock eyes with the Captain. Catch your breath. The whistle is about to blow.

Chapter 17

The Two-Minute Warning: Pigskins of Life

"You win with people, not with talent."

— Woody Hayes | Legendary head coach at Ohio State University (1951-1978), known for winning five national championships and 13 Big Ten titles.

THE CLOCK IS TICKING: THE TWO-MINUTE WARNING The scoreboard reads: DOUBT (28) vs. FAITH (28). The clock stops. You hear the deafening silence of 70,000 (Heavenly) fans holding their breath. It's the two-minute warning. You're holding the ball—the "pigskins of life"—the unresolved questions, the silent prayers, the moments where God's goodness seemed to walk off the field.

You've fought hard, pushing past the Gates of Hell with Rhema thought, weathering the stifling defense of past hurt and misunderstanding. You've broken free from the rigid narratives of the Pew and the Pulpit, but now, standing in the truth of Our Oneness, the ultimate pressure is on. Can you trust God in the red zone of your life? Is He really good enough to deliver a win when the answers are nowhere in sight?

The game isn't over, but it feels tied, and you're exhausted. This isn't the time for a time-out; it's the time for a Game Plan.

COACH'S HUDDLE: FAMOUS FOOTBALL WISDOM In this crucial moment, we look to the wisdom of the legends—those who know how to turn a tied game into a historic victory. Let these famous coach quotes be your rally cry, your new play-calling strategy:

In Him, all the fullness of Deity resides in a human body. He proves that human life is tailor-made for God. (The word, Deity, theotes, godhead/deity, is feminine. Jesus exhibits what the Father, Son and Spirit is like, in human form. The word resides, katoikeō means to dwell in, to inhabit. While the expanse cannot measure or define God, their detailed likeness is displayed in human skin. We are complete in Him. Jesus mirrors our wholeness and endorses our true identity. He is "I am" in us.) — Apostle Paul | Colossians 2:9-10 (Mirror Study Bible with commentary)

1. **On Persistence (The Ground Game)**

"You win with people, not with talent."

— **Woody Hayes** | (1913–1987) was a legendary American college football coach

• *The Play:* Stop relying on your own talent (or effort) to solve the mysteries of God. Victory comes from connecting with the Person of Jesus, the very essence of God's goodness. The persistent ground game is about relational knowing, not intellectual solving.

2. **On Facing Doubt** (The "Ego" Defense)

"The will to win is important, but the will to prepare is vital."

— **Joe Paterno** | Legendary head coach at Penn State (1966-2011), the winningest major-college coach in history.

• *The Play:* Ego suited-up in doubt and unanswered questions is a powerful defense. The preparation isn't about finding the answers; it's about conditioning your heart—it's practicing Communion and Stillness—so that when the pressure hits, your instinct is to run toward, not away from, the Coach (Jesus).

3. On Taking Action (The Charge Forward)

"When you get to the end zone, act like you've been there before."

— Vince Lombardi

The Play: This is a call to Sonship—to knowing Who Jesus says that I AM? over What would Jesus do? You already have the DNA of a winner (a child of God). Charge forward. As a Son or Daughter, stop hoping for a future victory; you already carry the access code. Heaven is your current residence—a reality secured by your identity—and this end zone is merely the next room you walk into. *God is fully at home in him. "Coach" Jesus exhibits God's happy delight to be human. (Delightful intent, "So spacious is he, so roomy, that everything of God finds its proper place in him without crowding." — The Message.)*

The Reflection: As "Coach" Jesus is fully at home in you. You are His address!

He initiated the reconciliation of all things to himself. Through the blood of the cross God restored the original harmony. His reign of peace now extends to every visible thing upon the earth as well as those invisible things which are in the heavenly realm. (The heavens, a place of elevation, a mountain, to lift, to raise, to elevate, "Not only that, but all the broken and dislocated pieces of the universe, people and things, animals and atoms, get properly fixed and fit together in vibrant harmonies, all because of his death." — The Message.) — Colossians 1:19-20 (Mirror Study Bible with commentary)

THE HAIL MARY: TYING UP THE UNANSWERED QUESTIONS A Hail Mary isn't just a desperate toss; it's a throw of absolute, unreserved faith into the hands of a receiver you trust will be there. Our Hail Marys are the "pigskins" of life—the things we can't control or understand. Let's tie them up:

• *The Pigskin of "Why?"*: The greatest unanswered question. Tie this up with the truth of How Good is God! *When you can't see the reason, choose to see the nature.* God doesn't need to explain His goodness; He just needs to display it. His character is the ultimate resolution.

• *The Pigskin of Identity:* The struggle between what the world says and what you feel. Tie this up with the revelation of Oneness with Jesus. The victory isn't about earning your purpose; it's about realizing your unity with Him. When the 'I AM' of God meets your 'I AM' identity, the game changes.

• *The Pigskin of Future Fear:* The anxiety of the next down. Tie this up with the power of Quantum Thinking (The reality that, in the Spirit, the future is as accessible as the past, and both serve the present moment of Christ's finished work). Stop playing the game linearly, only reacting to what's in front of you. Begin to operate from a place of finished faith, where the victory is already secured in the realms of creation. See the touchdown before you run the play.

• THE FINAL DRIVE: GETTING THE PIGSKIN ACROSS THE GOAL LINE You have two minutes. The play-calling is simple: We are moving the ball through Relational Discernment—hearing the Rhema Mind (the Spirit's voice) over the Logos Mind (the logical, rule-bound mind).

• 1st Down: Develop Your Spiritual Senses. This is your quick slant route. Stop relying solely on your physical sight and logic. Ask Jesus, *"What do You see right now?"* Engage the senses of your spirit.

• 2nd Down: Live Spiritually BRAVE. This is your power run up the middle. You are called to be Bold, Ready, Authentic, Valuable, and Empowered. The defense of doubt hates a player running full speed.

• 3rd Down: Take a Radical Step of Obedience. This is your tight spiral pass. Don't wait for certainty; act on the next small instruction you hear from the Coach. Faith is the forward motion; let the clarity catch up with the momentum. What if we had to kick a punt? What if the ball was intercepted? And it was time to call in Special Teams!

• 4th Down: Restoration of All Things. This is the final plunge into the end zone. The ultimate confidence that gets the pigskin across the goal line is not that you have solved God, but that you are a part of *What's my part: Restoration of All Things.* Your part is simply to believe in the goodness of God enough to run the play He calls. CONCLUSION The whistle blows. The final score is FAITH (35) vs. DOUBT (28). You didn't get all the answers, but you got the win. You realized the goodness of God isn't found in the resolution of your problems, but in the presence of the Coach on the sideline. Now, take the final step across the goal line and truly experience Heaven—not after the game, but right here, right now.

ACTIVATION

The whistle has blown. The game is tied. You are standing in the Two-Minute Warning of your own life. The questions ("pigskins") are heavy in your hands. This activation is about executing the final drive—moving from "hoping" for a win to "walking" in the victory.

A Direct Conversation with Jesus

1. The Ground Game (Persistence) "You win with people, not with talent." You have been trying to "talent" your way through this season—using your intellect, your strength, your resources. Jesus is calling for a ground game of relationship. Ask Him: *"Lord, where have I been relying on my 'talent' to solve a problem instead of Your presence? I am handing off the ball to You.* Show me what it looks like to win this down with 'people' (connection with You) rather than effort."

2. The Preparation (Communion) "The will to prepare is vital." The pressure of the Two-Minute Warning reveals your preparation. If you feel panic, it's a signal to return to the locker room of Communion. Ask Him: *"Jesus, I feel the pressure of [Name the Situation]. I am calling a time-out right now to prepare my heart. As I take a moment of stillness, remind me of Who resides in me. I am Your address. Make Yourself at home in my anxiety and displace it with Your peace."*

3. The End Zone (Identity) *"Act like you've been there before."* You are not a rookie; you are a Son/Daughter. You have the DNA of the King. Ask Him: *"Lord, I am charging forward. I am stepping into the End Zone of [Name the Promise or Desired Outcome]. I choose to act like I belong here. What is the one 'Radical Step of Obedience' (3rd Down) You are asking me to take today to prove that I believe the victory is already mine?"*

Reflect and Respond

Take a moment to record the "Play Call" you received. What is the specific audible God called for your life right now?

____

____

____

____

Next Step

Identify one "Pigskin" (unanswered question) you have been carrying. Write it down on a piece of paper. Literally ball it up like a football. Now, physically throw it—a "Hail Mary"—and declare: *"I am tying this up with the goodness of God. I trust the Receiver."*

Prayer and Contemplation

Father, thank You that the clock is never truly running out on me because I live in the "Forever Frequency" of Your love. I thank You that even when the score feels tied, You have already secured the win. I choose to run the play. I choose to trust the Coach. And I choose to cross the goal line with my head high, knowing that Heaven is my home field. In Jesus' name, Amen.

PLAY SHEET | EXHORTER

Exhorter Edition
Redemptive Gifts Summary

THE TWO-MINUTE WARNING: PIGSKINS OF LIFE
This chapter is the ultimate "Rally Cry." It is designed to mobilize the team when the energy is low and the stakes are high. It speaks the language of the Exhorter—the gift of "Encouragement" and "Mobilization." The Exhorter is the one who can look at a tired team and say, "We are not done yet!" This chapter is the spark plug that ignites the final drive.

THE DNA WRISTBAND AUDIBLE: CHAPTER PLAY-CALL

1. **The Green Dot Helmet** (Individual Redemptive Gift): **Exhorter** The frequency for this play is set to the Exhorter. This is your gift of "Influence" and "Reality."

2. **You are hardwired to bridge the gap between the "Playbook"** (theory) and the "Field" (reality). The Exhorter in you is being activated to take the "Pigskins" of life—the messy, unresolved issues—and turn them into fuel for the next drive. You are being called to be Spiritually BRAVE enough to "Act like you've been there before," leading yourself and others across the goal line not with perfection, but with momentum.

3. **The Coaches' Booth** (Legacy Anchor): Famous Football Wisdom In the "Booths" of your spiritual legacy, the voices of Hayes, Paterno, and Lombardi serve as the "Cloud of Witnesses." You apply this anchor by realizing that you are part of a long lineage of victors. The wisdom of the "Coach" is the Exhorter's greatest tool. When you feel the pressure of the Two-Minute Warning, you don't need a new theology; you need a "Word in Season." These quotes remind you that the principles of victory—Persistence, Preparation, and Identity—are universal constants in the Kingdom.

4. **The Play-Call from God**

"Child, check your helmet—I am shouting the 'Victory Chant' into your spirit. I see you looking at the scoreboard, calculating the odds, and feeling the weight of the 'Tie Game.' I am calling an audible: The Clock is Mine! I watched My Son, Jesus, run the ultimate Two-Minute Drill on the cross so that you would never have to fear the final whistle. You aren't a 'Spectator' hoping for a win; you are the 'Star Player' carrying the ball of My Glory. That is the C♡♡Lness

of our Oneness. When you feel the 'defense of doubt' closing in, I want you to remember that I have given you the

'Special Teams' of Heaven—the Restoration of All Things. Stop believing the lie that the game is over just because you are tired. Your DNA is hardwired for the Fourth Quarter Comeback. Be Spiritually BRAVE enough to throw the 'Hail Mary' of your unanswered questions to Me. I am the Receiver who never drops the ball. I am so good that I have already painted 'VICTORY' in the End Zone of your future. Run the play, Child. The crowd is cheering, the path is clear, and the trophy is yours."

5. The Audible (The Timeline of Now) The enemy wants you to remain "clock-conscious," paralyzed by the fear of running out of time. The Audible is this: Eternal Overtime! Right now, on the timeline of today, I am removing the "Panic of the Clock" from your brain. I am releasing the power of Finished Work Confidence. You are not racing against time; you are walking in Kairos. How Good is God!

REFORMATION DATA: THE ARCHITECTURE OF YOUR VICTORY To understand the "field" you are playing on, consider how to apply these "Exhorter" principles to your own "Final Drive":

- **The "Ground Game" Reality:** The Exhorter knows that high-flying theology doesn't win games; "boots on the ground" relationships do. Apply This: When you are stuck, stop reading books and start talking to Jesus (The Person). The ground game is Intimacy.
- **The "Ego" Defense:** Doubt often wears the mask of "Intellectualism" (Ego). Apply This: The Exhorter dismantles this by shifting from "Understanding" to "Preparing." Don't try to figure it out; just get your heart ready for the ball.
- **The "Hail Mary" Trust:** Sometimes, you just have to throw the ball. Apply This: Take the issue you cannot control (the "Pigskin") and physically release it to God. Trust that His "Hands" are bigger than your "Understanding."

HOW GOOD IS GOD!

FOREWORD

The date: October 25, 1964.

The game: Minnesota Vikings versus San Francisco 49ers.

Jim Marshall of the Vikings recovered a fumble and ran 66 yards in the wrong direction. He crossed his own line, scoring a safety for the 49ers. It remains one of the most famous plays in NFL history.

It was the moment of a one-in-a-thousand chance to get an advantage in the game. A golden opportunity to make a difference, expending energy and talent. Then he runs the wrong way and is remembered as the biggest goof in football history.

If that sounds familiar to you, that shows me you're in the game of life. And without proper coaching from those who have experienced this life, we can often run the wrong way.

When God sovereignly crossed my path with Kristen Wambach, I instantly knew I was in the presence of someone who not only knew her Lord in a deeply personal way but also understood the spirit world and how to live successfully as we follow Christ. I am honored to be included in presenting this amazing insight Kristen has laid out for us, so we may be victors in our journey in God's love and life. I have watched her minister out of the depths of her heavenly experiences, and because of that, my life has supernaturally increased.

The anointing that Kristen Wambach exhibits as a spiritual coach is evident in the pages of this book. And as a quarterback, she has passed to you, by the spirit of revelation, divine truth that will empower you to cross your personal goal line that God has placed within you.

I love the statement in Acts 13:36 about David: that he served God's will, purpose, and counsel in his own generation. Some say, "How can you believe that David fulfilled God's will when he made major stumbles in life?" The key to David's success, and our own success in this cosmic spiritual football game that God has placed us in, is that when we fumble the ball like David, we quickly repent, submit to the purpose He has given us, and run in the right direction toward the will of God for you in your generation.

Listen to how the Amplified Bible states this truth in Hebrews 10:36:

"For you have need of patient endurance (to bear up under difficult circumstances without compromising), so that when you have carried out the will of God, you may receive and enjoy to the full what is promised."

Kristen has accomplished something wonderful by taking us from the locker room to the practice field and into the big game. With the spirit of a coach and the wisdom of a pastor, Kristen has now prepared us for the final chapter.

Will we take the Holy Spirit's direction and run with it?

Hebrews 12:1 directs us to let go of the weights and the things that stumble us. Then we will be able to run life's marathon race with passion and determination, for the pathway has already been marked out for us.

Coach Kristen has given us a path to run on and a game to win.

So the ball is in our hands now. Will we carry it across the line to victory?

I perceive that this book, *How Good Is God* by Kristen Wambach, will send a tremor of faith and strength through the body of Christ, making a difference in the years to come.

Dr. George Watkins Prophet, Pastor, Evangelist

About the Foreword Author:
Dr. George Watkins is a seasoned prophet, pastor, and evangelist, and the director of George Watkins Ministries. Having pastored for twenty-nine years, his lifelong quest is to see the Kingdom of God rule on earth with power. He is the host of the Faith Producers International podcast and the author of several books. With a ministry spanning over twenty nations, Dr. Watkins carries a unique apostolic and prophetic mandate to equip the Body of Christ for the supernatural and to fulfill God's personal plan for their destiny. To Kristen, he is not only a mentor but a deeply treasured Spiritual Father who has profoundly shaped her life and heavenly experiences. You can find more of his teachings at georgewatkinsministries.com.

Enjoy this YouTube Video: Dancing on the Edge with Dr. George Watkins —
Hosted by Interviewing Jesus Podcast.

I could sit and listen to George's (GOD) stories for hours. ENJOY!

HOW GOOD IS GOD!

Chapter 18

The Fabulous Turnaround:

Consuming the Face Bread of Oneness

"During my eighteen years in the league, I came to bat almost 10,000 times. I struck out about 1,700 times and walked maybe 1,800 times. You figure a ballplayer will average about 500 at-bats a season. That means I played seven years without ever hitting the ball."

— **Mickey Mantle** | New York Yankees Legend and Hall of Famer.

Did we really arrive here? Is everything finally on the page? Did we argue, call names, debate the hard questions, and cry through the answers? We did. Because God is just that Good—and you and I, we knew it all along.

Well then, somebody must have been BRAVE.

Pause for a moment. How many of us could "bat" for seven years without ever hitting the ball and still mentally seat ourselves, day in and day out, with the legendary? As Sons and Daughters of the Most High, are we anything but legendary?

Has God's internal preparation in you and me prepared us to continue the conversation without falling back into a dogma of "seen" text versus the faith to discover the unseen?

THE UN-FINISHED BUSINESS

I looked over at The UnFinished Book sitting on my desk—my first printed copy.

The first. The one Don and I carried to celebrate at our favorite restaurant in Depoe Bay. I have a picture of him holding it, opened to the last page, stamped: *PROOF COPY.*

Inside that cover held years of conversations with the Lord. During the designing of that cover art, I had purposely turned the "F" in "UnFinished" backward.

It was my secret monument to my struggle with dyslexia—a visual sign of a life that felt backward, frustrated, and out of tune with the blueprint. But as I stood at the finish line of this book, I heard the Lord clear as a bell:

"Kristen, turn the F around. You don't do that anymore. Dyslexia is no longer a problem you deal with. Your brain has been re-programmed to accurately read, see, and perceive the writing on the wall." The "F" is now Fabulous. The "Un" is gone.

THE MIRROR LIFE

Look in the mirror. Not the one where you hunt for unbecoming things that need a tweezers' help, but the reflection. Together we have journeyed through hell's gates, felt the cold weight of the pews, climbed the ornate steps of the pulpits, and stepped beyond the pearly gates. Now, look at Our reflection, Our opportunity.

What has shifted? How Good is God? Is the Gospel gorgeous, simple, and completely restoring, from the beginning to the end? What would happen if you took just one small step through that rent veil? It's only about three and a half inches—the breadth of a hand. If you step "in-to" and through, until your body becomes entirely immersed in the Holy of Holies, I guarantee the "stuff"—the limits we place on us—won't step through with you. On the other side, you aren't repairing a broken person; you are discovering a Consummate Masterpiece.

THE DATA OF THE LOST GENERATION
Now that our thinking about God's Goodness is expanded and breathing... Breathe in. Breathe out.

There is a particular prophecy that you and I are very familiar with. It stirs our souls and baffles our wonder. The Billion Soul Harvest, shared with the body of Christ through Prophet Bob Jones (1930–2014), a foundational figure in the modern prophetic movement and the "Kansas City Prophets."

"He said I am going to bring 1 billion youth to myself in one of the greatest awakenings of all time. I'm going to glorify Myself beyond anything that has ever happened that's ever been done in scripture... One billion youth, over half the population of the world is under 18. One billion at once." — **Prophet Bob Jones** (Shared via Prophetess Patricia King)

I honor their ministries and how they have stewarded the glorious voice of the Lord. But here is my "Oneness" pondering. With the heart of a Servant, I'm going to use a "Butterfly Net," and with the design and purpose of the Prophet, I am going to swoop deep on the "right-side-of-the-boat."

What if God was calculating the harvest not just by the calendar ahead, but by the timeline of Eternity?

The Billion-Soul Search: 12–25 Demographic (approx. 1675–2026) If we ask the question, "Where are the billion?" and we look at the global mortality of youth (ages 12–25) to establish the cumulative threshold of one billion lives shortened, the data tells a story of a harvest field we may have missed.

- **1950 to 2026 (Modern Era):** In this 76-year period, approximately 150 to 170 million individuals aged 12–25 died.

- **1850 to 1950 (Industrial/War Era):** This century saw higher mortality rates due to the World Wars, the 1918 Flu pandemic, and less advanced medicine. Approximately 250 to 300 million youth lives were shortened in this window.

- **1675 to 1850 (Pre-Industrial Era):** To reach the full billion, the research must encompass the high-mortality centuries where infectious disease, famine, and constant conflict were the norm. In these centuries, while the global population was smaller, the percentage of youth who died before age 25 was often as high as 40–50%.

Yes, the logical stats would change, as many already knew Him before their untimely death. But for those who didn't? Grace is still speaking, dear family. Grace does not stop at the grave.

RHEMA THOUGHT: THE STREETS OF SHEOL

Our Rhema thought declares this: Since all doctrine is determined by the experience of our Lord, this is our invitation to preach the Gospel of His Goodness to those Billion souls. He holds the keys, which means the gates of Sheol are accessible. We must take captivity captive! We have wrongly assumed that this massive prophetic harvest was bound inside earthly, linear time.

The easiest street ministry I have encountered to date is on the streets of Sheol! The gates are not locked from the outside. If you found yourself sinking into this 'flame' and a family member suddenly walked through those gates to speak with you, moving about in the flame unbound and unharmed... obviously, the love of God sent them. And Love would need no words.

— **Kristen Wambach** | Mothers and Daughters

I leave my testimony with you. And please feel free to ask for assistance. Just sayin!

THE BRAVE SEND-OFF: THE 100-YARD KISS

You are an immortal being with a servant's mission. You aren't just saved; you are sent. In the "Schools of Jesus' Humanity," we learned that the Kingdom isn't a history lesson; it's a game played on the field of the "Eternal Now."

"I firmly believe that any man's finest hour, the greatest fulfillment of all that he holds dear, is that moment when he has worked his heart out in a good cause and lies exhausted on the field of battle — victorious."

— **Vince Lombardi** | Legendary Head Coach of the Green Bay Packers and namesake of the Super Bowl Trophy.

Step beyond the veil. Dwell there. Never pray another prayer from the "outside" looking in. Squeeze in between the Father and the Son at the right hand of power.

That is the ultimate kiss from the 10 x 53 1/3 yards (the exact dimensions of an NFL End Zone). You are no longer driving down the field; you are standing in the Holy of Holies of the Game.

How good is God?

Go find out—and take the world with you.

ACTIVATION

THE READY SCRIBE'S CONCLUSION: THE FABULOUS TURNAROUND This is the culmination of every conversation we have had in these pages. It is no longer about the Author's testimony, but about Your Testimony in Him. Reach across the geography of this book and hear His voice.

A Direct Conversation with Jesus

1. **The Finished Testimony** *"Child, I am the Resurrection and the Life. I am the one who stood in the tomb and folded the head-cloth to tell you I am not finished with you. Do you see the 'Un' removed from your story? I am the one who turned your 'F' around. I am not here to impress you; I am here to persuade you about YOU. Do you believe that My victory is your actual identity?"*

2. **The High Priest's Replacement: "***I am the Bread of Life. Every time you eat, you are celebrating My incarnation in you. When I replaced the showbread in the Tabernacle, I was setting the stage for our Oneness. I am the one who stands inside the person across from you. Will you join Me in replacing their stale bread with the 'Hot Bread' of My presence? Will you see them through My eyes?"*

3. **The Eternal Now Rest** *"My cross is your cross. It was the Great Exchange where I carried away the distance so there is only the embrace. You don't have to die daily to find Me; I died once and for all so you could live. I am the Coach in your headset, calling the play from the End Zone. I am already standing at the finish line. Are you ready to step through the veil and find that **We have been ready for this all your life?"***

Reflect and Respond

- The Mirror: Look past the "skin" of your behavior. Look past the labels. *Can you see the "Consummate Masterpiece" that Jesus sees?* He is the Mirror of your heart—what does He say about who you are?
- The Tabernacle: Reflect on the 100-yard map. You are no longer defending your goalpost; you are occupying the domain. *Where are you standing on the field of God's goodness today?*

____

____

____

____

Next Step

Identify one "Grave Cloth" or "Skin" of tradition you are still wearing. Physically mimic the act of "unwrapping" it. Declare: "I've been ready for this all my life!" and take your first step onto the luxurious grass of the End Zone.

Prayer and Contemplation

Father, I thank You that the "Un" is gone. I am a finished work. I digest Your goodness until it becomes my very DNA. I choose to live from the Portico of OMG and to walk in the authority of a Son. I thank You for the Fabulous Turnaround. Amen.

PLAY SHEET | MERCY

Mercy Edition
Redemptive Gifts Summary

THIS CHAPTER IS THE GRAND FINALE. It resonates with the frequency of the Mercy gift—the gift of "Fulfillment" and "Transcendence."

The Mercy is the only gift designed to travel into the "mess" of Sheol and the "glory" of the Throne Room without changing clothes. This chapter calls you to stop living on the timeline of earth and start living in the timeline of Eternity.

THE DNA WRISTBAND AUDIBLE: CHAPTER PLAY-CALL

1. The Green Dot Helmet (Individual Redemptive Gift): **Mercy** The frequency for this play is set to the Mercy. This is your gift of "Intimacy" and "Atmosphere." You are hardwired to sense the presence of God in the most unlikely places—even the grave. The Mercy in you is being activated to "Preach to the Lost" seen and unseen, by simply Being. You are being called to be Spiritually BRAVE enough to believe that the "Turnaround" is not just for the living, but for the "Billion" who are waiting for the Face-Bread of Oneness.

2. The Coaches' Booth (*Legacy Anchor*): *The Book of Life*: In the "Booths" of your spiritual legacy, the ultimate anchor is *the Lamb's Book of Life*. You apply this by realizing that your name isn't just on a roster; it is etched in the heart of the Father. This anchor reminds you that when the clock runs out, the game doesn't end—it transitions.

3. The Redemptive Gift "Mercy" understands what Coach Vince Lombardi meant when he described the ultimate victory:

"I firmly believe that any man's finest hour, the greatest fulfillment of all that he holds dear, is that moment when he has worked his heart out in a good cause and lies exhausted on the field of battle — victorious."

True victory is not a trophy that collects dust. It is the peace of a heart fully poured out. "Success isn't forever and failure isn't fatal" because the final score isn't about what you achieved.

The true victory is simply being with Him.

4. The Play-Call from God

"Child, check your helmet—I am speaking the 'Omega Frequency' into your spirit. I see you standing at the edge of the End Zone, wondering if it is safe to cross over into full Glory while your feet are still on the earth. I am calling an audible: Step In!

I watched My Son, Jesus, tear the veil from top to bottom so there would be no more 'outside.' You aren't a 'Visitor' in My Kingdom; you are a 'Resident.' That is the C♡♡Lness of our Oneness. When you feel the grief of a

lost billion, or a single soul, I want you to remember that My Mercy is wider than history and deeper than the grave. Stop believing the lie that death has the final word. Your DNA is hardwired in Resurrection. Be Spiritually BRAVE enough to consume the 'Face-Bread' of My presence and become the Bread for the world. I am so good that I turned the worst Friday in history into the greatest Sunday of all time. Run the play, Child. The Turnaround is complete. Welcome Home."

5. The Audible (The Timeline of Now) The enemy wants you to remain "mortality-conscious," limited by the dates on a tombstone. The Audible is this: The Fabulous Turnaround! Right now, on the timeline of today, I am removing the "Fear of the End" from your brain. I am releasing the power of Endless Life. You are not finishing the book; you are just starting the story. *How Good is God!*

REFORMATION DATA: THE ARCHITECTURE OF YOUR TURNAROUND

To understand the "field" you are playing on, consider how to apply these "Mercy" principles to your own "End Zone":

• **The Sheol Strategy:** The Mercy knows that Love can go where logic cannot. *Apply This:* Don't limit your prayers to the living. Release the goodness of God into your family line, past, present, and future.

• **The Face-Bread Consumption:** You become what you eat. *Apply This:* Stop feeding on the "stale bread" of religious duty. Feast on the "Hot Bread" of His presence every morning. This is the fuel for the turnaround.

• **The 10 x 53 1/3 Kiss:** The End Zone is the place of intimacy. *Apply This:* When you score a victory, don't just spike the ball. Squeeze in between the Father and the Son. The goal isn't the points; the goal is the Embrace.

The Film Room & Locker Room Notes:

Chapter-by-Chapter References & Reader Notes

THE FILM ROOM

Chapter-by-Chapter References

Every great playbook has an index, and every winning team reviews the film. This section serves as your practical reference guide for the entire book.

Instead of hiding the endnotes in tiny print, we brought them into the Film Room. Here, you can easily track down the specific origins of the concepts, quotes, and scriptures used in each chapter. For each chapter, you will find:

TIMELINE 101

- Vince Lombardi & Bill Belichick: The "Dream & Do" voices on the Emmaus road.
- Jesus Quote (Synthesized by Kristen Wambach): "Do not carry the memory of yesterday's failures, nor postpone your inheritance for tomorrow's striving..."
- Luke 24 (Conceptual Reference): The Emmaus Road journey.
- Matthew 16:19 (Conceptual Reference): The Keys to the Kingdom.
- (Note: As no direct Bible verses were quoted in this introductory chapter, specific translations are not listed here.)

GOD TEXT MESSAGE DELIVERED

- "The world speaks in broadcasts; God speaks in whispers..." — Kristen Wambach
- Secretariat (2010): Dialogue between Lucien Laurin and Penny Tweedy regarding redemption and unexpected destiny.
- Seabiscuit (2003): Dialogue by Tom Smith on the value of broken things.
- The Sandlot (1993): The Ham Porter vs. Phillips confrontation (The definition of "Offense").
- **Cheat Sheet** Did you find the 'J" man within 249 offense:5th column from the left, 10th row down!
- "Communion is God's ordained delivery system..." — Pastor Joseph Prince
- Napoleon Hill: Think and Grow Rich (Reframed as acknowledging the inheritance in Christ).

- 1 Kings 19:11–12 (NIV): God in the gentle whisper.
- Jeremiah 33:3 (NIV): "Call to me and I will answer you..."
- 1 John 2:27 (TMT): The Christ-anointing that teaches all things.
- John 6:53 (ESV/Standard): Eating the flesh and drinking the blood of the Son of Man.
- John 6:53 (Mirror Study Bible): "You have no real life in yourselves until you consume the flesh... fully assimilating and realizing our co-association and oneness."
- Philemon 1:6 (Mirror Study Bible): "The communication of your faith becomes effective in the accurate knowledge of every good thing..."

WORDS THAT MOVED MILLIONS
- "When you die, if you get up to the Pearly Gates... The dash is that little line between the year you were born and the year you died." — Linda Ellis (Often quoted by Paul "Bear" Bryant).
- "God has gone to great lengths to protect our ability to say no..." — Wm. Paul Young (The Shack).
- "What God has in us, is gift wrapped to the world..." — Rob Lacey (Couriers, Communicators, Counselors, and Coaches).
- The Inspiration: Margaret Becker concert in Portland.

- Redemptive Gift Study Resources: Nancy Benz, Mike Parsons, and Arthur Burk.
- The Bestseller Timeline: Research context mapping the "written revivals" (e.g., The 5 Love Languages, Jesus Calling, The Purpose Driven Life, The Shack).
- Jeremiah 1:5 (TPT): "Before I shaped you in the womb... You are my prophetic gift to the nations."
- Ephesians 4:11 (Conceptual): The Ministry Gifts functioning as edifiers.
- Romans 12 (Conceptual): The seven Redemptive Gifts.
- Ephesians 1:7-10 (Mirror Study Bible): "His blood is the ransom that secures our redemption... His grace communicates a wisdom and discernment of our worth."
- Romans 5:12 (Mirror Commentary): "Sin is to live out of context with the blueprint of one's design; to behave out of tune with God's original harmony."

THE FINGER OF GOD: AIMING YOUR HARD-WIRED PURPOSE

- Coaching Quotes: Referenced as the ongoing call to action driving the timeline forward.
- Psalm 119 (Conceptual Reference): The biblical foundation underpinning the "written revivals" of our time.

THE CONDUCTOR: PROPHET

- "A good coach will make his players see what they can be, rather than what they are." — Ara Parseghian, Legendary College Football Coach.
- The Shack (2007) by William P. Young.
- Super Bowl XLII (2008): The New York Giants overthrowing the undefeated New England Patriots.
- Psalm 119 (ESV / Standard): "My soul is consumed with longing for your judgments at all times."

THE RHYTHM SECTION: SERVANT

- "The first thing a coach needs to know is that he's a servant." — Bill Parcells, Hall of Fame NFL coach.
- The Purpose Driven Life (2002) by Rick Warren.
- Super Bowl XXXVI (2002): The New England Patriots defeating the St. Louis Rams.

• The historical context of the post-9/11 search for meaning and stability.
• Psalm 119 (ESV / Standard): "My soul clings to the dust; give me life according to your word!" and "I will run in the way of your commandments when you enlarge my heart!"

THE FIRST CHAIR VIOLIN: TEACHER
• "Winning is a habit. Unfortunately, so is losing." — Vince Lombardi, Legendary NFL Coach.
• The Prayer of Jabez (2002) by Bruce Wilkinson.
• Super Bowl XXXVIII (2004): Quarterback Tom Brady methodically leading his team to a game-winning field goal.
• The historical context of the early 2000s widespread interest in self-improvement and unlocking potential.
• Psalm 119 (ESV / Standard): "The law of your mouth is better to me than thousands of gold and silver pieces" and "teach me your statutes."

THE TRUMPET: EXHORTER
• "Coaching is the universal language of change and learning." — Pat Summitt, Hall of Fame Basketball Coach.
• Jesus Calling (2004) by Sarah Young.
• Super Bowl XLIII (2009): Larry Fitzgerald's exhilarating last-minute touchdown run that electrified the stadium.
• The historical context of 2004, a time when many were seeking intimacy and personal connection with a God who felt distant.
• Psalm 119 (ESV / Standard): "Oh, how I love your law! It is my meditation all the day."

THE HARP: GIVER
• "The difference between a successful person and others is not a lack of strength, not a lack of knowledge, but a lack of will." — Vince Lombardi, Legendary NFL Coach.
• Heaven is for Real (2010) by Todd Burpo.
• Super Bowl XLIV (2010): The New Orleans Saints claiming victory, serving as a unifying, collective gift of healing and joy for a city still rebuilding from Hurricane Katrina.
• The historical context of 2010, a time when personal stories with extraordinary claims were highly sought after.

• Psalm 119 (ESV / Standard): "I love your commandments more than gold, more than fine gold."

THE CELLOS AND BASSES: RULER

• "I'm a great believer in luck, and I find the harder I work the more I have of it." — Thomas Jefferson
• More than a Carpenter (1977) by Josh McDowell.
• Super Bowl XIII (1979): The Pittsburgh Steelers dynasty.
• The historical context of academic and cultural skepticism.
• Author's timeline event: The simultaneous arrival of a used copy inscribed to "Morris" and a text message from her son, Joseph, receiving the same book on the same day.
• Psalm 119 (ESV / Standard): "Your righteousness is forever, and your law is truth."

THE FLUTE OR OBOE: MERCY

• "You can accomplish anything you want in life if you don't care who gets the credit." — Zig Ziglar, Motivational Coach.
• The Five Love Languages (1995) by Gary Chapman.
• Super Bowl XXIX (1995): The San Francisco 49ers dynasty.
• The historical context of 1995, a period marked by rising divorce rates.
• Psalm 119 (ESV / Standard): "Let my cry come before you, O Lord; give me understanding according to your word!"

HE LEFT HIS FINGERPRINT: OPUS

• "Talent is God-given. Be humble. Fame is man-given. Be grateful. Conceit is self-given. Be careful." — John Wooden, Legendary UCLA Basketball Coach.
• Matthew 9:28 (NIV / ESV): "Do you believe that I am able to do this?"
• Luke 5:22 (NAB): "What are you thinking in your hearts?"
• Luke 24:17 (CEV / Paraphrased): "What are you talking about?"

THE SNAP: CROSSING THE LINE OF SCRIMMAGE

• "You don't play to the crowd; you play to the clock. And when the clock runs out on doubt, the only voice that matters is the Coach's voice in your headset." — Kristen Wambach

• (No direct scripture verses are quoted in this transitional section.)

INTRODUCTION

• "I've observed that if individuals who prevail in a high competitive environment have any one thing in common besides success, it is failure—and their ability to overcome it." — Bill Walsh, Head Coach, San Francisco 49ers.

• "Ability is what you're capable of doing. Motivation determines what you do. Attitude determines how well you do it." — Lou Holtz, Head coach, New York Jets.

• "We would accomplish many more things if we did not think of them as impossible." — Vince Lombardi, Legendary NFL Coach.

• "Each person holds so much power within themselves that needs to be let out..." — Pete Carroll, Super Bowl Winning Head Coach.

• "If I'm wrong, the life of Christ I live today, will show me the truth and share it, tomorrow." — Kristen Wambach, Mother of four incredible sons.

• "I've been ready for this my whole life." — Rudy, from the film Rudy.

• Julian Fellowes, Maggie Smith, and Judi Dench: Thematic references to romantic prose and historical mansions.

• Ephesians 4:4-5 (Standard / Paraphrased): "One Faith | One Body | One Baptism | One Spirit"

• Romans 8:38-39 (KJV / NKJV): "Neither death or life or angels or principality... shall be able to separate us from the love of God."

• Revelation 22:17 (Standard / KJV): "The Spirit and the Bride say, 'Come.'"

NOTE FROM THE AUTHOR: HAVE YOU EVER SAT IN A GLORY MOMENT?

• "The way to enter into that revival is through praise and worship..." — Ruth Ward Heflin (1939–1998).
• Brené Brown, Research Professor and Author: Defining the profound difference between adaptive guilt and destructive shame.
• The Author's Timeline: The transition from ballet to the piano bench, the writing of a deeply personal song about abortion, and the intentional choice to throw it away.
• (No direct scripture verses are quoted in this section.)

THE PLAYBOOK: COACHING CHURCH | THE DIVINE STRATEGY

• "I am not gonna coach you to who you are. I'm gonna coach you to who you should be someday." — Doc Rivers, NBA Coach.
• "Children were seen, not heard." (Referencing the pre-Boomer era).
• Sense and Sensibility (1995 film adaptation).
• The Generation of Questions: The Baby Boomer generation as "first responders" who questioned quiet faith.
• The Author's Timeline: Raised with three brothers, raising four sons, and writing The UnFinished Book.
• Watchman Nee, The Normal Christian Faith,
• John 15:16 (Mirror Study Bible): "I did not begin in you; you began in me..."
• Romans 8:37-39 (Mirror Study Bible): "On the contrary, in the thick of these things our triumph remains beyond dispute..."

COACHES ARE PLAYERS FIRST

• "Coaches who can outline plays on a blackboard are a dime a dozen. The ones who win get inside their players and motivate." — Vince Lombardi
• "A coach is someone who tells you what you don't want to hear..." — Tom Landry, Coach of the Dallas Cowboys
• The Synthesis: Lombardi gets you inside the player, Romans gets you inside Christ, and Landry forces you to see the true self.

• Romans 12:2-6a (Mirror Bible): "Do not allow current religious tradition to mold you into its pattern of reasoning..."

THE COACHED | PLAYER

• "For me, winning isn't something that happens suddenly on the field... Winning is something that builds physically and mentally every day..." — Emmitt Smith.
• "A winner is someone who recognizes his God-given talents, works his tail off to develop them into skills..." — Larry Bird.
• "Competing at the highest level is not about winning. It's about preparation..." — Joe Torre.
• The Ultimate Definition: A synthesized, inferred quote regarding the spiritual and eternal dimensions of winning.
• Matthew 6:19-20 (Synthesized Paraphrase / KJV influence): Building treasures where moth and rust cannot corrupt.
• Matthew 5:16 (Synthesized Paraphrase / NIV influence): Letting your light shine before others.
• Hebrews 12:1-2 (Synthesized Paraphrase / NIV influence): Running the race with perseverance.

THE COIN TOSS: HEADS OR TAILS?

• Matt Hasselbeck (2003 Wild-Card Playoff Game): Uttering the infamous "We want the ball, and we're going to score" line after winning the coin toss against the Green Bay Packers, only to throw a game-ending interception to Al Harris.
•   (No direct scripture verses are quoted in this section.)

Chapters 1-5

The Film Room & Locker Room Notes

CHAPTER 1: THE ART OF WRESTLING WITH GOD
- "Talent sets the floor, CHARACTER sets the ceiling." — Bill Belichick, New England Patriots.
- "Take notes on your own thoughts." — Myron Golden, Business Consultant & Author.
- Sun Tzu, *The Art of War*: Ancient wisdom teaching that the best battles are won before they are fought by understanding yourself and your environment.
- *The Patriot* (Film): Graphic display of Revolutionary War "Line Infantry" or "Line Strategy" tactics, prioritizing firepower over maneuverability by standing shoulder to shoulder in the open.
- Modern American Football: The evolution of Adaptive Tactics, where a quarterback reads the defense and changes the play on the fly.
- *The Shack* by William Paul Young: Functioning as the "Coaches' Booth" legacy anchor for the Prophet's redemptive gift.

- Genesis 32:30 (TPT): "So Jacob named the place Penuel (face of God), saying, 'I have seen God face-to-face, yet my life has been spared!'"
- Genesis 32 (Conceptual Reference): Jacob wrestling with God/the stranger in the wilderness until dawn, having his hip dislocated, and receiving the name Israel.

CHAPTER 2: SONSHIP AUTHORITY
- "The only sign we have in the locker room is from The Art of War: 'Every battle is won before it is fought.'" — Bill Belichick, Legendary NFL Coach.

- H.E.L.L. (Harness Eternal Lessons Liberally): A motivational locker room acronym breaking down actionable leadership principles.
- Sun Tzu, *The Art of War* (Synthesized Application): A conceptual quote suggesting that true battles for spiritual gates are fought with illumination, dissolving the illusion of separation.
- *More Than a Carpenter* by Josh McDowell: Functioning as the "Coaches' Booth" legacy anchor for the Ruler's redemptive gift.
- Isaiah 53:6 (Conceptual Reference): Like sheep, we have gone astray.
- Ephesians 1:3-4 (Mirror Translation): "Jesus is God's mind made up about you! Before the foundation of the world, God lavished every blessing heaven has upon you in Christ. He always knew in His love that He would present you again face-to-face before Him in blameless innocence."
- Genesis 1:28 (Conceptual Reference): The mandate to subdue the earth as the natural expression of unfallen Sonship Authority.
- 1 Corinthians 1:30 (Mirror Study Bible): "Of God's doing are we IN CHRIST..."
- Psalm 24:1-7 (TPT): "Yahweh claims the world as his... The King is (has come) Coming! So wake up, you living gateways!"
- Hebrews 12:28-29 (Mirror Bible): "We are fully associated in this immovable Kingdom; an authority that cannot be challenged or contradicted."
- Psalm 68:18 / Ephesians 4:8-9 (NASB): "When He Ascended on high He led captive the captives and He gave Gifts to people."
- Romans 8:38-39 (Mirror Bible): "This is my conviction; no threat... has what it takes to separate us from the love of God unveiled in our Lord, Jesus Christ."
- Romans 1:17 (Mirror Study Bible Commentary by Francois du Toit): "Herein lies the secret of the power of the Gospel; there is no good news in it until the righteousness of God is revealed."
- Matthew 16:15 (Standard / Conceptual): "Who do you say that I am?"

- Mark 4:40 (Standard / Conceptual): "Why are you so afraid? Do you still have no faith?"
- Matthew 20:32 (Standard / Conceptual): "What do you want me to do for you?"

CHAPTER 3: HE THAT COMES FACE TO FACE

- "There's no traffic past the extra mile." — Paula Abdul, American singer & Choreographer.
- *Pride and Prejudice* (2005 film): The famous scene where Keira Knightley (Elizabeth Bennet) stands on a cliff in England's Peak District (Stanage Edge), gazing mystically at the horizon.
- *Persuasion*: A pun referencing the Jane Austen novel.
- "It's not the will to win that matters—everyone has that. It's the will to prepare to win that matters." — Paul "Bear" Bryant, Legendary Alabama Football Coach.
- *The Shack* by William Paul Young: Functioning as the "Coaches' Booth" legacy anchor for the Prophet's redemptive gift.
- John 6:36 (Mirror Commentary by Francois du Toit): "Jesus said, I am the bread of life... I'm not here to impress you with me. I'm here to persuade you about you."
- John 6:36-39 (Mirror Translation by Francois du Toit): "Everyone whom the Father has given me will come face to face with me... My rescuing mission will conclude in their joint-resurrection."
- John 5:39-47 (Mirror Translation by Francois du Toit): "You scrutinize the Scriptures tirelessly... yet I am what the Scriptures are all about."
- John 8:43 (Standard / Conceptual): "Why do you not understand my language?"
- Mark 10:38 (Standard / Conceptual): "Are you ready for the baptism I am to undergo?"
- Matthew 12:48 (Standard / Conceptual): "Who are my mother and my brothers?"

CHAPTER 4: MOTHERS AND DAUGHTERS (FIGHT, FLIGHT, OR FREEZE)

- "She has played every position... A mother's love is the unshakeable foundation... Without that, no trophy, no victory, means a thing." — MOM!

• The Party Line: An early telephone system used as a metaphor for how the Holy Spirit can intercept and direct the course of prayers.

• "Most of the mistakes in thinking are inadequacies of perception rather than mistakes of logic." — Edward de Bono, Authority on Creative Thinking.

• *The Five Love Languages* by Gary Chapman: Functioning as the "Coaches' Booth" legacy anchor for the Mercy's redemptive gift.

• Jeremiah 1:11-13 (NIV): "'What do you see, Jeremiah?' 'I see the branch of an almond tree,' I replied. The word of the Lord came to me again: 'What do you see?' 'I see a boiling pot, tilting away from the north,' I replied."

• Proverbs 25:2 (Standard / Conceptual): "It is the glory of God to conceal a matter, But the glory of kings is to search out a matter."

• Psalms 68:18 / Ephesians 4:8 (Conceptual Reference): The assignment taking the author into Sheol to preach the gospel of love.

• Luke 16:19-31 (Standard / Conceptual Paraphrase): The story of the Rich man and Lazarus. "And he cried out, Father Abraham, have mercy on me and send Lazarus to dip the tip of his finger in water to cool my tongue, for I am sinking into this flame!"

• Romans 8:38-39 (Mirror Bible): "This is my conviction; no threat whether it be in death or life... has what it takes to separate us from the love of God unveiled in our Lord, Jesus Christ."

• John 5:6 (Standard / Conceptual): "Do you want to get well?"

• Mark 5:9 (Standard / Conceptual): "What is your name?"

• John 21:16 (Standard / Conceptual): "Do you love me?"

CHAPTER 5: FIRST LOVES: A 4 MINUTE MILE

• "He smiles at me, and I am suddenly seventeen again—the year I realize that love doesn't follow the rules, the year I understood that nothing is worth having so much as something unattainable." — Jodi Picoult, *My Sister's Keeper*.

• "What Breaking the 4-minute mile taught us about the limits of conventional thinking" (Harvard Business Review by Bill Taylor): Referencing Roger Bannister breaking the impenetrable track-and-field barrier to teach us what it takes to break new ground.

• "The future for me is already a thing of the past / You were my first love and you will be my last." — Bob Dylan, *Bye & Bye*.

• 2023-2024 Suicide Statistics: 49,316 deaths in the U.S. (11th leading cause of death), 80% male, 2nd leading cause of death for ages 10-34, and over 720,000 globally.

• "The Bible is not completely void of teachings. However, all the teachings rest on the person Christ Jesus... The doctrines are absolutely based upon the person and bound to the person. This is genuine Christianity." — Watchman Nee, *The Normal Christian Faith*, Chapter 6.

• *Heaven is for Real* by Todd Burpo: Functioning as the "Coaches' Booth" legacy anchor for the Giver's redemptive gift.

• John 4:7-8 (MTB): "Beloved, love always includes others, since love springs from God... To love is to know God; to know God is to love. Not to love, is not to know God."

• Acts 1:12-20 (NIV): "With the payment he received for his wickedness, Judas bought a field; there he fell headlong... Everyone in Jerusalem heard about this, so they called that field in their language Akeldama, that is, Field of Blood."

• Psalm 69:22-28 (Standard / Conceptual Reference): "May their table become a snare... May their eyes be darkened so they cannot see... May they be blotted out of the Book of Life and not listed with the righteous."

• John 20:13 (Standard / Conceptual): "Woman, why are you crying?"

• Luke 24:5 (Standard / Conceptual): "Why do you look for the living among the dead?"

• Matthew 21:16 (Standard / Conceptual): "Have you never read?"

Chapters 6-10

The Film Room & Locker Room Notes:

CHAPTER 6: THE ANATOMY OF ANGER: A SOUL'S FINAL RIGHT

- "Go to Heaven for the climate, Hell for the company." — Mark Twain
- "I'd walk through hell in a gasoline suit to play baseball." — Pete Rose
- "You may all go to Hell, and I will go to Texas." — Davy Crockett
- "The safest road to hell is the gradual one - the gentle slope, soft underfoot, without sudden turnings, without milestones, without signposts." — C.S. Lewis
- "It is easy to go down into Hell; night and day, the gates of dark Death stand wide; but to climb back again, to retrace one's steps to the upper air- there's the rub, the task." — Virgil, *Aeneid* (Book VI: "Facilis descensus Averno...").
- "The hottest place in Hell is reserved for those who remain neutral in times of great moral conflict." — Unknown
- "I hold it to be the inalienable right of anybody to go to hell in his own way." — Robert Frost
- "I am afraid that the schools will prove the very gates of hell, unless they diligently labor in explaining the Holy Scriptures and engraving them in the heart of the youth." — Martin Luther
- "I'm going to let God be the judge of who goes to heaven and hell." — Joel Osteen
- "If I'm going to Hell, I'm going there playing the piano." — Jerry Lee Lewis
- "Marines don't die. We just go to hell and regroup." — Christopher Hopper, *Gods and Men*.
- *More Than a Carpenter* by Josh McDowell: Functioning as the "Coaches' Booth" legacy anchor for the Ruler's redemptive gift.

- 1 Corinthians 15:26 (KJV): "The last enemy that shall be destroyed is death."
- 1 Corinthians 15:26 (Mirror Study Bible): "Resurrection life will finally triumph over every definition of death."
- Psalm 68:18 (Standard / Conceptual Reference): He received gifts from men, even the rebellious.
- Ephesians 4:7-10 (NIV): "But to each one of us grace has been given as Christ apportioned it... (What does 'he ascended' mean except that he also descended to the lower, earthly regions? He who descended is the very one who ascended higher than all the heavens, in order to fill the whole universe.)"
- Luke 16:24 (NLT): "The rich man shouted. 'Father Abraham, have some pity! Send Lazarus over here to dip the tip of his finger in water and cool my tongue. I am in anguish in these flames.'"
- Matthew 16:18 (Standard / Conceptual): Jesus says to Simon Peter, "and on this rock I will build my church, and the gates of hell shall not prevail against it."
- Matthew 16:17-19 (The Passion Translation Paraphrase): "You are favored and privileged Simeon... I give you the name Peter, a stone. And this rock will be the bedrock foundation on which I will build my church—my legislative assembly... I will give you the keys of heaven's kingdom realm to forbid on earth that which is forbidden in heaven, and to release on earth that which is released in heaven."
- Matthew 7:3 (Standard / Conceptual): "Why do you see the speck in your brother's eye, but do not consider the plank in your own eye?"
- Matthew 20:15 (Standard / Conceptual): "Is it not lawful for me to do what I wish with my own things? Or is your eye evil because I am good?"
- John 21:22 (Standard / Conceptual): "What is that to you? You follow me."

CHAPTER 7: SO SAD U SEE: UNRAVELING THE ANCESTRAL BIND

- "The scroll was signed in dust, long, long ago..." — A poetic verse opening the chapter.
- "Yeshuat Hashem k'heref ayin." (The salvation of God is like the blink of an eye) — Pesikta Zutreta.
- Pesikta Zutreta: A collection of Jewish religious commentary (Midrash) compiled in the 11th century CE by Rabbi Toviyah ben Eliezer.
- Jewish Mindset vs. Traditional Christian View on Salvation: Contrasting the Jewish concept of inherent purity and conscious moral choice with the traditional Christian doctrine of Original Sin and inescapable moral incapacity.
- The Folded Head Cloth (Cultural context): Referencing the belief that a master folding his cloth at the table signaled to servants that he intended to return.
- *Mary Poppins* (Original Film): Used as a visual metaphor for the royal carousel horse breaking free to canter into the picture and liberty of life.
- The Sadducees (Historical context): The Jewish sect that did not believe in the resurrection ("So Sad, You See").
- *The Prayer of Jabez* by Bruce Wilkinson: Functioning as the "Coaches' Booth" legacy anchor for the Teacher's redemptive gift.
- John 20:6-7 (Mirror Translation): "Then Simon Peter also arrived and went straight into the tomb and took a long look at the grave clothes lying there. He also noticed that the cloth that was wrapped around the head of Jesus, was not lying with the other strips of linen cloth, but neatly rolled up separately."
- 2 Corinthians 5:14-15 (Mirror Bible): "The love of Christ constrains us and resonates within us; leaving us with only one conclusion: when Jesus died, every individual simultaneously died..."

• John 6:36 (Standard / Conceptual Reference): "But even though you have seen me, you are not persuaded... And the only way that I can persuade you about you is to take you with me into your death and darkness and overcome your fear and hell and birth you again into newness of life in my resurrection!"

• 2 Corinthians 3:14-16 (Conceptual Reference): The veil that covers the hearts of people when the Old Covenant is read, which is lifted when one turns to the Lord.

• Matthew 22:23, Mark 12:18, Luke 20:27, Acts 23:8 (Conceptual Reference): Identifying the Sadducees as those who say there is no resurrection.

• 2 Corinthians 5:1 (NIV): "Now we know that if the earthly tent we live in is dismantled, we have a building from God, an eternal house in heaven, not built by human hands."

• Mark 10:51 (Standard / Conceptual): "What do you want me to do for you?"

• John 3:12 (Standard / Conceptual): "If I have told you earthly things and you do not believe, how will you believe if I tell you heavenly things?"

• 1 Corinthians 3:16 (Standard / Conceptual): "Do you not know that you are God's temple and that God's Spirit dwells in you?"

CHAPTER 8: THE READY SCRIBE: GREEN AND GROWING, NOT RIPE AND ROTTING

• "You're either green and growing or ripe and rotting. Get a moving target. You have to be in motion. The moment you think you've figured it out, you've stopped growing." — Lou Holtz, Former NCAA and NFL Head Football Coach.

• Earthing / Grounding: The concept of physical contact with the Earth's surface transferring free electrons into the body to neutralize free radicals and reduce chronic inflammation.

• Norms (Local Aurora, Oregon Market): A pin-marker location for the author receiving her first prophetic word.

• The Evolution of the Pew: The historical transition from active worship in the Tabernacle (which contained no chairs) to fixed wooden pews, which were often rented or owned by wealthy families, creating divisions based on status.

• *The Shack* by William Paul Young: Functioning as the "Coaches' Booth" legacy anchor for the Prophet's redemptive gift.

• Psalm 45:1 (Author Inspired / Paraphrased): "My heart is not merely composing a good song; it is bursting with the finished matter of our King! ...it is the fluent pen of a ready scribe..."

• Mark 7:13 / Matthew 15:6 (Conceptual Reference): "The traditions of men make the Word of God of no effect."

• Psalm 45:1 (KJV): "My heart is indicting a good matter: I speak of the things which I have made touching the king: my tongue is the pen of a ready writer."

• 1 Corinthians 3:16 (Standard / Conceptual): "Do you not know that you are God's temple and that God's Spirit dwells in you?"

• Matthew 20:6 (Standard / Conceptual): "Why do you stand here idle all day long?"

• Matthew 16:15 (Standard / Conceptual): "Who do you say that I am?"

CHAPTER 9: THE SHROUD AND THE ALTAR: UNWRAPPING THE LIVE BODY

• "A revival is nothing else than a new beginning of obedience to God." — Charles Finney, Father of Modern Revivalism.

• Pastor Tommy Barnett (Endorsement Note): Author, Co-Pastor Dream City Church Phoenix, Founder of the Los Angeles Dream Center.

• Pastor Tommy Barnett's Legacy Note: At the age of 60, he ran across the Mojave Desert (the equivalent of a marathon per day for 19 days) to raise funds to open the Dream Center.

- Martin Luther (1483–1546): Described as "The Hammer," who tore down the veil of a "pay-to-sit" salvation system and put the Word into the hands of the common man.
- John Calvin (1509–1564): Described as providing "The Structure," seeking a settled foundation but inadvertently authoring a cessationist view that boarded up the windows to the supernatural.
- Huldrych Zwingli (1484–1531): Described as "The Simplifier" of the Swiss Reformation, stripping active participation (statues, music, altars) out of buildings to leave only the grounded weight of the Word.
- Catherine of Siena (1347–1380): A mystic who proved reformation begins in the Secret Place, calling the highest authorities back to spiritual integrity.
- All Saints' Church in Wittenberg, Saxony-Anhalt, Germany: The historical and spiritual location where the author met Martin Luther in a vision.
- *Tomorrowland* (2015 Film): Used as a comparison for how the author was able to see into different timelines (steering the "earth wheel").
- The Dual Nature of the Human Journey (Leviticus 16 Geometry): The first thief mirroring the Lord's Goat (Yom Kippur), and the second thief mirroring the Azazel (Scapegoat).
- *Jesus Calling* by Sarah Young: Functioning as the "Coaches' Booth" legacy anchor for the Exhorter's redemptive gift.
- Luke 22:19 (Standard / Conceptual Reference): "Do this in remembrance of me."
- 1 Corinthians 11:29-30 (Mirror Bible): "Anyone who partakes of this meal in an indifferent manner... eats and drinks judgment upon themselves...
- The human body of Jesus represents the judgment of every single human life... This is the reason why many of you are suffering unnecessarily with weaknesses and illnesses, and many have already died."

• John 11:44 (Mirror Bible): "And the dead man appeared with his hands and feet swathed in linen cloths also his face was covered in a cloth. Jesus said to them, 'Unwrap him and so that he can move around freely.'"

• 1 Corinthians 15:52-53 (Mirror Bible): "This will happen in an instant, in a blink of the eye: the final trumpet will sound, then the dead shall be awoken out of their sleep and we, who are still alive, shall be instantly changed into a different kind of body. For this corruptible must be clothed with incorruption and this mortal must be clothed with immortality."

• Luke 23:43 (Standard / Paraphrased): "I promise you— this very day you will enter paradise with me."

• Matthew 16:15 (Standard / Conceptual): "Who do you say that I am?"

CHAPTER 10: THE GATES OF HEAVEN: THE GEOGRAPHY OF SIMPLE

• "If you can't explain it simply, you don't understand it well enough..." — Vince Lombardi.

• "If you can't explain it to a six-year-old..." — Albert Einstein.

• Learning to ride a bike (Metaphor): Used to describe experiencing heaven—not just reading about it, but feeling the "In-With-in" reality of the Father's hand on the seat.

• Santa Claus, the Easter Bunny, and the Tooth Fairy: Cultural references used to contrast make-believe with the truth of the Gospel.

• The 100-Yard Map of Oneness: A spatial breakdown of spiritual progression, mapping the Parables of the Kingdom from the defensive stance to the scoring reality of rest and union.

• John 1:1 (Author Inspired / Paraphrased Commentary): "In the beginning—the first in order, time, place, or rank | is to find the Word—Living word with a name, filled in intelligence... already present there with God, face to face, mirror, no beginning no end. The Word is (His name) IAM..."

• John 14:9 (Standard / Conceptual): "If you have seen Me, you have seen the Father..."

• The Topography of Heaven (Conceptual): Stepping through the veil of His flesh, encountering types and shadows of the Tabernacle.

• Matthew 13:31-32 (Conceptual Reference): The Parable of the Mustard Seed (The 10 Yard Line).

• Matthew 13:33 (Conceptual Reference): The Parable of the Leaven / Yeast hidden in the meal (The 20 Yard Line).

• Matthew 13:44 (Conceptual Reference): The Parable of the Hidden Treasure in a field (The 30 Yard Line).

• Matthew 13:45-46 (Conceptual Reference): The Parable of the Pearl of Great Price / Merchant seeking beautiful pearls (The 40 Yard Line).

• Matthew 13:47-50 (Conceptual Reference): The Parable of the Dragnet cast into the sea (The 50 Yard Line).

• Matthew 22:1-14 (Conceptual Reference): The Parable of the Wedding Feast (The 60 Yard Line).

• Matthew 13:52 (Conceptual Reference): The Parable of the Householder bringing out treasures New and Old (The 80 Yard Line).

• Matthew 13:3-9, 18-23 (Conceptual Reference): The Parable of the Sower / Seed finding Good Ground (The End Zone).

Chapters 11-15

The Film Room & Locker Room Notes:

CHAPTER 11: "HELLO" SCARED, MAD, ANGRY, DONE: YOU ARE BRAVER THAN THE SUM OF YOUR SECRETS

• "Everyone has that moment I think, the moment when something so momentous happens that it rips your very being into small pieces..." — Kathleen Glasgow, *Girl in Pieces*.

• "May your choices reflect your hopes, not your fears." — Nelson Mandela.

• "Pure logical thinking cannot yield us any knowledge of the empirical world; all knowledge of reality starts from experience and ends in it." / "Information is not knowledge. The only source of knowledge is experience. You need experience to gain wisdom." — Albert Einstein, *Ideas and Opinions*.

• "To uncover your true potential you must first find your own limits and then you have to have the courage to blow past them." — Picabo Street, Former American World Cup alpine ski racer and Olympic gold medalist.

• "If you put shame in a petri dish, it needs three ingredients to grow exponentially: secrecy, silence, and judgement." — Brené Brown.

• "You are braver than the sum of your secrets." — K. Wambach.

• "A coach is someone who tells you what you don't want to hear, who has you see what you don't want to see, so you can be who you have always known you could be." — Tom Landry, Dallas Cowboys.

• "Football is an incredible game. Sometimes it's incredibly cruel. And that's the sport. If you can handle the pain, if you can handle the disappointment, then eventually you have to get up, and keep moving, and fight, and believe, and try to win." — Urban Meyer, Celebrated American former college football coach.

• Magnum P.I.: A cultural reference used to describe the hometown boy's dark eyes and brows.

• The Lovejoy Center in Portland: The historical location referenced in the author's timeline.

- *The Shack* by William Paul Young: Functioning as the "Coaches' Booth" legacy anchor for the Prophet's redemptive gift.
- 2 Corinthians 1:21-22 (Standard / Conceptual): "Now it is God who establishes both us and you in Christ. He anointed us, placed His seal on us, and put His Spirit in our hearts as a guaranteeing pledge of what is to come."
- Romans 6:22-23 (MTB): "Consider your life now; there are no outstanding debts; you owe sin nothing... The reward of the law is death; the gift of grace is life. The bottom line is this: sin employs you like a soldier for its cause and rewards you with death; God gifts you with the highest quality of life all wrapped up in Christ Jesus our Leader."
- Acts 7:20-31 (NASB / Condensed): "It was at this time that Moses was born... But when he was approaching the age of forty, it entered his mind to visit his brethren..."

- Deuteronomy 32:18 / Romans 3:23 (MTB): "You have forgotten the Rock that begot you and have gotten out of step with the God who danced with you."

- John 3:16 (Standard / Conceptual): "For God so LOVED the world that He gave His only begotten Son that whosoever believes in Him shall not perish but will have everlasting life."

- John 3:16 (Mirror Translation Bible): "The entire cosmos is the object of God's affection. And He is not about to abandon His creation - the gift of His Son is for mankind to realize their origin in Him who mirrors their authentic birth..."
- Matthew 20:1-16 (NASB / Condensed): "For the kingdom of heaven is like a landowner who went out early in the morning to hire laborers for his vineyard... So the last shall be first, and the first last."

- 1 Corinthians 3:16 (Standard / Conceptual): "Do you not know that you are God's temple and that God's Spirit dwells in you?"
- Matthew 7:11 (Standard / Conceptual): "If you, then, being evil, know how to give good gifts to your children, how much more will your Father who is in heaven give good things to those who ask Him?"
- Luke 8:45 (Standard / Conceptual): "Who touched me?"

CHAPTER 12: EIGHT DAYS TO HEAVEN | THE RESURRECTION OF I LOVE YOU

- "It is easier to build strong children than to repair broken men." — Frederick Douglass (1818–1895) | Social reformer, abolitionist, orator, and writer.
- "I've said it before, but it's absolutely true: My mother gave me my drive, but my father gave me my dreams. Thanks to him, I could see a future." — Liza Minnelli.
- "As we express our gratitude, we must never forget that the highest appreciation is not to utter words, but to live by them." — John F. Kennedy.
- "HARD" (Metaphor): Broken down as h↔d (two chairs facing each other) with "ar" sandwiched between (Him ar Daughter, Her ar Dad).
- The Author's Father: Described through his military service (Korean War, World War II, 11th Airborne, 127th Combat Engineers, Mascot "The Angels") and his personal habits (fanatical organization, tucked-in shirts, feeding the dog with a fork).
- "TAPS" (Extinguishing Light): The 24-note bugle call played at military funerals.
- The 1800s Silver Dollar (Family Legacy): A physical anchor and heirloom passed down from the grandfather to his grandsons, used by the author's son (Joseph) while deployed in Afghanistan to make a crucial decision at a crossroads.

• *The Five Love Languages* by Gary Chapman: Functioning as the "Coaches' Booth" legacy anchor for the Mercy's redemptive gift.

• *The Anchor*

• Hebrews 4:12 (NIV): "For the word of God is alive and active. Sharper than any double-edged sword, it penetrates even to dividing soul and spirit, joints and marrow; it judges the thoughts and attitudes of the heart."

• Hebrews 4:12 (Mirror Study Bible): "The message God spoke to us in Christ, is the most life giving and dynamic influence in us, cutting like a surgeon's scalpel... to the dividing of soul and spirit; ending the dominance of the sense realm and its neutralizing effect upon the human spirit."

• John 11:25 (Standard / Conceptual): "I am the resurrection and the life."

• Matthew 16:15 (Standard / Conceptual): "Who do you say that I am?"

•

CHAPTER 13: GODS FAVORITE CHARITY: THE CURRENCY OF THE HALL OF FAME

• "To have the kind of year you want to have, something has to happen that you can't explain why it happened. Something has to happen that you can't coach." — Bobby Bowden, Legendary College Football Coach.

• "You never really understand a person until you consider things from his point of view... until you climb into his skin and walk around in it." — Atticus Finch in Harper Lee's novel *To Kill a Mockingbird*.

• "The NFL Draft measures potential in a moment; greatness is measured in decades..." — Kristen Wambach.

• Highway 99E / Aurora Colony / The "Train House": The historical setting in Oregon built by descendants of the Oregon Trail.

• *Miracle on 34th Street* (Original film with Maureen O'Hara and Natalie Wood): The courtroom scene where the United Postal Service forwards backlogged letters to prove the identity of Kris Kringle.

• St. Teresa of Avila (the "Doctor of Prayer"): Her teachings on the "Interior Castle" and paying God a compliment by asking great things of Him.

• *Mysteries, Marvels and Miracles: In the Lives of the Saints* by Joan Carroll Cruz: Quoting a bank employee regarding lost bank notes (*res nullius*) providing a heavenly supply for miracles.

• Smith Wigglesworth: Mentioned regarding the tangible, weighty atmosphere of his prayer meetings.

• "The real glory is being knocked to your knees and then coming back. That's real glory. That's the essence of it." — Vince Lombardi.

• *The Purpose Driven Life* by Rick Warren: Functioning as the "Coaches' Booth" legacy anchor for the Servant's redemptive gift.

• Matthew 17:26 (Standard / Conceptual): "... go to the sea, and cast in a hook: and that fish which shall first come up, take: and when thou hast opened its mouth, thou shalt find a stater [coin]: take that, and give it to them for me and thee."

• Hebrews 4:16 (Amplified Translation): "Let us then fearlessly and confidently and boldly draw near to the throne of grace..."

• Hebrews 4:16 (Mirror Translation): "For this reason we can approach the authoritative throne of grace with bold utterance."

• Throne(s) of Authority (Conceptual References): Revelation 3:21, Matthew 19:28, Luke 22:30, Revelation 4:4, and Revelation 20:4.

• John 10:9 (Standard / Conceptual): "...going in and out and find pasture."

• Matthew 6:25-26 (Standard / Conceptual): "Look at the birds of the air, that they do not sow, nor reap nor gather into barns, and yet your heavenly Father feeds them."

- 1 John 2:5-8 (Mirror Translation): "Whoever treasures the 'Logos'—the logic of God's authentic thought—is standing in the place where Agape love is fully realized in its most complete context."
- Divine Knowledge/Happenstance (Conceptual References): John 1:47-48, John 4:16-18, Matthew 17:24-27, Luke 5:4-6, Mark 14:13-15, Matthew 21:2-3, John 11:11-14, Mark 2:8, John 6:64, Luke 22:10-12.
- Genesis 32:22-32 (Conceptual Reference): Jacob wrestling with the Angel of the Lord, receiving the name Israel, and the touching of his hip socket.

CHAPTER 14: RECLAIMING THE TABLE: DISOWNING THE CURSE, EMBRACING THE BLESSINGS | AMELIA

- "Today I will do what others WON'T, so tomorrow I can accomplish what others CAN'T." — Jerry Rice, Widely regarded as the greatest wide receiver in NFL history (San Francisco 49ers).
- "Aunt Ruth's Spiced Plum Cake" (Metaphor): A recipe representing generational maladies, physical ailments, and inherited family traits passed down through a maternal 1940s black-and-white metal recipe box.
- "Don't give up at half time. Concentrate on winning the second half." — Paul "Bear" Bryant.
- "A man who has no imagination has no wings." — Muhammad Ali, Iconic American professional boxer and three-time world heavyweight champion.
- *The Wizard of Oz* (Film Reference): "I don't think we are in Kansas anymore," referencing the transition into deep spiritual vision.
- "Git-R-Done!" — A catchphrase popularized in the 1990s by comedian Larry the Cable Guy.

• "There's always something in the game you wish you would have done different. That's why players improve, because they learn from what they did before..." — Gordie Howe ("Mr. Hockey"), Iconic Canadian professional ice hockey player (Detroit Red Wings).

• *More Than a Carpenter* by Josh McDowell: Functioning as the "Coaches' Booth" legacy anchor for the Ruler's redemptive gift.

• John 3:16 (Conceptual Reference): Drawing a line under faith and questioning inherited traditions.

• Galatians 3:13 / Deuteronomy 21:23 (Mirror Translation): "Christ redeemed us from the curse as consequence of our failure to keep the law. In his cross he concentrated the total curse of the human race upon himself."

• Luke 9:23 (Mirror Translation): "Joining me in close companionship in your daily walk, involves perceiving my mission as fully representing you."

• Ephesians 4:7-9, Ephesians 2:5-6, Colossians 3:1-3, Ephesians 1:4 (Mirror Bible / Conceptual References): Relocating us face to face with the Father and being co-quickened, co-raised, and co-seated in His Executive authority.

• Genesis 3:14 (NLT): "Because you have done this, you are cursed more than all animals, domestic and wild."

• Genesis 3:17 (NLT): "Since you listened to your wife and ate from the tree... the ground is cursed because of you."

• Genesis 4:11 (Standard / Conceptual): "Now you are cursed and banished from the ground, which has swallowed your brother's blood."

• Psalm 6:2 (NLT): "Heal me, LORD, for my bones are in agony."

• Habakkuk 3:16 (NLT): "I trembled inside when I heard this; my lips quivered with fear. My legs gave way beneath me, and I shook in terror."

• Proverbs 17:22 (KJV): "A merry heart doeth good like a medicine: but a broken spirit drieth the bones."

- Psalm 42:10 (NASB): "As a shattering of my bones, my adversaries taunt me..."
- Psalm 31:10 (NASB): "For my life is spent with sorrow... My strength has failed because of my guilt, And my body has wasted away."
- Proverbs 12:4 (NLT): "...a disgraceful woman is like cancer in his bones."
- Psalm 38:3 (NLT): "Because of your anger, my whole body is sick; my health is broken because of my sins."
- Job 33:19 (NLT): "Or God disciplines people with pain on their sickbeds, with ceaseless aching in their bones."
- Proverbs 14:30 (NLT): "...jealousy is like cancer in the bones."
- Jeremiah 20:9 (NLT) / Lamentations 3:4 (NLT): "...It's like a fire in my bones!" / "...He has broken my bones."
- Psalm 32:3 (NLT): "When I refused to confess my sin, my body wasted away..."
- Psalm 109:18 (NIV): "He wore cursing as his garment; it entered into his body like water, into his bones like oil."
- Mark 10:51 (Standard / Conceptual): "What do you want me to do for you?"
- Mark 5:30 (Standard / Conceptual): "Who touched me?"
- Mark 10:21 (Standard / Conceptual): "What do you lack?"

CHAPTER 15: NDE · PDE = PAST DEATH EXPERIENCES IMMORTALITY

- "In this lifetime, you don't have to prove nothin' to nobody - except yourself. And after what you've gone through, if you haven't done that by now, it ain't gonna never happen. Now go on back." — Fortune, the head groundskeeper at Notre Dame Stadium in the movie *Rudy* (1993).
- *Rudy* (1993 Film): The story of Rudy Ruettiger's perseverance to play for the Notre Dame football team, including references to Coach Dan Devine and Ara Parseghian.

- "5 feet nothin', a 100 and nothin', and you got hardly a speck of athletic ability." — A famous quote from the film *Rudy*.
- Ancient Roman Triumphs (Historical Context): Referencing the victory parades where an abundance of perfumes and wreaths of sweet-smelling flowers were used to diffuse a sweet aroma, symbolizing the success of the cross.
- "I've been ready for this my whole life." — Rudy from the film *Rudy*.
- *The Shack* by William Paul Young: Functioning as the "Coaches' Booth" legacy anchor for the Prophet's redemptive gift.
- Galatians 5:1 (MTB): "Christ has set us free to live a free life. So take your stand! Never again let anyone put a harness of slavery on you."
- Romans 10:9 (LBT): "If you openly declare that Jesus is Lord and believe in your heart that God raised Him from the dead, you will be saved."
- John 3:16 (NASB): "For God so loved the world, that He gave His only begotten Son, that whoever believes in Him shall not perish, but have eternal life."
- Colossians 2:13-14 (LBT): "You were dead in sins, with no hope at all, but God gave you new life with Christ! (He forgave you all your sins!) He took away the list of sins and shortcomings we had failed to keep, and nailed it to the cross."
- Romans 8:11 (NASB): "But if the Spirit of Him who raised Jesus from the dead dwells in you, He who raised Christ Jesus from the dead will also give Life to your mortal bodies through His Spirit who dwells in you."
- 1 Peter 2:24 (TPT): "He personally carried our sins in His own body on the cross so that we would be dead to sin and alive to righteousness. Our healing flows from His wounds, for by His stripes we were healed."

- Romans 6:4 (TMT): "Through the action of baptism we were immersed into His death; so that just as Christ was raised from the dead by the Father's glory, we also should live in a new dimension of Life."
- Romans 5:9-10 (NASB): "Much more then, having now been justified by His blood, we shall be saved from the wrath of God through Him..."
- Romans 10:4 (NASB): "For Christ is the end of the law for righteousness, so that everyone who believes will be justified."
- Romans 8:1-2 (NASB): "Therefore there is now no condemnation for those who are in Christ Jesus. For the law of the Spirit of Life in Christ Jesus has set you free from the law of sin and death."
- Ephesians 2:8-9 (TPT): "For it was by grace you were saved. It was not the result of your own actions, but God's gift to you..."
- Colossians 1:20 (NASB): "and through Him to reconcile all things to Himself, having made peace through the blood of His cross..."
- John 6:35, 48, 51 (TPT): "Jesus replied, 'I am the Bread of Life. Come every day and you will never be hungry...'"
- John 7:37-39 (TPT): "On the last and greatest day of the feast, Jesus stood and spoke in a loud voice to the crowds: 'All you thirsty ones, come to me! Believe in me and drink!'"
- John 10:10 (TPT): "The thief comes only to steal and kill and destroy; I came that they may have Life, and have it abundantly."
- 2 Corinthians 2:14-17 (Mirror Study Bible): "I am overwhelmed with gratitude. Wherever my travels take me I am so aware that God leads us as trophies in his victory parade. What he knows to be true about us diffuses through us like a perfume of sweet aroma everywhere we go..."
- John 3:1-7 (Mirror Study Bible): The story of Nicodemus the Pharisee coming to see Jesus under the cover of night.
- John 19:38-40 (Mirror Study Bible): Joseph of Arimathea and Nicodemus making a bold announcement of their love by bringing spices to prepare Jesus' body for burial.

• Genesis 2:7 (NASB): "Then the Lord God formed man of dust from the ground, and breathed into his nostrils the breath of life; and man became a Living Being."

• John 11:25-26 (Standard / Conceptual): "I am the resurrection and the life... And whoever lives and believes in Me shall never die. Do you believe this?"

• John 3:12 (Standard / Conceptual): "If I have told you earthly things and you do not believe, how will you believe if I tell you heavenly things?"

• Mark 8:29 (Standard / Conceptual): "But who do you say that I am?"

• Romans 6:8 (Standard / Conceptual): "If we died with Christ, we believe we will also live with Him."

Chapters 16-18

The Film Room & Locker Room Notes:

CHAPTER 16: I LOVE IT, TOO! THE BLUEPRINT TO THE FIRST ESTATE

• "The best way to predict your future is to create it." — Abraham Lincoln, 16th President of the United States.

• *The Young Victoria* (Film Reference): Queen Adelaide saying to Queen Victoria, "A man that has no work is ridiculous. Let him share your work!"

• "Lunatic, Liar or Lord?" — A coined phrase from a well-respected book (referencing C.S. Lewis's trilemma).

• "I was merely thinking God's thoughts after Him. Since we astronomers are priests of the highest God in regard to the book of nature, it benefits us to be thoughtful, not of the glory of our minds, but rather, above all else, of the glory of God." — Johannes Kepler, Mathematician and Astronomer.

- "You cannot hope to sweep someone else away by the force of your writing until it has been done to you." — Stephen King, *On Writing: A Memoir of the Craft*.
- "To do things you've never done before, you have to do things you've never done before." — Sean Payton, Super Bowl-winning NFL head coach (New Orleans Saints).
- *The Shack* by William Paul Young: Functioning as the "Coaches' Booth" legacy anchor for the Prophet's redemptive gift.
- Romans 8:19-21 (ESV): "For the creation waits with eager longing for the revealing of the sons of God..."
- Ezekiel 28:12b-15 (Standard / Conceptual): "You were once the consummate model of perfection... Your ways were blameless from the day I created you."
- 1 John 3:8 (TPT): "But the one who indulges in a sinful life is of the devil... The reason the Son of God was revealed was to undo and destroy the works of the devil."
- Genesis 1:28-31 (TPT): "And God blessed them in his love, saying, 'Reproduce and be fruitful!...'"
- Romans 10:9 (Standard / Conceptual): "...that if you confess with your mouth the Lord Jesus and believe in your heart that God has raised Him from the dead, you will be saved."
- 2 Peter 2:4 (Weymouth New Testament): "For God did not spare angels when they had sinned, but hurling them down to Tartarus consigned them to caves of darkness..."
- Proverbs 25:2 (Standard / Conceptual): "It is the glory of God to conceal a matter; to search out a matter is the glory of kings."
- 1 Corinthians 13:13 (TMT): "Now persuasion and every pleasurable expectation is completed in agape... Love defines my eternal moment."
- 1 Kings 11:38 (New Heart English Bible): "It shall be, if you will listen to all that I command you... that I will be with you, and will build you a sure house..."
- Ephesians 6:12 (KJV): "For we wrestle not against flesh and blood, but against principalities, against powers..."

- Romans 6:8 (Standard / Conceptual): "If we died with Christ, we believe we will also live with Him."
- Ephesians 6:10, 13 (NKJV): "Finally, my brethren, be strong in the Lord and in the power of His might... having done all, to stand."

CHAPTER 17: THE TWO-MINUTE WARNING: PIGSKINS OF LIFE

- "You win with people, not with talent." — Woody Hayes, Legendary head coach at Ohio State University (1951-1978).
- "The will to win is important, but the will to prepare is vital." — Joe Paterno, Legendary head coach at Penn State (1966-2011).
- "When you get to the end zone, act like you've been there before." — Vince Lombardi.
- Famous Football Wisdom (Coach's Huddle): Synthesized coaching principles applied to spiritual persistence (The Ground Game), facing doubt (The "Ego" Defense), and taking action (The Charge Forward).
- The Hail Mary / Pigskins of Life (Metaphor): Using the concept of a desperate, unreserved pass to represent tying up unanswered questions (Why?, Identity, and Future Fear) and trusting the Receiver.
- The Final Drive (Football Metaphor): Applying football downs (1st: Spiritual Senses, 2nd: Spiritually BRAVE, 3rd: Radical Obedience, 4th: Restoration of All Things) to the process of getting the "pigskin" across the goal line through Relational Discernment.

- Colossians 2:9-10 (Mirror Study Bible with commentary): "In Him, all the fullness of Deity resides in a human body... Jesus exhibits what the Father, Son and Spirit is like, in human form."
- Colossians 1:19-20 (Mirror Study Bible with commentary): "He initiated the reconciliation of all things to himself. Through the blood of the cross God restored the original harmony."

CHAPTER 18: THE FABULOUS TURNAROUND: CONSUMING THE FACE BREAD OF ONENESS

- "During my eighteen years in the league, I came to bat almost 10,000 times. I struck out about 1,700 times and walked maybe 1,800 times. You figure a ballplayer will average about 500 at-bats a season. That means I played seven years without ever hitting the ball." — Mickey Mantle, New York Yankees Legend and Hall of Famer.
- *The UnFinished Book*: The author's first printed copy, featuring a backward "F" as a monument to her struggle with dyslexia.
- "He said I am going to bring 1 billion youth to myself in one of the greatest awakenings of all time..." — Prophet Bob Jones (1930–2014), a foundational figure in the modern prophetic movement, shared via Prophetess Patricia King.

- The Billion-Soul Search Data: A demographic estimate of global youth mortality (ages 12–25) from 1675 to 2026 to locate the billion souls.

- "The easiest street ministry I have encountered to date is on the streets of Sheol!..." — Kristen Wambach, *Mothers and Daughters*.
- "I firmly believe that any man's finest hour, the greatest fulfillment of all that he holds dear, is that moment when he has worked his heart out in a good cause and lies exhausted on the field of battle — victorious." — Vince Lombardi, Legendary Head Coach of the Green Bay Packers.
- 10 x 53 1/3 yards: The exact dimensions of an NFL End Zone.
- The Book of Life: Functioning as the "Coaches' Booth" legacy anchor for the Mercy's redemptive gift.
- John 11:25 (Standard / Conceptual): "I am the Resurrection and the Life."
- John 6:35 (Standard / Conceptual): "I am the Bread of Life."

- Luke 9:23 (Mirror Translation / Conceptual): "My cross is your cross."
- Matthew 27:51 / Hebrews 10:19-20 (Conceptual Reference): The rent veil and stepping into the Holy of Holies.
- Revelation 21:27 (Conceptual Reference): The Lamb's Book of Life.

Bible Translations

1. The Franchise Quarterback: The Mirror Translation (MSB / MTB / TMT) by Francois du Toit
- **The Verdict:** Hands down, this is the MVP of your book. You don't just quote it; you actively celebrate it. In Chapter 3, you stated that du Toit's commentary has "become an internalized narration of new life communion for me."
- **How You Used It:** I used the Mirror to do the heaviest theological lifting in the book—defining our Co-Inclusion in Christ, the Resurrection, the "death of death," and the First Estate. It is your go-to translation for pulling the "Rhema" out of the "Logos."
2. The Star Receiver: The Passion Translation (TPT)
- **The Verdict:** Coming in at a very strong number two, TPT is your go-to translation for emotion, identity, and victory.
- **How You Used It:** I used it right out of the gate in Chapter 1 for the foundational *Penuel* (face of God) verse, and leaned on it heavily in Chapter 15's "Checklist of Life" to express the abundant, flowing, and passionate nature of God's love (e.g., *Rivers of Living Waters, Bread of Life*).
- The Offensive Line: New American Standard Bible (NASB)
- **The Verdict:** When you needed an undeniable, structurally sound, and historically accurate foundation to build a play upon, you called on the NASB.

• **How You Used It:** I used extensively in Chapter 15 to anchor the "Checklist of Life" (Romans 8, Colossians 1) and to define the "Laborers in the Vineyard" in Chapter 11. It provided the solid, classic grit to back up your modern revelations.

4. The Defense: New Living Translation (NLT)

• **The Verdict:** The NLT is your situational powerhouse for making the "hard" things easy to understand.

• **How You Used It:** I used it almost exclusively in Chapter 14 when you were diagnosing the "Anatomy of a Curse." You used the NLT to break down all the scriptures related to bone diseases, fear, and sorrow so the reader could clearly understand exactly what Jesus absorbed on the cross.

• The Trusted Veterans: NIV & KJV

• **The Verdict:** These are your classic, legacy translations. You didn't overuse them, but you brought them in when you needed a familiar, resonant anchor.

• **How You Used It:** I used the **KJV** perfectly for the majestic, poetic mandates like the "Ready Scribe" (Psalm 45:1) and the reality of spiritual warfare (Ephesians 6:12). You used the **NIV** for foundational anchors like the "Living Sword" (Hebrews 4:12) and Christ descending to the lower regions (Ephesians 4).

• The Color Commentator: The Message (MSG)

• **The Verdict:** Used sparingly but effectively to bring a modern, conversational punch to deep theology.

• **How You Used It:** I dropped it into Colossians 1 and 2 in Chapter 17 to describe how "roomy" God is in human skin, and in Chapter 16 to explain the practical reality of judging angels and everyday matters (1 Cor 6:2-3).

• The Special Teams (The Niche Translations)

• These translations were brought in for highly specific, specialized plays where you needed a very particular word or nuance:

• **Amplified Translation (AMP):** Used in Chapter 13 to expand the definition of boldly approaching the Throne of Grace (Hebrews 4:16).

• **New Heart English Bible (NHEB):** Used in Chapter 16 specifically because it perfectly translated the promise of the "Sure House" (1 Kings 11:38).

• **Weymouth New Testament:** Used in Chapter 16 for its exact wording regarding the angels cast down to *Tartarus* (2 Peter 2:4).
 • **LBT (Living Bible / Life Bible):** Used in Chapter 15 to bring a straightforward, triumphant tone to the promises of salvation and forgiveness (Romans 10:9, Col 2:13-14).

Acknowledgements

The Co-Captain: To my husband, Don Wambach. You have allowed me the freedom to grow, change, and change again. It is a Liberty Gift I am deeply grateful for. I love you.

The Coaching Staff: To Laure Fabre (Editor, Translator, & Friend), John Bugni (Co-Editor & Friend), Susan Schoonover (Co-Editor & Friend), Dr. George Watkins (Prophet & Spiritual Father), and Brendon Burchard & the GrowthDay Staff (Leadership & Coaching).

The Home Team: To my Dad, who saw this book before I did, and my Mom, Erla Richards, for the life you sowed into me. To my sons—Joseph, Jace, Jacob, and Justin—my daughters-in-love, Erika and Kate, and my dear granddaughter, Liesel. To Suzanne, for your loyal friendship. Thank you all for witnessing and walking out the life of Christ I now live daily.

The Divine Sponsor: And to Heaven. Who could pen a single thought without the breath of conversation and the picture of majesty?

About The Author

KRISTEN WAMBACH is a spiritual investigative journalist, an ordained pastor, and the CEO of Rabbitrail Supply. As the host of the *Interviewing Jesus Podcast*, she helps a global audience move beyond religious exhaustion into a face-to-face reality with the Father.

With over thirty years of spiritual investigation, Kristen specializes in sharing "spiritually brave" activations that help believers rewrite their lives with supernatural wisdom. She is dedicated to closing the gap between Heaven and Earth—from the boardroom to the living room.

A longtime resident of the Pacific Northwest, Kristen has called the region home since childhood, drawing inspiration from its rugged beauty to coach others through their own spiritual wilderness. Married to Don for 43 years, she is a mother of four and remains a student of the undeniable goodness of God.

Connect with Kristen:
- **Website:** KristenWambach.com
- **Podcast:** Interviewing Jesus
- **Social:** https://linktr.ee/kristenwambach

Tehillah - תהלה